This book is dedicated to all those
descended from the family of
Irish Masons who migrated to
Australia in 1839

THE MASON STORY

Helen Malcher

The Mason Story
Author — Helen Malcher

© Helen Malcher 2015

For information and alterations, visit the website:
www.masonstory.com

ISBN: 9780646927138

The facts are as close as possible to correct, taking into account the inaccuracies and omissions of historical records and family members' memories. Some errors and differences of opinion will have occurred as stories are passed through generations of the family, and new facts will continue to come to light. We welcome additions and corrections, which can be sent to the contacts above.

All rights reserved. This book may not be reproduced in whole or part, stored, posted on the internet, or transmitted in any form or by any means, electronic, mechanical, photocopying, recording, or other, without permission from the author of this book.

1821 census
1901 census
Birth, Deaths & Marriages registers
Conversations with as many Irish locals as would permit it
Lewis Topographical Dictionary, 1849
Local History Library, Cahir
National Library of Ireland
Parish maps
Shipping Records
State Library of NSW
Genealogical Society records
Plus stories, memories, pictures and corrections from family members, for which we are most grateful.

Abbreviations:
BC / MC / DC — Birth, marriage and death certificates.
m1, m2 — First and second marriages.
Numbers in Family Trees — 1st, 2nd, 3rd etc generations shown in the table.

Authors / Contributors:

Helen (Mason) Malcher — daughter of Victor Mason,
granddaughter of William and Priscilla Mason,
great-granddaughter of the migrating John Mason III.

Terry Mason and **Monica (Murphy) Mason** — great-grandson and his wife of the migrating Oliver Mason, whose writings, recollections, contributions, illustrations and research of Oliver's side of the family have been extensive and invaluable.

Other Researchers:

Jan (Mason) O'Donnell — sister of Helen Malcher, daughter of Victor Mason, granddaughter of William and Priscilla Mason, great-granddaughter of the migrating John Mason III, for her memories of the life of our family.

Robyn Mason — daughter of Hilton Mason, granddaughter of
William and Priscilla Mason, great-granddaughter of the migrating John Mason III, whose contributions have been most appreciated.

Bob Mason — son of Arthur Edmund Mason, grandson of the migrating John Mason III, for his memories and contributions on his family.

Bill Mason — son of Eric Mason, grandson of William and Priscilla Mason, who was prepared to write his own family's story.

Patricia Keevers — daughter of Margaret Mason Keevers, granddaughter of Charles (Vin) Mason, great-granddaughter of James,
and great-great-granddaughter of the migrating Oliver Mason.

And the essential production team:

my daughters
Vicki Malcher and **Alex Fullerton**

Without their assistance, this book would not have been possible.

The story of the family of
John Mason I
Irish father of Australian descendants
b. c1760, d. c1798 in Tipperary
whose sons migrated with their children to
Australia on the *China* in 1839

The Mason family settled in the Hunter River
area, later moving to Tamworth, and produced
many progeny into the present generation.

Where only brief information about any family member
has been found, it is included in the lists of
descendants, particularly in the family trees.

Names are spelt variously in records.

Contents

Chapter 1 The Family Migrates 1
   The bare facts of the first migrating family 1
   Ireland and Tipperary..2
   The Land They Left 3
   The Famine...5
   From Ireland to Botany Bay — the *China* 8
   Settling in — A Snapshot of Morpeth 11

Chapter 2 John Mason I, Charles Mason and Patrick Arthur Mason...................15
   John Mason I..15
   Charles Mason and Joanna Quiggly..15
   Patrick Arthur Mason and Catherine Hanlon 17

Chapter 3 John Mason II, III and their descendants 19
   John Mason II and Joanna Quigley..19
      (Mary, John III, Oliver, Margaret, Johanna, Daniel)
     John Mason III and Mary Hickey/Maria Maher...21
       (John IV, Cornelius, Matilda, Johanna — children of Mary)
       (Oliver Peter, Patrick, Dan, Will, Arthur — children of Maria)
     Maria Maher and her family...26
       Oliver Peter Mason and Annie Bezant 28
       Dan Mason and Maud Smith 30
       Will Mason and Priscilla Smith..33
        (Arthur, Ethel, Vic, Jack, Eric, Hilton, Bob Mason)
     Priscilla Smith..36
     — William Smith, father of Priscilla (Smith) Mason 38
     — William Smith's first wife Louisa and their seven children 38
     — Lt. Colonel Grove White, father of Louisa Smith...38
     — Ann Smith, mother of Priscilla (Smith) Mason)..41
     — Mary Ethel Smith, sister of Priscilla (Smith) Mason 43
       Arthur William Mason..44
       Vic Mason and Cath Hogan 48
      Cath Hogan   55
     — Norm Hogan, brother of Cath (Hogan) Mason...58
     — Hogan, great-grandfather of Cath (Hogan) Mason 59
       Jan Mason and Cy O'Donnell 61
       Helen Mason and Harry Malcher 67
        Vicki Malcher..69
        Alex Fullerton...70
          Flynn and Ella Mitchell 70
        Chris Malcher and Giang Truong...71
        Oliver and Emily Malcher 71
       Jack Mason and Mella McCare..72
        Clarice Mason Reid 73
          Ross, Glenn and Brett Reid..73

Eric Mason and Thelma Davies	78
Bill, John, Dennis, Eric Mason	78
Bill Mason and Anne Benjamin	79
Sharon and Glenn Mason	81
Hilton Mason and Thelma Denny	83
Pamela, Lyn and Robyn Mason	83
Bob Mason and Audrey Parker	85
Bill, Sue, Linda and Terece Mason and children	85
Arthur Edmund Mason and Maude Bailey	88
Peg, Jack, Bob and Dorothy Mason	88
Daniel Mason	97

Chapter 4 The migrating Oliver Mason 99

Oliver Mason and Ann Fitzgerald	100
Descendants of Oliver Mason	104
(John, Patrick Arthur, James, Oliver, Charles, Edward, Charles, Joseph and children)	
John Mason and Ada Burnes	104
Oliver Patrick Mason	104
Robert Joseph Mason	105
Ann Mason	105
John Leo Mason	105
Zillah Mason	105
Mary Philomena Evans	105
James Edward Mason	105
Joseph Charles Mason	105
Edward John Mason	105
Ada Mason	105
Patrick Arthur Mason and Margaret Toohey	105
Hannah Smalley	106
Bartholomew Mason	106
Veronica Johnson	106
James Mason and Jane Purtell	106
Mary Therese Purcell	106
Patrick Daniel Mason	106
Sister Dolores	107
Margaret Mason	107
Jack Mason	107
Ruby Mason	107
Sister Thomasene	107
Vin Mason	107
Gus Mason	107
Blandine Mason	108
Irene Mason	108
Dorothy Mason	108
Oliver Mason and Elizabeth English/Nora Dunn	108
Charles Gerald Mason	109
Edward Terence Mason	109
Charles Mason	109
Joseph Paul Mason and Catherine Purtell	109

Jack Mason	109
Brother Herman	110
Ronald Joseph Mason	110
James Aubrey Mason	110
Joseph Mary Hillary Mason	110
Sister Mary Consiglio	110
Charles Mason and Catherine Morris	111
(Oliver Alphonsus, May, Sr Irenaeus, Sr Regis, Dick, Morrie, Jim, Rene, Clem)	
May Mason	114
Sister Mary Irenaeus	114
Sister Mary Regis	115
Dick Mason	115
Morrie Mason	116
Jim Mason	116
Rene Mostyn	117
Clem Mason	118
Oliver Alphonsus Mason and Netta Garrett/Rosemary Lollbach	119
(Mick, Chick, Leila, Pat, Br Claudius, Terry, Claire, Anne, Cath — children of Netta)	
(Colleen, Josephine, Judith, Tony, James Oliver — children of Rosemary)	
Mick Lyons	125
Terry Mason	126
Monica (Murphy) Mason	132

Chapter 5 The migrating Mason daughters and their families 137

Mary Mason and Thomas Sheridan	137
Joanna Mason and Charles Tighe	140
Margaret Mason and Patrick Creevey	141

Chapter 6 Family Bible..147

Chapter 7 The Full Mason Family Tree..151

Noteworthy

Widows	22
War Service	105
The Religious	111
The Railways	124
Three Convicts	145

Chapter I

The Family Migrates

The bare facts of the first migrating family

The **Mason** family of two parents and six offspring migrated to Botany Bay in 1839. They were an unusually complete, even old, family to choose to migrate as a unit. **John II**, at 46, was nearing the end of his expected life span, and **Joanna**, two years older at 48, was even closer to the average life expectancy for women in those tough and troubled times.

The 'pull' factor from the colony at Botany Bay was that it was at that time geared towards such units — stable families, of healthy workers — 'whole family' immigration. They were also either stronger, more close-knit as a unit, or had a degree more financial security than other agricultural labourers from Tipperary.

John III and **Oliver**'s later stories suggest some **Mason** males had assets, acquired property quickly and had a quite visible strength of character and personality, not noticeably dissipated through generations — or at least till the generation known by this writer, that of **John III**'s great-grandchildren. Many of their descendants also married strong women.

The migrating Irish Mason family and their later husbands and wives

1 **John Mason** II b. 1787 d. 10 Jan 1858 m. 1811 **Joanna (Johanna) Quigley** b. 1792 d. 6 Apr 1857
  2 **Mary Mason** b. 1813 d. 3 Mar 1873 m. **Thomas Sheridan** 1840 b. 1796 d. 11 Aug 1858
  2 **John Mason III** b. 1816 d. 12 Oct 1879 m1. **Mary Hickey** 14 Jan 1850 b. 1827 d. 21 Aug 1860
  m2. **Maria Maher** 3 Aug 1863 b. 1844, d. 27 May 1905
  2 **Oliver Mason** b. Feb 1818 d. 7 Apr 1885 m. **Ann Fitzgerald** 21 Jan 1853 b. 1825 d. 1 Aug 1891
  2 **Joanna Mason** b. 5 Apr 1823 d. 1885 m. **Charles Tye/Tighe** 20 Jun 1841 b. 1803 d. 1850
  2 **Margaret Mason** b. 5 Apr 1825 d. 8 Apr 1870 m. **Patrick Creevey** b 15 Apr 1844 1809 d. 23 Jan 1871
  2 **Daniel Mason** b. 1832 or 1834 d. ?

Chapter 1: The Family Migrates

Ireland and Tipperary

Maps of Ireland as a whole and County Tipperary.

Cashel, Cahir, Tipperary, Golden, all on the River Suir, to Waterford, the embarkation point on the south coast.

John III and **Oliver Mason** came from Golden village, population 268 in 2002.
Golden, (Ecclesiastic) Parish of Golden, (Administrative) Parish of Relickmurry & Athassel, Poor Law Union of Tipperary., Barony of Clanwilliam, County Tipperary.

Their father **John II** listed his homeplace as Cashel, Diocese Town, Parish of St. John the Baptist, Poor Law Union of Cashel, Barony of Middlethird, County of Tipperary, about 3 Irish miles away.

Their mother **Johanna** was from Cahir, population 3668 in 1849.
Cahir, Parish of Cahir, Poor Law Union of Clogheen, Barony of Iffa & Offa West, County Tipperary

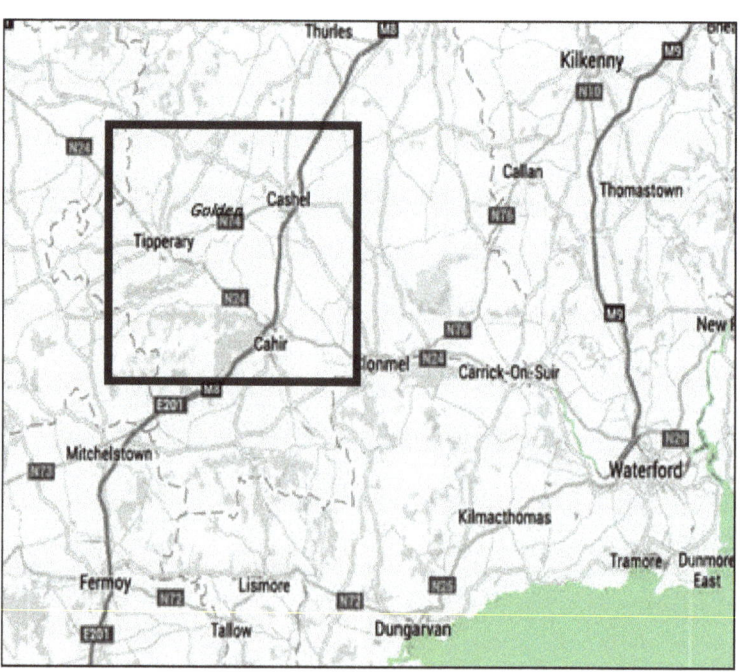

Chapter 1: The Family Migrates

The Land They Left

Ireland, and particularly Tipperary, the County from which our family came, is a green and pleasant land, lush and ripe looking. A pleasure to see.

But still it did not produce a livelihood or a sufficiency of food or work for the poor in southern Ireland in the early 19th century, when our family left it. That period saw the development of a quite horrendous famine, which killed thousands of Irish, releasing them from the dire straits in which they lived. It also initiated a wave of thousands of Irish to America and Australia.

Our **Mason** family was early in this movement, leaving for Botany Bay in 1839.

John III and his brother **Oliver Mason** lived, until they arrived in Australia in 1839, in Tipperary in the tiny village of Golden, in the South Riding of County Tipperary only 3½ Irish miles west of the Diocese township of Cashel, and 82 miles southwest of Dublin. The father, **John Mason II**, formerly of the nearby town of Cahir (pronounced 'Care'), and mother **Joanna (Quigley) Mason** of Cashel, all Catholics, lived in the cathedral township of Cashel, where their children were born. In 1839 the **Mason** family made the courageous decision, taken with more foresight (and considerably earlier) than most of their contemporaries, to leave economically prostrate Ireland, for the new and unknown land of Botany Bay (Australia).

The whole combined family of eleven migrated:

> **John II** and **Johanna**, (aged 46 and 48 at the time)
> sons **John III** and **Oliver**, at 23 and 21,
> daughters **Mary**, **Joanna** and **Margaret**, at 26, 16, 14,
> and **Daniel**, probably 7.

> **John II's** brother **Charles** and his wife **Joanna (Quigley)**
> and their baby daughter **Margaret**
> migrated on the same ship, the *China*

The County of Tipperary was considered to be one of the poorest counties in southern Ireland at the time. Mostly pastoral, it was producing crops not for its starving population, but for the *British* market!

There is a vast lack of data of the many who chose (albeit with few alternatives available to them), to leave their native land and travel half way across the world to a country of which they knew little or nothing. To understand something of their life and times therefore, one must resort to establishing as much as possible about the area, parish, village or society in which they lived. For this, the County libraries within those parishes have been found to be goldmines. Each of them, in this writer's experience, contains at least one local historian, *fascinated* by his subject, who offers, at the exhibition of any interest by a visitor, a vast gamut of local colour, stories, ideas, facts and figures.

As a family of healthy, working migrants, this family would appear to support historian Patrick O'Farrell's assessment in his 1986 *The Irish in Australia*, that it was not those who were truly starving, at the bottom of the poverty scale, who migrated, since those had neither energy nor capability to plan and execute such a massive step. It was the slightly better-off agricultural worker, unbound by land (or later, with only failed land available to him), who could find the finances, wherewithal and strength to manage to victual himself and his family on the journey to the port of embarkation and beyond. The fact that they were assisted was probably the reason they took on the journey and transplantation.

However no matter how assiduous the search of parish or general records, either here in Australia or in Ireland, there is very little hope of discovering the background of individual Irish landless labourers beyond, at most, about 1800. At best one can manage some of the ambience of the time, place and people, which we have tried to do.

John and his brother **Oliver**, at 23 and 21, moved to **Golden** to get work, which they found as labourers in one of the flour and oatmeal mills there. Such mills provided most of the available work for young healthy males at the time, in the days before much of Ireland's industry. However, when these Tipperary young men arrived here they registered themselves as a ploughman and a labourer — which either disproves their mill work, or shows them as being receptive to their perception of the needs of the new land.

Later information has shown that their grandfather, **John Mason I**, who did not migrate, labelled himself as a 'farmer', and the shipping records for his family label him a labourer. This probably meant that farming skills were part of that family. The landless poor in Ireland were subject to the government, the landowners, dramatic unemployment, and the lack of a supporting welfare system. We could well have been wrong about the mill employment!

The village of Golden is tiny, holding in the 1980s the original store, one now-defunct mill, an old stone bridge and tower on the River Suir attesting to slightly greater prosperity earlier, and a monument to courage and conflict on the site at the time of 'The Troubles', the history of which the area is inordinately proud. There is also a small Catholic chapel, and a larger Church of Ireland church, in the grave yard of which there are (astonishingly to this writer) many of the older *Catholic* graves, a fact confirmed by the old gravediggers there.

Golden village is an old post-town, part of the Golden Vale of rich agricultural land. It was also considered the most troubled area in all Ireland.

The picturesque Golden Vale, Tipperary, Ireland, in which lies the village of Golden.
Green and lush, but unsupportive of its starving population in the early 1800s.

At the 1821 census, Golden held 104 families, a total of 616 persons, in 121 houses, of which 17 were uninhabited. The concept of one family to a house, comparatively rare in rural Ireland, therefore, almost existed in this small community. Only 203 of the inhabitants were employed, 87 in trade and manufacture and 65 in agricultural pursuits. With 80 children registered as being at school there (50 boys, 30 girls), about half the child population was not accounted for. However, taking into account the women, very young children and the aged, for whom no statistics were taken, Golden in the context of the time and period would seem to be fairly prosperous.

The standard of education in the time and in the area was not high. Even now, the rural Irish Catholic schools observed by the writer in the 1980s, ran at a rudimentary level Australia bettered only in the 1930s. There was little perceived necessity (or opportunity) for potential farm or mill labourers to linger in school. Yet in 1839 the decision was made for the whole Mason family to migrate, all eleven of them. This decision was courageous, taken in the years during and following the famine.

So they travelled on a boat down 'their' River Suir (pronounced Shoor) to Waterford, the port of embarkation, to take their assisted passage on the *China* in May 1839. Memories in the area still extend to grandparents subscribing to Wakes for emigrants to either of the 'New Worlds'. The purpose of such a wake was to provide food and sustenance to the migrants for the long voyage, not the least difficult part of which was that to the port of embarkation.

Yet there is no comprehension on the part of 21st century inhabitants of Golden of Australian (and American) interest in our Irish ancestry — though they are quite cheerful about putting that interest to good financial use for themselves if at all possible.

The Famine

1849 Famine victims

A sad farewell — and then forgotten

In the middle of the 19th century — officially dated from 1845 — Ireland suffered a massive famine, which had been building steadily through the previous years. Called the 'Irish Potato Famine' because of the dependence of the whole community on that food, it caused literally thousands of Irish emigrants to leave their homeland before and during the catastrophe, to go to America (the majority) and to the unknown Botany Bay. For these thousands, very few official records exist. For the extremely poverty-stricken — and there were many of those — who were forced by circumstances into the work houses run by the Poor Law Unions, some scant records do survive. Only for the very, very poor in the work houses, or the much richer estate owners and the landed gentry, is it easier to find extant records for an individual or family, and even in some cases for their property or estate. Our family was not recorded in any of these groups.

There was actual destitution well before the actual famine from failure of the potato and wheat crops. One, quoted from the Poor Enquiry of 1835, in its cold bureaucratic language, is horrifying in its unvoiced recognition of a society that has come to the stage of deserting its children to their fate and an almost certain death. The following report took evidence from the rectors, priests and wealthier tradesmen in the Parish of Carrick:

There has been one newborn child exposed in Newtown Parish in a field, and one in Carrick parish. The practice is for them to be taken round from house to house, and they stay only one night: they mostly die: it cannot well be otherwise. The child in Newtown parish is given out to nurse, and is supported by voluntary subscriptions.

All the children exposed in this neighbourhood, except the one in Newtown parish, have died. The church warden never takes charge of deserted children or orphans in this parish: he refused in the last case to provide for the child in Carrick parish, stating that he had no funds, but made no attempt to change the levy.

Some legislative interference is very much wanted to make the present law relating to deserted children effective, as it is now a dead letter in Carrick.

The migrators were by no means the weakest or poorest in Ireland. It required courage, strength, some finances, initiative and health, to pull up roots and trek to the nearest port, or to England, and set off to make a new life in an unknown land at the other side of an unknown world. For the **Masons** it required scratching together sufficient funds, food and clothing for the journey, expensive travel to the port of embarkation (in their case Waterford on the Irish south coast), and £5 each for the passage to Australia itself, assisted though it was. That the **Masons** managed these hurdles for all eleven of them (the families of **John II** and his brother **Charles**) must stand as evidence that some were more fortunate, and to a very slight degree better off, than their luckless neighbours. The savage effects of the potato 'blight' or disease, felt much earlier, must be considered as part of the impetus for the **Mason** family leaving their homeland in 1839. And their home county of Tipperary was one of the heaviest hit Irish counties, by both famine and emigration.

The deaths and emigration, making permanent changes in the country's demographic, political and cultural landscape, make modern historians regard this as a dividing line in Irish history. One third of the population was entirely dependent on the potato for food, and the loss of successive annual crops thus had a traumatic effect. As Catholics — as were 80% of the Irish population — our family was even more disadvantaged, Catholics having only recovered some of their rights in 1829.

This mud, thatched cottage is probably indicative for the slightly better-off Irish in the 19th century, though many were at a level far below this — homeless and starving.

The pull factor from the colony at Botany Bay was that it was at that time geared towards assisting the immigrations of family units — whole family immigration. Between 1832 and 1859, 70% of representatives of Ireland in the British Parliament were landowners or the sons of landowners — *not* representative of the majority of the population, the agricultural poor. The poor had, one English leader said in 1844 — *a starving population, an absentee aristocracy, an alien church, and in addition the weakest executive in the world*. The **Masons**, we believe, were not in this condition — or they could not have afforded the trip to the port of embarkation and the voyage to Australia. We don't know the extent of their assets or income, unfortunately. When they got here, they managed to achieve much better conditions.

Ireland had a rapidly increasing population — despite starvation. Three-quarters of her labourers were unemployed, housing conditions were appalling, and the standard of living unbelievably low. This was in contrast to Britain, beginning to enjoy the modern prosperity of the Victorian and industrial ages.

The Commissioners could not *forbear expressing our strong sense of the patient endurance which the labouring classes have exhibited under sufferings greater, we believe, than the people of any other country in Europe have to sustain*.

But little was done. Two-thirds of the eight million population in 1841 depended on agriculture for their survival, but rarely received a working wage. They had to work for their landlords in return for the patch of land they needed in order to grow enough food for their own families, and only the potato could be grown in sufficient quantities. It had become a base food of the poor, especially in winter, and a staple food all year round for farmers — one of the main reasons the emergence of the potato blight had such devastating effects in Ireland, and far less effect in other European countries.

Grazing land for cattle (for the *English* market) occupied much of the acreage, leaving the native population virtually dependent for survival on that potato, growing abundantly in less favourable soil. The potato was also used extensively as a fodder crop for livestock immediately prior to the famine, and approximately 33% of production was normally used in this way, rather than providing food for the Irish poor.

Writings at the time included condemnation of the British government, which had exacerbated the problem by continuing, under the Corn Laws, to export corn (grain) grown in Ireland out of the country, as the people starved. John Mitchel, one of the leading political writers of the Young Ireland group, wrote that the people *watched as their food melted in rottenness off the face of the earth, all the while watching heavy-laden ships, freighted with the yellow corn their own hands have sown and reaped, spreading all sail for England*.

Records show Irish lands exported food even during the worst years of the Famine. The poor had no money to buy food and the government did not ban exports, and as the problem worsened and poor tenants were unable to pay their rent, landlords began clearing them off their land, evicting them even from the hovels to which they'd been reduced.

> Estimated potato crop: 1844 — 14.862 million tons
> 1845 — 10.063 million tons
> 1846 — 2.9 million tons
>
> This shows a dramatic and devastating drop over two years, from which Ireland did not recover until after 1859.

The potato crop failure was universal throughout the country. In both 1841 and 1844 potato crop failure was widespread, and the unreliability of the potato crop was said to be an accepted fact in Ireland. On top of this, came the blight — universal and incurable, destroying well over a third of the entire country's crop. The proximity of these dates to their departure demonstrate how clear the problem must have been to our family, to encourage them, with the assistance of the Australian government, to take the huge step in 1839 of starting a new life elsewhere. It was still most unusual for families to migrate together — the **Masons** were rare in this.

The famine in Ireland boded ill for the future, too. Between 1841 and 1851, the number of 1-5 acre blocks reduced from 44.9% of the whole to 15.5%. Further figures prove that the smaller blocks were being integrated into the larger holdings. Historian Dr Patrick Power set acreage at 60 acres as the turning point for survival, making this the eradication of the small-farmer class.

From the Australian point of view, Irish immigrants accounted for one-quarter of Australia's overseas-born population in 1871. Large numbers of Irish priests, nuns and brothers followed other Irish immigrants to Australia from the earliest years of European settlement in order to provide Catholic education to their children. Towards the end of the 20th century about 20% of Australian students were in Catholic schools established largely by those Irish clerics.

DINNER ON BOARD THE FIRST EMIGRANT SHIP FOR NEW ZEALAND.

This illustration of dinner (and sleeping quarters) in the interior of one of the immigrant ships at that early period shows a little more of the crowding and lack of space and comforts endured by those on board for 145 days. It is however probably comparable to the conditions they left behind them, and perhaps not too much unlike the conditions they were coming to. They sailed direct from Waterford to the Cape of Good Hope for supplies and water, then down to Botany Bay, arriving in Sydney on 19 December 1839

Chapter 1: The Family Migrates

From Ireland to Botany Bay — the *China*

The *China*'s passengers on their journey were mostly assisted immigrants from Tipperary, and were probably well known to each other by the time they arrived in Australia. Coming from the family's hometowns of Cahir, Cashel and Golden, they came down the River Suir, which flows through those towns and near the rich agricultural land of the Golden Vale, down to Waterford, from whence their ship sailed. The fare for the overseas trip was only £5 per person, which was difficult enough for them to accumulate, but this was what 'assisted migration' meant — this amount they had to produce. The balance was a partial funding, paid to the ship's master by the Australian government, for their human cargo. They still had to conform to the Australian rules of minimum and defined pieces of clothing for each — none of which would have been cheap.

The *China* left Waterford on Ireland's south coast on 28 Jul 1839 with our family, bound for agricultural employment in the Hunter Valley in New South Wales. They left behind them violence, poverty, potential starvation, and a total lack of opportunity. It is sad that we can only find circumstantial evidence to see how all this touched their lives. Attempts have been made, notably by historian Patrick O'Farrell, to shed light on the experience that was an emigrant ship in the 1830s to the end of the century, but what letters survive are by nature those of literate, better educated, less impoverished emigrants, giving little detail of life of the poor, southern, Irish catholic in steerage. And in the case of the **Mason** family, they left absolutely no family behind them. Yet they had their own support system. Study of the shipping records for the *China* and the sponsor network in the Hunter Valley establishes that they made strong relationships with (or already had relationships with) at least two other Tipperary families on board. In later years the families attended each other at births, deaths, and marriages, and even intermarried. This mutual moral support does not appear to have been rare.

The ship *China* was itself tiny by 21st century standards — 618 tons, compared to 1140 tons for the Freshwater class of ferries on Sydney Harbour. It carried 263 emigrants and took 145 days for the journey.

**Disposal of Mason migrants from the *China*, 20 December 1839.
From the ship's records of C O'Brian Esq, Surgeon RM (Royal Marines)**

Disposal	M / F
Married	40 / 43
Single	42 / 49
Children over 14 years	10 / 4
Children 7 to 14 years	26 / 15
Children under 7 years	20 / 13
Souls on board	**262**

Abstract by trade	Av. wages £/Term/Rations
Male:	
6 ploughmen	25 / Year / Yes
32 Ag. labourer	22 / Year / Yes
1 Dom. servant	32½ / Year / Yes
Female:	
10 Farm Servants	12 / Year / Yes
22 House servants	14 / Year / Yes
1 Laundress	14 / Year / Yes
8 Nursemaids	12 / Year / Yes

Births and Deaths:
5 births on board
3 deaths on board
2 deaths in barracks
1 birth in barracks

- **John Mason II** engaged to Wm. Bucknell, of Patersons River, at a wage of £21 per year, with rations.
- **Chas Mason** engaged to Wm. Bucknell, of Newtown, at a wage of £21 per year, with rations.
- **John Mason III** and **Oliver**, aged 23 and 21, also engaged to Wm. Bucknell, of Patersons River, at a wage of £21 per year, with rations.
- **Mary (26)** and **Johanna (16)** of Cashel to Mr Harper in Sydney at £16 and £10 respectively, with rations.
- **Michael Power** of Tipperary, 22, and wife, 21, to Wm. Bucknell, of Patersons River, at a wage of £21 per year, with rations.
- **Cornelius Ryan**, farm labourer, 22, to Wm. Bucknell, of Patersons River, at a wage of £21 per year, with rations.
- **Ellen Ryan**, dairymaid, 24, 'gone with her brother to Patersons River'.

Many of these Irish men and women met on the ship coming out, or, being from Tipperary, knew each other in Ireland. Certainly by the time they got to Patersons River their lives and their families were intermingled

The Disposal of the Masons on arrival December 1839

This record (translated below) accounts for **John Mason II** and his wife **Joanna**, with their two youngest children (**Margaret** and **Daniel**), plus **Charles Mason** (John II's younger brother) with his wife, all on the *China*. The older offspring of **John Mason II** — **Mary, John III, Oliver,** and **Johanna** — are recorded as single adults, being 16 and over. Most passengers on this ship were from Tipperary, Ireland.

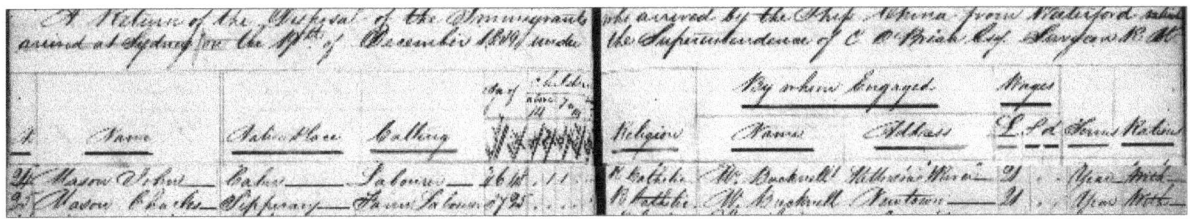

A return of the disposal of the Immigrants who arrived by the Ship 'China' from Waterford which arrived at Sydney on 19th December 1839 under the Superintendence of C O'Brian Esq, Surgeon RM

Name	Native Place	Calling	Age		Children		Religion	By Whom Engaged		Term / Rations
			Self	Wife	>14	>7		Name	Location	
Mason, John	Cahir	Labourer	46	48	1	1	RC	Wm Bucknell	Patersons River	£21 Year /with rations
Mason, Charles	Tipperary	Farm Labourer	27	25	-	-	RC	Wm Bucknell	Newtown	£21 Year /with rations

The China in Sydney 1839-40

Medical Report of the passengers on the Masons' voyage on the *China*, 1839

VERBATIM

China 1839 — MEDICAL REPORT

618 ton, Capt. Archibald Phillips: Waterford, 28 July 1839
to Sydney, 20 Dec 1839

Details of the Journey of the Ship CHINA from Waterford: O' Brien MD Surgeon Superintendent. Archibald Philips Master. Tonnage 618 Tons

Port from which vessel sailed   Waterford
Date of sailing   28th July 1839

Adults		Children			Total
Males	Females	1 to 7	7 to 15	Over 15	
81	87	40	45	7	263

No of males embarked	Adult	81	
	Children	52	
No of Females embarked	Adult	87	
	Children	43	
		263	
Died on Board Males	Adults	0	
	Children(infant)	2	
Female	Adults	1	
	Children	0	
Landed		260	

Name of Principal diseases which reoccurred on board	Fever, Dysentery, Diarrhoea Difficult Dentition, Cynanche Tonsillaris (abscess about the tonsils), scorbutus Incipient early scurvy)
General state of vessel on arrival in respect to health	Very Healthy Vessel in perfect order in reference to cleaning & ventilation and only one person in the sick bay
Length of passage In days	145 days including 7 days at the Cape.
Date of Arrival	19th December 1839
Number of children born aboard	5

We called at the Cape for fresh provisions, vegetables, water which was of the greatest Benefit to the People. In the Evenings when the weather permitted there was music and dancing. These occupations entertained them and prevented [idleness].

Stating whether and where church service was performed on board by the respective number of Protestants and Catholics; whether school was established on board; how many attended; what regulations were established for the preservation of health and cleanliness. Those occupations were recommended and encouraged.

Divine Service was performed regularly every Sunday and when the weather was unseasonable was held between Decks. The comparative Number of Protestants and Catholics were **Prot 50 Caths 210** making the total of 260 landed at the Emigrant Barracks. We had a school established a few days after our sailing when the children had recovered from the sea sickness & 2 Very Efficient School Masters were appointed, the average number of pupils were 60 in constant attendance so made considerable progress in reading and spelling. The Principal Part of people's time was taken up in cleaning their Berths & utensils & keeping the deck and water closets in good order.

Chapter 1: The Family Migrates

Settling in — A Snapshot of Morpeth

The Mason family settled in the East Maitland/Morpeth/Patersons River valley. The area just out of Morpeth is flat, lush and green — a flood plain. It was called Phoenix Park, possibly after the Park of the same name in Dublin, and because of its frequent flooding, remains to this day green and fertile, much closer to the Ireland they knew than the drier land nearer Sydney. Morpeth lies across river from Phoenix Plain. It is here, presumably, which had most of the producing fields of the establishment belonging to the gentleman settler Dunmore Lang. The area was extremely vulnerable and susceptible to floods, though that added to its fertility.

By 1839 when **John Mason** and his family arrived, Morpeth was just becoming conscious of itself. The government had previously offered a grant of 100 acres to Dunmore Lang, which he had refused. He later took up a similar grant from Governor Brisbane to found Dunmore (another Tipperary place name) on a rise overlooking the plain. When the **Mason** family arrived, or by 1870 when they had left, Morpeth had several important commercial buildings supporting its river trade on the Hunter River — the St James Church, Dunmore Public School (in Largs village), Campbell's Bond Stores, all in Morpeth before the **Masons** arrived, and a Courthouse, which arrived a little later, in 1862. It also had Queens Wharf on the Hunter River, to receive the steamers coming up river with supplies, and a punt across river to the Phoenix Park/Plain, where the fertile land supported the large number of workers under the auspices of Dunmore.

Morpeth was the township around which most of the **Masons** of the first migrating generation clustered. First step on the site had been made by a Lt. Edward Close in 1821, when he migrated here after the Peninsula Wars. He built a Gentleman's Residence named *Closebourne*, and a personal avenue to the St James Church he completed in 1838. By 1873, when most of the **Mason** family had left, Morpeth had several important commercial buildings supporting its river trade on the Hunter River. There is little evidence of **William Bucknell's** property *Brecon*, to which the **Masons** had been allocated.

We also have little evidence of the lifestyle or place of the **Masons** in this area — though we know they were there. They left in c1870 to make their home in Tamworth.

PHOENIX PARK

Phoenix Park is a flood plain, nestling in a nearly-closed circle of the serpentine Hunter River. It is rich, fertile country, and flat flat flat. Still only sparsely dotted with houses, it is totally covered with neatly set-out agricultural tilled areas and some stock. It shows evidence of the residents coping with the frequent floods by houses being constructed on raised knolls above the expected flood levels. The road itself through the plain from the Dunmore House side to the Morpeth side was already raised some three metres above the natural surface. The levies throughout the Phoenix Plain area give an indication of the recognition by the farming community of the value of the floods, but also of the necessity of containing them.

Tamworth lies in the Peel Valley, discovered on 1 Sept 1818 by John Oxley, who was quite lavish in his praise of its fertility. The area consisted of grazing runs from the 1830s (though illegally, since it was outside the Nineteen Counties proclaimed by Governor

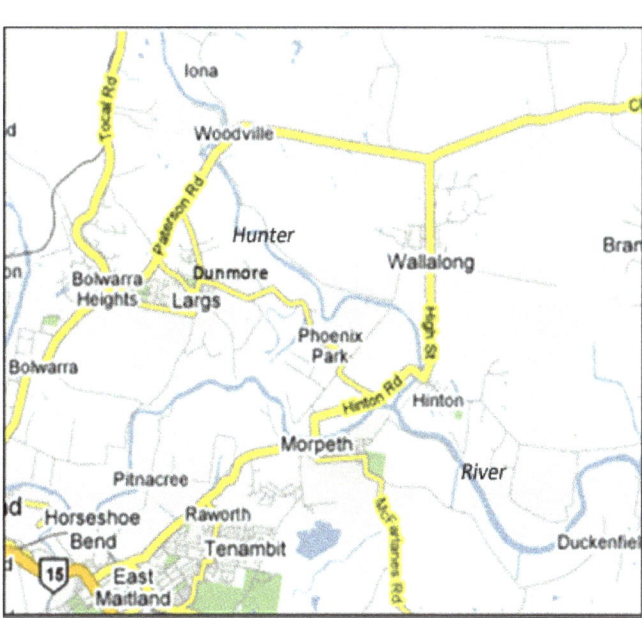

The Maitland / Morpeth / Phoenix Park / Dunmore / Largs / Swan Reach / Hinton / Paterson River area on the Hunter River where the Masons settled from late 1839 to about 1877.

Chapter 1: The Family Migrates

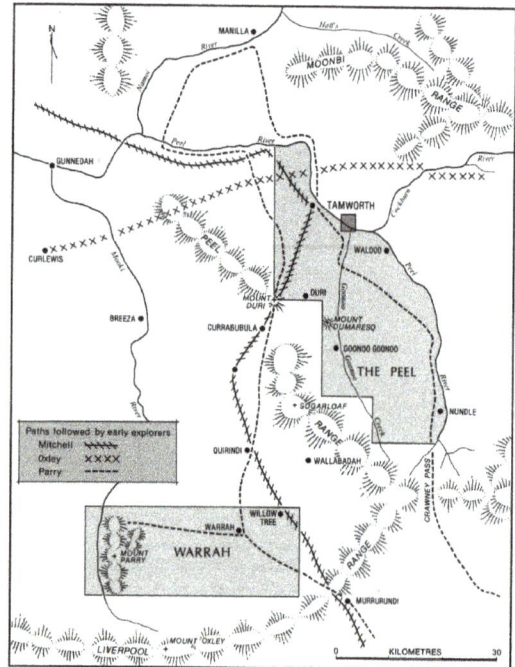

The second AAC grant, partly centred around Tamworth, after the grant near the sea was found to be impossible for sheep.

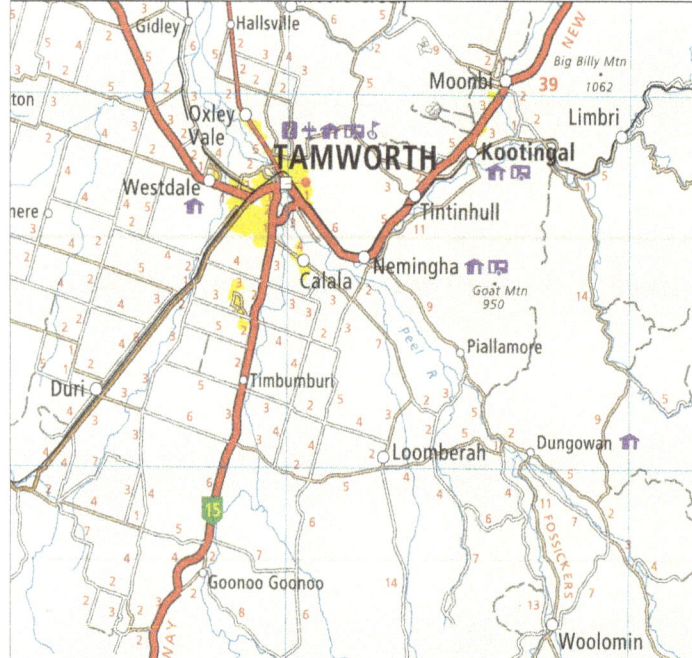

A more modern map of Tamworth and surrounds, including Oxley Vale (formerly part of Woolamol), Goonoo Goonoo, Nemingha, Tintinhull, Calala, Dungowan and the Cockburn River which follows the New England highway heading northeast.

Darling). The first run was Wallamaul, also known as Wallamore and more recently Woolamol, now renamed Oxley Vale, a suburb of the modern city of Tamworth.

The **Mason** family moved up to Tamworth — a developing town by 1870 — after being in the Maitland/ Morpeth/Phoenix Park area. **Margaret (Mason)** and **Patrick Creevey** went to Dungowan, in the Tamworth area in the late 1860s, and **Oliver Mason** and his family *bought* land from the Woolamol AAC site (northwest of Tamworth). We had not known they had assets. The **John Mason** family followed them to Tamworth by 1870 to 1873.

By about 1834, the Australian Agricultural Company (AAC), whose founders included John Macarthur, owners (by negotiation with the government) of a vast tract of land at Port Stephens, decided it needed better territory (and more water) for its huge sheep flocks. It acquired over 300,000 acres of land which became known as Goonoo Goonoo (pronounced gunna-g'noo) on the Liverpool Plains, south of the present town of Tamworth. It also acquired acreage in the same general area, called Warrah and The Peel. The company's only access to the coast for supplies (and the area was not self-sufficient even in food for some number of years) was over the mountains into the Hunter Valley, then out (or in) through Morpeth to the river traffic on the Hunter. From the first the AAC sent scores of workmen to build buildings, herd sheep, drive pack mules and sheep over the 'Peel Line', the track across the mountains to the Liverpool Plains. They thus increased the number of the people in the valley working on their new properties. Its building program ensured town development in what had virtually been only a coaching station, and as an indication of growth, two pubs were licensed in 1847. As early as 1835 the AAC's and other activities at Goonoo Goonoo and Calala (a second station) had encouraged the establishment of the first store. In 1855 the first teacher was posted to the National (or Public) School.

By 1850, NSW had a sheep population of 13 million, the basis of supply of half of *British* total wool needs. This burgeoning of the sheep economy came from a steep increase in the British market. During the 1820s freight costs to Britain declined, and competition increased for wool sales after the Napoleonic wars. However, the market for medium cloth, which was what the Australian sheep industry was producing, increased dramatically, to the considerable benefit of graziers here, as Roger Milliss argues in *Tamworth: City on the Peel*.

When the **Masons** arrived from Morpeth, where they had first settled, in about 1870, Tamworth had a population of just over 1500. It had a position as a 'river port' making it central to trade, a Catholic and a Church of England church, a police force (most of whom were Irish), courthouse, newspaper, post office, five hotels, 'numerous good dwelling houses', a postman, stores and a place of entertainment (the 'Little Paradise Gardens'). The bullock dray still survived as a means of transport beyond the turn of the century.

Tamworth was called a city in 1876. By 1878 the train line reached Maitland from Sydney, thus massively encouraging the growth of the area, and ensuring that Morpeth would virtually die, since the rail went on another route. One commentator at the celebrations to mark the coming of the 'iron horse' was moved to comment on the existence of no less than 40 hotels by that time, for a population estimated at 3000. The river was bridged again in 1881, more employment was available in the town with the establishment of a flour mill in 1883, and street electrification came on 9 Nov 1888.

During the 1870s and 1880s, Tamworth went through a quite exponential growth period, from a cluster of slab and timber houses, with the occasional more solidly-constructed church or hotel. It is difficult to establish where in this ranking the **Masons** would have fitted. Their experience was agricultural, though by the end of the century the **Mason** men were well ensconced in urban-type occupations and houses. **Oliver Mason** may well have had an urban-type house in the 1870s. Certainly he had urban addresses when he died in 1885.

By 1885, there was a quite dramatic change in the appearance of Tamworth: many more large brick commercial buildings, better laid-out streets, and a definite appearance of a town which had come of age — probably due in no small way to the coming of the railway. It had survived (and been enriched by) the gold rush of 1856, much increasing the population in the valley. It had also survived devastating floods in 1864 and 1872 — and would again in 1910. It had its first 'Show' in 1873.

Until 1883 in Tamworth, when the new West Tamworth Public School was established, there was only a small and very crowded denominational school in Tamworth. That year, after community pressure, the government school was constructed, intended to cope with some 250 children. By that stage many of the sons of **John** and **Oliver** were too old for school, so their education must have been very *ad hoc*, with little help from **John**'s wife, their illiterate mother.

Calala, the original cottage, now Tamworth Historical Society premises. Timber construction and bark roof. The brick chimney fireplace is probably a more recent addition, for safety.

A Cobb & Co coach — when the Masons travelled en masse, with family and goods, to Tamworth in 1870, they probably used this mode of transport.

Part of the problem of researching Irish ancestors of present day Australians from Ireland is that so many of them were landless labourers. As such the official records for them either in Parish records or in official documents are extremely rare. Only the land owners and, as one goes further back in time, only the greater land owners, have official records that can easily trace a family further back than the early 19th or late 18th century. We are extremely fortunate that we have been able to go back with our family of **Masons** as far as this. Yet we have new information that **Oliver Mason** (at least) had sufficient funds during this period to a) *buy* 182 acres on the Woolamol site, and b) *own* a hotel with food and stabling in Morpeth. Search continues on this aspect.

In the 1860s and 1870s, the very rare photos of Tamworth display a scattered cluster of slab and timber houses, with the occasional more solidly constructed building of a church or hotel. The much larger number of photos taken in 1885, however, show a quite dramatic change in appearance: many more larger brick commercial buildings, better laid-out streets, and a definite appearance of a town which has 'come of age' — probably due to the coming of the railway, and street electrification.

Of all immigrants to Australia in the 19th century, 25 per cent were said to be Irish (David Fitzpatrick, in Colm Keirnan, ed *Ireland and Australia, 1984)*. They came in families, and Irish women migrated as often as men — there was, therefore, something of a balance in the Irish immigrants in a land short of women. They also did not 'huddle together defensively in residential enclaves' (though the family ties, particularly out of the city, were strong). And one third of policemen were Irish!

The broader **Mason** family and its offspring lived, farmed and worked in Tamworth for many years, only spreading in the generation of the grandchildren of **John** and **Oliver Mason.**

Chapter 2

John Mason I, Charles Mason and Patrick Arthur Mason

We have chosen that this history cover only the direct family of **John Mason II** and **Johanna Quigley**, plus **Oliver Mason** and their family, who migrated here. The **Charles** and **Joanna (Quiggly) Mason** family, though related, are not in that direct line, and will not be covered in this history. **Patrick Arthur Mason** claimed to be related to this family, however that has not been verified.

John Mason I: b. 1760 d. c1803

EARLIEST KNOWN MASON OF THIS FAMILY
HUSBAND OF MARGARET O'CONNOR
STAYED IN TIPPERARY
A FARMER, OUTSIDE CAHIR, TIPPERARY

John Mason I and his wife **Margaret O'Connor**, residents of Tipperary, Ireland, were the parents of the migrating family, and did not themselves migrate, dying well before departure date. **John** was defined as a 'farmer' on the death certificate of his son **Charles**, but little else is known of them, except that they were Catholic, as were the migrators, and had two sons, **Charles** and **John**, both of whom married and came to live in Australia. The father had died in about 1803, and could therefore have had no input to the decision for the sons to sail to the other, unknown, side of the world. His only known bequest to his family was that he was *a farmer*, and that therefore his family had farming skills — important in their new life.

Charles Mason: b. 1798 d. 13 Sep 1865

JOHN MASON II'S BROTHER
M. JOHANNA QUIGGLY IN CASHEL, TIPPERARY 1838, ARRIVED ON THE CHINA 19 DEC 1839
LIVED IN CAHIR, TIPPERARY, SON OF JOHN MASON AND MARGARET O'CONNOR
THEIR BABY DAUGHTER MARGARET WAS ALSO ON BOARD
DIED 13 SEP 1865, DC 4580/1865

On the same ship (*China*, 1839) with **John Mason II** and his wife **Joanna (Quigley) Mason** and their sons and daughters, was another couple — **Charles Mason** and his wife **Johanna (Quiggly) Mason**. The similar names for both the couples make for some real difficulties in sorting out the families!

Charles' and **Johanna's** daughter, **Margaret** (recorded as 'Mary' on the shipping record), aged 25 at her father's death, and illiterate, was the one who gave the information for his Death Certificate. She was born in Tipperary, and appears as a baby in the shipping records of the *China* before the ship sailed. For **Charles'** death certificate also, in 1865, she was still **Margaret Mason** — marrying **Michael Walsh** at nearby Patricks Plain three years later, in 1868 (MC 3123).

Charles and **Johanna Mason** were, according to **Charles'** death certificate, married in 1838 in Cahir, Tipperary not long before they boarded the *China*. On arrival in Australia on 19 December 1839 they were assigned, as were our family, to **William Bucknell**, though they went to Bucknell's Newtown property, rather than to his place at Paterson's River, where the

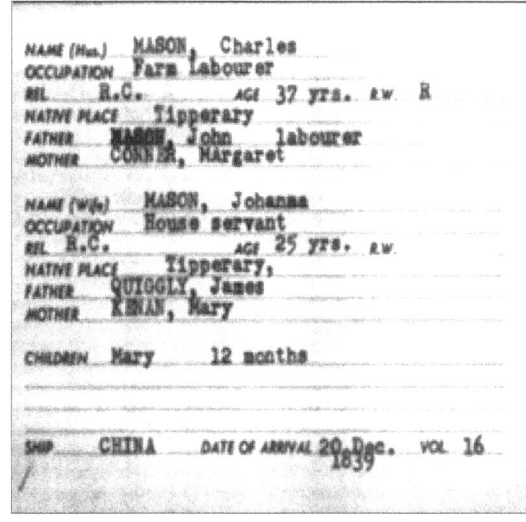

Charles & Joanna Mason's record on the China

others were allocated. **Charles'** death certificate in 1865 records Charles as being 67 years old, a carpenter, with parents '**John Mason**, Farmer, and **Margaret O'Connor**', as does **John Mason II**'s death certificate, so **John II** and **Charles** are definitely brothers. That they each married a **Johanna Quiggly** is extraordinary, but appears to be true. **Charles'** wife **Johanna** was said to be 25 on landing in the *China*, so she would have been born in about 1814, and he in 1798.

Birth records of Charles and Johanna Mason's children

Reference	Name	First Name	Father	Mother
1838, Ireland No record	Mason	Margaret	Charles	Joanna
1841/1414 133/1841	Mason	Mary	Charles	Joanna
V1843/135 134/1843	Mason	John	Charles	Johanna
V1844/1579 62/1844	Mason	Bridget	Charles	Johanna
V1847/3570 64/1847	Mason	Ellen	Charles	Johanna
V1848/212 66/1848	Mason	Johannah	Charles	Johannah
V1851/2180 68/1851	Mason	Charles	Charles	Johannah
V1854/62 71/1854	Mason	Janet	Charles	Johanna

Death Record of Charles Mason

DC Reference	Name	First Name	Father	Mother	Died
004580/1865	Mason	Charles	John	Margaret	Morpeth

Patrick Arthur Mason: b. c1825 d. 1899

M Catherine Hanlon 1856 d 1914

Extensively researched by Patricia Keevers

The record for **Patrick Arthur Mason** is not consistent or very credible. He claims for himself that he was a son of the migrating **John Mason II**, that he was born in 1825 in Ireland, and was omitted from the list of incoming migrants on the *China* in 1839. He certainly appears in no records to support this claim.

He was on his deathbed and in an asylum for the homeless when he repeated those claims. Neither **John Mason**'s nor his brother **Charles'** record on the *China* include **Patrick**, nor does he appear in the full list of immigrants from Ireland. He also claims his mother was a Matilda Baynes, a name that does not appear anywhere in our history. He claimed to be from Cork, but our family is all from Co Tipperary.

However, his argument is reinforced by it being a **John Mason** who sponsored his wedding to **Catherine Hanlon** (from Co Monaghan) in 1856 in **Morpeth**, in the general area that our **John Masons** lived. **Patrick** also claimed on his deathbed to have been 60 years in the colony, which in 1899 matches the date of the *China* in 1839. His birthdate is harder to establish — if he was in fact 86 at his death in 1899, as the gaol records claim, he was born in 1813 (not 1825), so he was 26 on his arrival, and thus 43 at his marriage.

Wedding Record:

Reference	Name	First Name	Wife	Location
1565/1856	Mason	Patrick Arthur	Catherine Hanlon	Maitland

Patrick was a confectioner and a baker, but his police record shows him often drunk and disorderly, in debt, and deserting his wife and their growing number of children. The police report at his first desertion of **Catherine** and their children about ten years later describes him as '*50 years of age, 5 feet 8 inches high, fresh complexion, red hair, beard and moustache, gray eyes, an Irishman, a baker*'.

Transcript: 1873 NSW Police Gazette

*NSW. Police Gazette 26 March,1873 Deserting Wives and Families Services & Co. Arrest of **Patrick Arthur Mason***

*Charged with deserting. A Warrant has been issued by the Bathurst Bench for the arrest of **Patrick Arthur Mason**, charged with deserting his wife, leaving her without means of support. Supposed to have gone to the fishery on the Darling River, 70 miles from Bourke.*

Patrick owned Clonmore Hotel in Morpeth from 1856, as attested by the listing below, and was declared bankrupt from 22 Nov 1861 to 17 Feb 1863.

Patrick Arthur evidently took his own life in Rookwood asylum — at the time a place for homeless and destitute men, and there is little support to his claim of being part of this family. He is included because there IS a doubt, by **John Mason** sponsoring his wedding to **Catherine.**

His wife **Catherine** bore all his failings, had no dealings with him after 1873, and eventually owned her own greengrocer businesses in and around Sydney. She died in 1914, having also supported her children through further financial crises.

Insolvency index:

Name	Location	Occupation	Date	Ref	Final Date
Patrick Arthur Mason	Black Creek	Storekeeper	22 Nov 1861	5664	17 Feb 1863

Publicans (owners) listing:

Name	First Name	Property	Location	Date	Ref	Catalogue
Mason	Patrick Arthur	Clonmore Hotel	Morpeth District	2 Sep 1856	1302	NRS 14403(7/1507); Reel 1239

Descendants of Patrick Arthur Mason

1 **Patrick Arthur Mason** b. 1825 d. 1899 m. **Catherine Hanlon** 1856 Morpeth NSW d. 1914
  2 **Johanna Mason** b. 1857 Maitland, NSW BC. 7927
  2 **Pallister A Mason** b. 1858 Murrurundi NSW BC. 9761
  2 **Ann Mason** b. 1861 No birth record found
  2 **Catherine Mason** b. 1863 Patricks Plain NSW BC. 12034
  2 **Margaret Mason** b. 1865 Bathurst NSW BC. 5555
  2 **Helen (Ellen) Mason** b. 1867 Mudgee NSW BC. 12481
  2 **John Mason** b. 1872 BC. 6605 Bathurst NSW

Chapter 3

John Mason II and III
and their descendants

John Mason II: b. c1793 d. 10 Jan 1858

Son of John Mason I and Margaret O'Connor. Catholic
Lived in Cashel, County Tipperary, Ireland till his migration
m. Joanna Quigley of Cahir, Tipperary 1811 b. 1791 d. 1857
Father to six children — Mary, John III, Oliver, Johanna, Margaret, Daniel
Migrated to NSW on the China, arriving after 145 days, on 19 Dec 1839 with his wife and children
John's brother Charles Mason, Charles' wife Johanna, and their under-one-year-old daughter Margaret joined them, also on the China
Settled first in the Morpeth area as a labourer, then moved to Tamworth

John Mason II, born about 1793, was the father of the family group who migrated to Australia from Tipperary. His father had been a farmer in Cahir, and he lived in Cashel, 3½ miles east of Golden, where his two adult sons, **John III** and **Oliver**, lived and worked. The family story belongs with the next generation, but as the father of the group, his input to the decision to migrate must have been large.

John II came with his entire family, all Catholics — his wife **Joanna Quigley**, at 48, three sons and three daughters — **John, Oliver** and **Daniel,** and **Mary, Margaret** and **Johanna**, as well as his brother **Charles Mason**, his wife **Johanna** and baby daughter **Margaret**, to Australia on the *China* in December 1839. There were a great many other Tipperarians also on board the same vessel.

John Mason II at 46 was most unusually old for a migrant, as was his wife, at 48. They came from County Tipperary where (if our connection of records is correct), there were at least their parents **John Mason I** (d. 1787) and his wife **Margaret O'Connor.** Appalling conditions in Ireland at the time must have provided the initiative, but how they accumulated enough to victual themselves to the coast, and pay the £5 each towards the trip, is impossible to speculate.

Bounty payments were made in London to shipowners and businessmen. These were the amounts for the trip to Australia to which the £5 from each of the travellers was added.
  £38 for man and wife, less than 40 years old
  £19 for a single man or woman
  £10 children
    (John Birmingham's *Leviathan*).

It was an extremely brave decision to collect them all, in a starving Ireland, and migrate to an unknown land on the other side of the world. They had to victual themselves down the River Suir to the embarkation point of Waterford, on the Irish south coast, onto the ship *China* for a trip that eventually lasted 145 days, to Botany Bay. They were 'assisted migrants', and thus the cost of their long sea trip was *only* £5 each — a great deal of money for a large family to find in those days. But they made it, on a small sailing ship, smaller than most of the current Sydney ferries, and very much overcrowded.

With a total lack of letters or diaries for this not-particularly-well-educated family, we have no personal information on their lives before they arrived in NSW, and must largely rely on the local history of the places they lived.

Golden — the home of the two adult sons of **John Mason II** — is still a picturesque village with typically Irish architecture and probably not more than 100 houses. The town centre is colourful and old, but the newer, much richer houses on the outskirts demonstrate a more luxurious way of life. The mill has gone, so has the poverty, and this is now quite a prosperous village. In 2014, it had changed considerably, based on the quite luxurious mansions outside the village. It's now in a totally different economic class to that seen by the 19th century population.

Golden held, when this writer visited in the 1980s, the original store, the now-defunct mill, an old stone bridge and tower on the River Suir attesting to slightly greater prosperity earlier, and a monument to courage and conflict on the site at the time of 'The Troubles', the history of which the area is inordinately proud.

Colourful Golden is no longer poverty-stricken in 2014. Large, luxurious mansions exist outside the town.

The **Masons** left, in 1839, an Ireland not quite descended into the savage, traumatic famine (officially dated later, from 1845) which, together with migration to Australia and the US, so very much reduced the Irish population in the 19th century.

The males of the family were employed directly from the boat as labourers, and the older girls as house servants to a Mr Harper, in Sydney. The males went up to settler **William Bucknell**'s property at Paterson River, north of Maitland and Morpeth at £21 per year with rations — the standard rate — taking the youngest two, **Margaret** and **Daniel**, 14 and 5, the older girls staying in Sydney. **William Bucknell** also employed **Charles Mason, Michael Power,** and **Cornelius Ryan**, all of Tipperary off the ship, and Cornelius' sister **Ellen** followed her brother. **Bucknell** was related to the explorer/politician **William Wentworth,** and had some land grants allocated to him. We do not hear later, though, of any contact between (or work done for) **Bucknell**'s properties by 'our' family, so we don't know how they lived or worked. The **Masons** and related **Mahers** formed a nucleus of the mutual community support system existing in the Hunter River district, for their respective families over the next (probably difficult) years, through births, christenings, deaths and marriages.

The oldest, 26 year old daughter **Mary,** a housemaid (who could not read or write), and 16 year old **Johanna**, a child's maid (who could read and write), defined themselves as being from Cashel, Tipperary. They earned £16 and £10 per year respectively, with rations, the difference being due to their ages.

Despite **Oliver** and **John** having (we believed) worked in the mills in Golden, Tipperary, they claimed when they landed here to be *agricultural labourers* — evidently this was seen to be what was required in this very new land. We did discover that **John Mason I**, their grandfather, had been a farmer in Tipperary, and it is more than probable that the boys did have farming skills. Certainly **Oliver** later proved to have business skills. They needed farming skills to advance as they did in this country.

John Mason II died in 1858, defined by his grandson **Charles Mason** as a farmer in 1885 (27 years after his death) on the death certificate of **John II**'s son **Oliver Mason**.

Chapter 3: John Mason II and III and their descendants

John Mason III: b. c1816 d. 12 Oct 1879

1ST SON OF JOHN MASON II AND MARGARET O'CONNOR. CATHOLIC
AGE 23, AN ASSISTED MIGRANT WHEN HE MIGRATED ON THE CHINA, ARRIVING 19 DEC 1839 WITH HIS WHOLE FAMILY.
BROTHER TO MARY, OLIVER, JOANNA, MARGARET AND DANIEL.
WORKED IN GOLDEN, TIPPERARY, UNTIL HIS MIGRATION
M1. MARY HICKEY, BORN IN IRELAND, 1850 BC V1850379 96 /1850, B.1827 D. 21 JUN 1860. FOUR CHILDREN
M2. MARIA MAHER, BORN IN IRELAND, 3 AUG 1863 B. C1845 D. 27 MAY 1905 TAMWORTH. FIVE CHILDREN
LIVED IN THE MORPETH AREA UNTIL ABOUT 1870, WHEN MOST OF THE FAMILY MOVED TO TAMWORTH.
DIED 12 OCT 1879, DC 173973 IN TAMWORTH. DC (BY WIDOW MARIA MAHER) SAYS BORN ENGLAND!
BURIED TAMWORTH CEMETERY, ROW BB42-6, IN FAMILY PLOT

Records indicate that **John Mason II**, father of **John III** and **Oliver Mason**, was the son of **John Mason** and **Margaret O'Connor**, of Cahir. Information (as yet unverified) has been given to us that if there is money on the woman's side of a marriage in Ireland, the male takes the women's surname, which may mean that **John** and **Margaret O'Connor** *were* married. The children in this case, however, are all named **Mason**, and there is little evidence of wealth in the migrating family.

The *China* left Waterford on Ireland's south coast on 28 July 1839, with **John Mason II's** family, including **John Mason II's** brother **Charles Mason** and his wife **Johanna** with their baby daughter **Margaret**. **Patrick O'Farrell** attempts to shed light on the experience that was an emigrant ship in the 1830s to the end of the century, but what letters survive are by nature those of literate, better educated, less impoverished emigrants, giving little detail of life of the poor, southern Irish catholic in steerage.

On 19 Dec 1839, on the vessel *China*, the complete **Mason** family landed in Sydney from Ireland — parents and six offspring aged between perhaps 7 and 26 (ages are, to say the least, indefinite). From these assisted migrants — Irish, landless labourers, largely uneducated, though the two adult boys could read and write — has stemmed a prolific and very diverse family, but with no written records for the early days except official ones. **Oliver Mason** showed already considerable signs of business acumen, though the evidence is sketchy.

John Mason III was employed by **William Wentworth Bucknell** of Patersons River from the boat at £21 per year plus rations (the standard rate) and went straight out to Maitland with most of the family, the sisters finding employment in Sydney and staying behind. By 1850 he was living in Swan Reach, and in Morpeth and Dunmore in 1854, recording his occupation as 'Labourer and Settler' — which carefully defined him as never having been a convict. By 1857 he defined himself as a farmer, as also in 1870 in faraway Singleton. He died in 1879 (DC 2213/1878)

Since **John I** (their grandfather) was listed as a farmer in Tipperary, one could presume that therefore the family had some farming skills, which they seemed to utilise when they arrived in the Morpeth area, and later in Tamworth.

Margaret and **Daniel**, listed as aged 14 and 7, were not allocated, but went with their parents to the Morpeth area — **Paterson's River**. **John II's** brother **Charles Mason** was also allocated to **William Bucknell**, to another of his properties, with wages of £21 and rations.

The **Mason** family settled in the flood plain of Phoenix Park. This flood plain may well have been a pull for them to settle there, but they actually had no choice in their placement, once having been 'disposed' off the ship to **William Bucknell** for work at his property, *Brecon*. We know little to nothing of where and how they lived in the period from their arrival in December 1939 to their departure for Tamworth in 1870, except that they seemed to be together, and left only officially-required information found in the publicly recorded births, deaths and marriages. Dunmore House, a major property in that valley, owned by a Scotsman, Dunmore Lang, had employment opportunities of its own, and was not infrequently used as an address by our family. Dunmore had been intended to be worked by Scottish protestants, but the **Mason family** and many on the ship with them were *Irish Catholics* - suggesting that perhaps the Irish Catholic presence was strong. The name Phoenix Park was the name of a popular park area in Dublin, and was given to the area where most of the settlers seemed to be. The sponsors of baptisms and marriages as recorded in the Newcastle Library Parish Registers also seem to have a predominance of Irish Catholics. There is, however, an absence of information on **William**

Bucknell's estate of *Brecon*, to which the family and others on board the *China* were assigned, except that Bucknell's venture failed very shortly after the Masons arrived.

John Mason III was one of the first to get himself settled. In 1850 he married (MC 379, Vol 96), the quite newly-arrived Irish-born Mary Hickey, daughter of Conor Hickey of Windermere, NSW, in the Catholic Church at East Maitland — the same area where the family had settled. This ceremony was witnessed by John's brother Oliver Mason and Mary's cousin (daughter of Tom Hickey, brother of Conor Hickey) Johanna Hickey. John was said to be 23 when he arrived, so now he was 34, and Mary was 21. His occupation was given as labourer/settler.

The sponsorship network, as with Oliver, who acted as sponsor many more times, is indicative of relationships in the very Irish Maitland area. Whilst at Hinton, John Mason sponsored the birth of his nephew Patrick Tighe on 21 Feb 1847 (son of his sister Joanna Mason and Charles Tighe) and his first wife's relative (possibly nephew) Thomas Hickey on 18 July 1858.

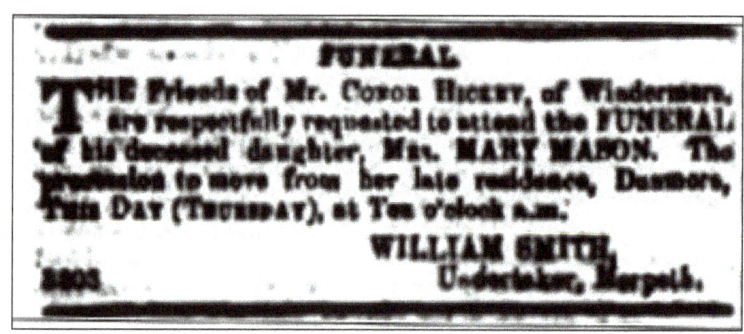

Mary (Hickey) Mason bore John four children, and died at only 33, on 21 Jun 1860 (Dunmore Landsale records) when they were still were living at Dunmore at that stage. Mary and John's four children came to Tamworth with John.

John Mason III remarried three years later on 3 Aug 1863. John was 47 years and old and his new wife Maria Maher was only about 19 and illiterate.

"The Friends of Mr. Conor Hickey, of Windermere, are respectfully requested to attend the FUNERAL of his deceased daughter, Mrs. Mary Mason. The procession to move from her late residence, Dunmore, This day (Thursday), at Ten o'clock a.m. William Smith, Undertaker, Morpeth" Sydney Morning Herald 1860

Widows

The surprisingly long list of long-surviving widows is astonishing in one family.
This list is of Mason women who comprehensively outlived their husbands.
Possession of assets doesn't seem to be a strong element in this list.
Perhaps it's just that the Mason males had the sense to marry strong women!

Maria (Maher) Mason, wife of John, **26** years a widow
Mary (Mason) Sheridan, wife of James **15** years a widow
Annie (Bezant) Mason, wife of Oliver Peter, **22** years a widow
Joanna (Mason) Tighe, wife of Charles, **35** years a widow
Priscilla (Smith) Mason, wife of William, **33** years a widow
Jane (Purtell) Mason, wife of James, **21** years a widow
Win (Fletcher) Mason, wife of Clem, concert pianist, **31** years a widow
Sarah (Rowling) Creevey, wife of John Creevey, **35** years a widow
Nora (Dunn) Mason, 2nd wife of Oliver, son of the migrating Oliver, **11** Years a widow
Thelma (Davies) Mason, wife of Eric Mason of Wollongong, died 1999, **31** years a widow (married Richard Hogan 1972-1981)
Emily Maude (Smith) Mason, wife of Dan Mason in Lismore, **15** years a widow

Descendants of John Mason III and Mary Hickey

1 **John Mason III** b. 1816 Golden, Tipperary, IRL. d. 12 Oct 1879 Ref 9059/1879 Occupation Labourer/ Settler. m1. **Mary Hickey** 14 Jan 1850 Swan Reach, Catholic Church, East Maitland, Witnesses **Oliver Mason**, East Maitland, **Johanna Hickey** [daughter of **Tom Hickey**, brother of **Conor Hickey**] b. 1827 Tipperary? d. 21 Jun 1860 Morpeth NSW
    2 **John Mason IV** b. 10 Dec 1852 BC 1080 Vol 70. d. 1858 DC 4071/1858 Maitland
    2 **Cornelius Mason** b. 2 Aug 1854 BC 1128 Vol 71. Morpeth d. 18 Sep 1934, Armidale m. **Janet Mitchell** 1 Jul 1878 MC 2213/1878 Cameron's Creek, Armidale. b. 1857 Armidale NSW d. 9 Jul 1933 Armidale NSW
        3 **Matilde Mary Mason** b. 5 Oct 1879 BC 0853, Armidale d. 5 Oct 1964 Neringah Home of Peace, Wahroonga NSW m. **Percival Charles Drew** 1905 Armidale, b. 1870 Armidale d. 21 Dec 1953 State Hospital, Lidcombe NSW
        3 **William George Mason**. Changed his name to **Thomas Mitchell Mason** b. 1881 BC 24360/1881 at Walcha (66km from Armidale) d. 24 Apr 1970 Armidale & New England Hospital, Armidale. m. **Mary Barry** 1905 near her home at Armidale
    2 **Matilda Mason** b. and d. <1857 Recorded on BC as Johanna Mason, b 1857
    2 **Johanna Mason** b. 23 Oct 1857 Windermere, near Lochinvar NSW Ref 8509/1857 registered Mait land. Witness Honora Hickey d. 20 Nov 1930 pulmonary tuberculosis, Coast Hospital Auxiliary, Randwick. M. **William Henry Hill** 28 May 1881 Sydney. Ref 731 / 1881 b. 18 Aug 1858 Pitt Town NSW d. 28 Sep 1888 Cholera, at his home Eden St, St Leonards [son of Henry Jacob Hill and Louisa Harvey]
        3 **William Hill** b. 1882 St Leonards. Ref 9335/1882
        3 **Edith Hill** b. 1884 Redfern Ref 9934/1884 d. 1964 Ref 30894/1964 m. **Frederick Mashford** 1902 St Leonards MC 7619/1902 d. 1946 Mosman NSW
        3 **Emily Hill** b. 1886 Sydney BC 470/1886 d. 23 Mar 1956 Newington State Hospital, Newington m. **John (Jack) Crighton** 1908 Chatswood d. 1955 Parramatta
        3 **John Hill** b. 1888 St Leonards BC 12931/1888 d. 1907
        3 **Arthur Edward Hill** b. 1889 d. 1969 Mater Hospital Crows Nest m. **Olive Irene Jahns** 1916 b. 1895 Tamworth d. 1956

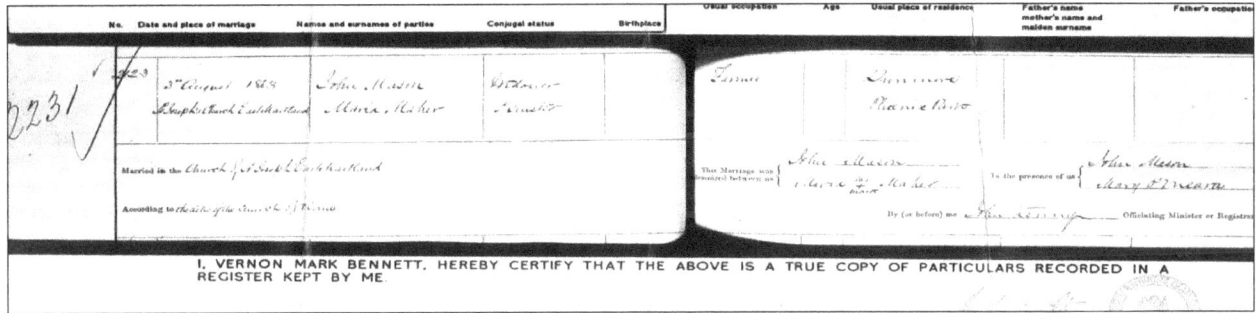

Marriage record of John Mason and Maria Maher, 3 Aug 1863, he a widowed Farmer of Dunmore, she (illiterate) of Phoenix Park

Children of John Mason III and second wife Maria Maher

1 **John Mason III** b. 1816 d. 12 Oct 1879 m1. **Mary Hickey** 14 Jan 1850 b. 1827 d. 21 Jun 1860 Morpeth m2. **Maria Maher** 3 Aug 1863 MC 379, Vol 96. b. 1844, d. 27 May 1905. Buried Tamworth Row BB42-6
    2 **Oliver Peter Mason** b. 29 Jun 1864 Morpeth d. 12 Apr 1935 BC 10971/1864 m. **Annie Bezant** 23 Apr 1905 b. 11 Jan 1862 d. 26 Dec 1957
    2 **Patrick P Mason** b. 20 April 1866 Morpeth BC 10986/1866 d. 17 May 1881 at only 15 years of age. Buried Tamworth Row BB42-75
    2 **Dennis (Dan) Mason** b. 7 May 1868 Patricks Plain BC 14785/1868 d. 10 Aug 1932 m. **Emily Maude Smith** 1893 b. 1871 d. 9 Apr 1947
    2 **William John Mason** b. 7 Aug 1870 Patricks Plain BC 15494/1870 d. 11 Jan 1935 m. **Priscilla Ann Smith** 25 Apr 1898 b. 24 Aug 1878 d. 23 Dec 1968
    2 **Arthur Edmund Mason** b. 29 Apr 1872 Morpeth d. 9 Sep 1939 m. 14 Nov 1917 **Maude Bailey** b. 9 Aug 1893 d. 25 Dec 1974

John III 's second wife **Maria Maher** was born 1844, so was 19 at her marriage. He was probably 42. She came out on the *Northumberland* with her brother **Denis Maher** and his wife **Margaret Boland** in 1862. **Denis** was born in 1830 in Thurles, Ireland (where **Maria** was also born) and died in a shunting accident on the railway in 1889. His daughter, **Florence Maher**, became **Sister Zita**, and died in 1939, but did have contacts with some of **John**'s brother **Oliver's** descendants.

That they stayed for 30 years in the lush area to which they were allocated — the Hunter River near Maitland / Morpeth / Dunmore / Phoenix Park — says their standard of living was acceptable to them. There they married and produced many children, who assisted the descendant families in their move to Tamworth in 1870. **Maria** died 27 May 1905, outliving her husband by some 26 years. According to family lore, she was an alcoholic in her later years and when her son **Arthur Edmund Mason** (her carer) left her to go on his honeymoon, she promptly drank herself to death.

The family's last stay before moving to Tamworth seems to have been in Morpeth, a river port on the Hunter established by Lt. Close in 1821. By the time the family moved to the district, Lt Close had also built himself a manor house and an avenue of trees to the St James Church, built in 1838 as a result of a vow made during the Peninsula Wars. Some town houses had been built around Queen's Wharf, and the Courthouse was built in 1862.

In about 1870 the families moved out to Tamworth, and we have no idea what living conditions were like there, Tamworth's surge of development being in its infancy. Their father, **John Mason II**, died in 1858, defined by his grandson **Charles Mason** in 1885 (well after the father's death) as a farmer on the death certificate of **John II**'s son **Oliver Mason**. The youngest sons, **William** and **Arthur** seem to have been born in Tamworth.

These houses may have been of the type lived in originally by the Mason clan, either on their arrival or later. The illustration on the right is considered to be a worker's house, of slab and other construction, with probably bark roofs — the corrugated iron shown here did not begin here till 1850s/1860s. These cottages are preserved in Castle Hill, Sydney.

John III died in Tamworth on 12 Oct 1879 at the age of 64, and is buried in the family plot at Tamworth General cemetery where most of the family lie. **Maria** was the (somewhat misinformed) informant at his death — she said her *Irish* husband was from England, that she didn't know his mother's name, that he was 67, thus 27 years old when they arrived in Australia and that he had lived here 52 years (which also calculates that he arrived here at 27). Our records show him to be at most 23 when he arrived.

Birth records of John Mason III's and Maria (Maher) Mason's children

BC Reference	Name	First Name	Father	Mother	Place	Died
10971/1864	Mason	Oliver P	John	Maria	Morpeth	1935
10986/1866	Mason	Patrick P	John	Maria	Morpeth	1881
14785/1868	Mason	Dennis	John	Maria	Patricks Plain	1932
15494/1870	Mason	William	John	Maria	Patricks Plain	1935
?/1872	Mason	Arthur E	John	Maria	Not Listed	1939

John Mason III's and Maria (Maher) Mason's death records, buried at Tamworth

DC Reference	Name	First Name	Father	Mother	Died
9059/1879	Mason	John	John	Unknown [Joanna Quigley]	Tamworth
6838/1905	Mason	Maria	John ?	Nora ?	Tamworth

Sacred to the memory of Mary Hickey, the beloved wife of John Mason. Daughter of Conor Hickey of Windermere, formerly of Borrisoleigh County Tipperary, Ireland, who died 22 June 1869, 33 years.
Requiescat in pace.
This is also the burying place of Conor Hickey and family

In loving memory of our dear parents Maria Mason who died May 27th 1905 Aged 58 years
John Mason who died Oct 12th 1879 aged 64 years.
Also Patrick Mason, beloved son of the above, who died May 17th 1881, aged 15 years.
Also Oliver Peter, beloved husband of Annie Mason, who died April 12th 1935, aged 70 years.
R.I.P.

Maria (Maher) Mason: b. c1845 d. 27 May 1905 and her family

2ND WIFE OF JOHN MASON III
M. JOHN MASON III 3 AUG 1863 B. 1816 D. 12 OCT 1879
SISTER TO DENIS MAHER B. C1830 D. 1889
AUNT TO DENIS' MANY CHILDREN D. 1905

Researched by Robyn Mason

John III's second wife **Maria Maher's** brother, **Denis Maher** and his wife **Margaret Boland**, came to Australia together on the *Northumberland* in 1862. Born in Thurles, Ireland (also **Maria's** birthplace). **Denis** died in a shunting accident on the railway in 1889. His daughter, **Florence**, became **Sister Zita**, dying in 1939, and did have contacts with some of **John's** brother **Oliver's** descendants.

The Maher family were prolific — though they don't seem to be exact in recording dates. **Denis'** children were numerous and **Maria** produced five.

The Maher family
Back row: unknown, Mary, Malcolm Vincent, Lena, Nora
Front row: Denis and Nora Maher with unknown child.
In Tamworth in the late 19th century

Death certificate of John Mason III
Maria (Maher) Mason was informant on her husband John Mason III's death certificate. John died 12 Dec 1879. Maria claims one male child deceased, of whom we know nothing, and says her Irish husband is from England! She also doesn't know his mother's name.

Denis and Maria's father, John Maher (also illiterate), left a handwritten Will, leaving his estate to Denis Maher, 'for his absolute use and benefit'. The 'interest arising from the investment of £400.06.06' was left 'in four equal proportions' to his daughters, Maria (Maher) Mason (age 33 when he died), Colleen Tobin (26), Ellen McMahon (24), and Nora Bowe (20)

Descendants of John Maher, father of Maria (Maher) Mason

1 **John Maher** b. 29 Aug 1812? Nenagh, Ireland d 15 Oct 1878. m. **Honora (Nora) Hogan** d. 4 May 1873
  2 **Denis Maher** b. 1846 Thurles, Tipperary d. 18 Sep 1918. Killed in shunting accident on railway. Buried Sandgate Cemetery Newcastle DC 1918/11413 m. **Margaret Boland** West Maitland NSW, age 24.
    3 **Kate Maher** b. 1871
    3 **Dennis Maher** b. 1873
    3 **Honora Maher** b. 1876
    3 **Ann Maher** b. 1878
    3 **Andrew Maher** b. 1881
    3 **Patrick Maher** b. 1885
    3 **Mary T Maher** b. 1886
    3 **Josephine I Maher** b. 1888
    3 **Matthew V Maher** b. 1890
    3 **Florence (Sister Zita) Maher** b. 1892 BC 25087/1892 Newcastle d. 17 Jun 1939 age 47 DC 9039/1939
    3 **3 males deceased**
  2 **Maria Maher** b. 1844, Thurles, Tipperary d. 27 May 1905 Tamworth. m. **John Mason III** 3 Aug 1863 Singleton, NSW. b. 1816 Golden, Tipperary, IRL. d. 12 Oct 1879 Tamworth DC 9059/1879 [son of **John Mason II** and **Joanna Quigley**]
    3 **Oliver Peter Mason**, b. 29 Jun 1864 d. 12 Apr 1935
    3 **Patrick P Mason** b. 20 Apr 1866, d. 17 May 1885
    3 **Dennis (Dan) Mason** b. 7 May 1868, d. 10 Aug 1932
    3 **William John Mason** b. 7 Aug 1870, d. 11 Jan 1935
    3 **Arthur Edmund Mason** b 29 Apr 1872 d. 9 Sep 1939
  2 **Catherine Maher** m. Tobin? b. 1852 Twin with Ellen
  2 **Ellen Maher** m. McMahon b. 1852
  2 **Honora Maher** m. Bowe b. 1854
  2 **Michael Maher** b. 1856

Oliver Peter Mason: b. 29 Jun 1864 d. 12 Apr 1935

FIRST SON OF JOHN MASON III AND MARIA MAHER
M. ANNIE BEZANT / BIZANT 1905 B. 11 JAN 1862 D. 26 DEC 1957
BROTHER TO PATRICK, DAN, WILLIAM, ARTHUR
BROUGHT UP YOUNGER BROTHER ARTHUR WHEN HIS FATHER DIED IN 1879

Children of Oliver Peter Mason

1 **Oliver Peter Mason** b. 29 Jun 1864 Dunmore NSW BC. Morpeth 10971/1864 d. 12 Apr 1935 DC. 7880/1935 Buried Tamworth Row BB42-6 m. **Annie Bezant** 23 Apr 1905 Tamworth. MC 10971 Witness brother **Arthur Mason** Tamworth Grave record. **Annie** was the sole beneficiary of **Oliver Peter Mason**'s will. [daughter of **Matthew Bizant** and **Ellen O'Connor**]
  2 **Mary Mason** b. 1908 Tamworth d. 1 Feb 1929 Aged 21. Marius St, Tamworth

---

Birth record of Oliver Peter Mason

Reference / Birth	Name	Father	Mother	Location
10971/1864	Mason Oliver	John	Maria	Morpeth

Oliver Peter was born in Dunmore, near Morpeth, in 1864, sponsored by his father **John Mason III**'s sister **Mary Mason** (who called him Alfred Peter in the documents). He moved with the family to Tamworth in about 1870, and lived there the rest of his life. Quite different from other males in his family, he took his responsibilities as oldest brother seriously, and when their father **John Mason** died in 1879, brought up his youngest brother, **Arthur Edmund**, eight years younger than himself. He worked as a painter in Tamworth, and later as a builder, quite successfully it would seem. His Probate (206252) gives evidence of properties he owned in Tamworth – 251, 253, 255 Marius Street, 202-204 Marius St, and 255 Hill Street - all brick cottages, described at the time of his death in Probate as '4 rooms, kitchen and offices'. He was obviously a man of property.

Oliver married **Annie Bezant** in 1905, at the age of 39, the ceremony witnessed by his young brother **Arthur**. Her parents were Austrian **Matthew Bizant** and Irish **Ellen (O'Connor) Bizant** (the spelling varies), from County Cork. The large family arrived in Australia in 1849 on the *Phoenician*, married in 1855 and roamed the country looking for gold. **Matthew Bizant** died at his daughter's residence in Marius Street Tamworth on 26 Dec 1917 at age 87. **Matthew's** wife **Ellen** died on 22 Jun 1918 at 86, and they are buried together in Tamworth General Cemetery.

Tamworth Cemetery Record for Matthew and Ellen Bizant

Surname	Name	Died	Age	Relationship	Religion
Bizant	Matthew	26 Dec 1917	87	Husband to Ellen, Father to Annie	RC
Bizant	Ellen	22 Jun 1918	86	Wife to Matthew Mother to Annie	RC

One of **Oliver Peter**'s responsibilities was his mother, **Maria (Maher) Mason**. Knowing she had a real drinking problem, he never gave her any money after his father died in 1879. But when he went away on his honeymoon, after his marriage to **Annie Bizant** in 1905, he did, and she promptly drank herself to death. **Oliver** and **Annie**'s only child **Mary** was born in 1908, dying at the age of 21 in 1929 with a spine problem.

When **Annie**'s husband **Oliver Peter** died in 1935 (Probate 206252), Annie moved in with her younger sister **Mary Vidler Bizant**, (1872-1957) widow of **Thomas Vidler** (married 1895). They lived together for 22 years, moving later to the nursing home Nazareth House, and are buried together at Tamworth cemetery, having both died in 1957.

Wedding Certificate Oliver and Annie Mason

MC	Husband	Name	Wife	Name	Place	Date
5317/1905	Mason	Oliver P	Bizant	Annie	Tamworth	23 Apr 1905

Death certificates Oliver and his daughter Mary Mason

Name	First Names	Died	Age	Place	Religion
Mason	Mary Agnes	1 Feb 1929	21	NSW	RC
Mason	Oliver Peter	14 Apr 1935	70	NSW	RC

Annie Mason, wife of Oliver Peter Mason, lived with her sister Mary Vidler as widows for 22 years to their death in 1957. Buried together.

Mary Mason, daughter of Oliver Peter Mason and Annie Bizant, died at the age of 21.

Dennis Michael (Dan) Mason: b. 7 May 1868 d. 10 Aug 1932

3RD SON OF JOHN MASON III AND MARIA MAHER, SPONSORED BY JAMES AND JOANNA MASON AT HANNAHTON
BROTHER OF OLIVER PETER, PATRICK, WILLIAM, AND ARTHUR E MASON.
MARRIED EMILY MAUD SMITH 1893 MC 84785 IN EAST MAITLAND B. 1871 D. 1947
PARENTS OF ONE SHORT-LIVED SON, ARTHUR B. 1900 D. 1902
COMMUNITY STALWART IN LISMORE
OWNER OF A LARGE MENSWEAR SHOP IN LISMORE — MASON & HAGUE
PROBATE 183650
RESIDED 124 CATHCART STREET LISMORE FOR MOST OF HIS LIFE

Researched by Robyn Mason

Born at Patricks Plain, registered at Singleton, on 7 May 1868, of 'parents of moderate means' (*Lismore Star*), Dan was the most successful of this generation of Masons. **Dan Mason** and **Emily Maud (Maud) Smith** married in 1893 — he was 25, she was 22 — in Armidale, where she had been born. They they later settled in Lismore, living at 124 Cathcart St, Lismore most of their lives.

Between 1910 and 1932 **Dan** and his wife were devoted to church and orphanages. All this energy may have been related to the fact that he and his wife only had one son, **Arthur**, born in 1900, who died very young, in 1902.

Just before his move to the district (and, the dates would appear to indicate, soon after the birth and possibly death of his only son), he and his wife had a two-year world tour, 1900-1902, after selling his first shop in Armidale, moving then to Lismore. On his death, he left behind a store bearing his name — Mason & Hague. It was built in 1916 and was situated on Woodlark Street, Lismore. Twice during the 28 years he was in Lismore he toured England. (Some of these dates and periods are inherently inconsistent. All from *Lismore Star* which declared in a lengthy and fulsome piece that **Dan** was community-minded).

The premises of Dan Mason's Mason & Hague store, in Woodlark Street, Lismore.

> In Woodlark Street, Messrs Mason and Hague conducted a Men's mercers shop stocked with all that was best and fashionable at the time. Mr Mason used to spread himself writing verses extolling the excellence of Hague and Mason's ties and assuring the public of the comfort and durability of the firm's stock of trousers. Friendship with Mr Mason is a pleasing memory.

HG Peak (in Lismore 1909-1910) writing in 1984.

Wedding Certificate of Dan and Emily Maud Smith

Ref / Year	Husband	First Name	Wife	First Name	Place
1824 / 1893	Mason	Dennis M	Smith	Emily M	Armidale

Birth and Death Certificates of son Arthur Mason

Ref / Year	Name	Father	Mother	Place
BC 8843 / 1900	Mason	Arthur H	Maud	Sydney
DC 11904 / 1903	Mason	Arthur H	Maud	Tamworth

Chapter 3: John Mason II and III and their descendants

OBITUARY

MRS. E. M. MASON
The death occurred in Lismore on Friday of Mrs. Emily Maud Mason at the age of 77. Fifty years ago she married Daniel Mason, who predeceased her by 15 years. The late Mr. Mason established and conducted a mercery business in Lismore for many years, and actively participated in public affairs. Mrs. Mason also was prominent in charitable organisations in Lismore and district for many years.

Robyn Mason (**Dan**'s great-niece) has discovered shipping records that show that **Dan** and **Maud Mason** took another trip to the US, presumably as a holiday, on the *Ventura* leaving Australia on 12 April 1922. He is described as a store keeper, with **Oliver Mason** as contact, and **Maud** as a housekeeper, with Mrs Rac Bone (unknown to us) as contact.

Travelling with them was **Miss Lenore Hague**, a 15 year old student, listed as **Dan** and **Maud**'s adopted daughter. She was actually the daughter of **Dan**'s partner in Mason & Hague, and provided company for **Dan** and **Maud** during their journey.

Dan Mason's letter to his nephew Jack, son of William and Priscilla, much marked by Jack having treasured it in his wallet all his life, agreeing to Jack's request for a loan.

Dan was involved in the movement to get the railway to Lismore, to establish the St. Vincent's Hospital, and to establish the agricultural college.

In 1932, during the Depression, **Dan**'s nephew **Jack Mason** (son of **William** and **Priscilla Mason**) hit a very bad period, and worked up his courage enough to ask his successful and philanthropic uncle **Dan** for a loan for his family. **Dan**'s warm response, dated only a few months before his death, granted his request, and wished him and his brothers well. **Jack** treasured that letter all his life.

According to the *Lismore Star* on the occasion of his death on 10 Aug 1932, **Dan** had come to the Lismore area 30 years before, at the age of 28 after the death of his father **John**. (His father **John III** is buried in family plot in Tamworth, having died in 1879, grandfather **John II** died 1858, which would not appear to support this story.) **Dan** worked in general stores, and gradually acquired his own men's outfitter's mercery store. His young brother, **Arthur**, was the chief mourner at his funeral.

Dan's Will was probated (ref 183650), and it may well have been **Jack**'s request that motivated the clause in **Dan**'s Will, quoted verbatim below. His list of property distinguishes him from the rest of the family.

*Each of the children of my brothers **Arthur Edmund Mason** and **William John Mason**, who being sons attain the age of 21 years, and being daughters attain that age or marry, £250, to be paid asap after my death.*
*Balance to my wife **Emily Maud Mason** for her own sole use and benefit absolutely.*
Estate £27,862 – probate granted.

Family lore has had **Dan** (stupidly, in the minds of some) leaving his money to the church at his death. **Bob Mason**'s recollection is that he left his money to his wife, **Maud**, who left it to the church: a nice difference. It still caused quite a flurry in the family. One online service upgrading that £250 in 1932 to 2013 makes it $12,500! It is by no means sure though that the boys actually received it. **Vic,** son of **William Mason,** and **Bob,** son of **Arthur E Mason,** don't recall getting it, for reasons we don't know. Examination of Probate shows that in fact **Dan** gave significant bequests to various members of the church, hospitals, etc, but the bulk of his not-inconsiderable estate was unequivocally bequeathed to his wife **Emily Maud Smith**.

Dan was a valued member of many community organisations:
Top: (with the crazy hats) The Lismore Bowling Club in 1912-1913
(Dan in the centre of the middle row).
Bottom: An undated pic of the same group (hatless) with Dan at the second top.
Dan Mason was an office bearer of this group from its beginning in 1908. He was also vice president of the local choral musical group.

William (Will) Mason: b. 27 Aug 1870 d. 1935

SON OF JOHN MASON III AND MARIA MAHER
M. PRISCILLA ANN SMITH 25 APR 1898, REG SINGLETON, B. 1878 D. 1968
PARENTS OF ARTHUR, SHORT-LIVED ETHEL, VIC, JACK, ERIC, HILTON, AND BOB MASON
GRANDPARENTS OF MANY MASONS

Little is known of **Will Mason** as a person — only as a husband of **Priscilla**, and father of six sons. He was born in Armidale, but was living in Tamworth in 1870-71 according to electoral rolls. He worked on the railways, as a guard and later a driver, all his working life. He was born in Patrick's Plains (now Jerry's Plains), about 38km northwest of Singleton, as was his brother **Dan** two years earlier, both sons of **John III** and **Maria (Maher) Mason**. John III was listed on the electoral rolls as a 'farmer' in 1870.

A rare photo of all the Mason boys and their wives at the family home at 206 Chapel Road, Bankstown. Early 1960s.
L-R Cath (wife of Vic), Jack and Mella Mason, Thelma Davies (wife of Eric), Thelma Denny (wife of Hilton), Audrey and Bob Mason, Eric Mason, Vic Mason, and in front Hilton Mason with their mother Priscilla (Smith) Mason

Priscilla and William Mason's sons, Father William Mason, at top, then Vic, Jack, Eric, Hilton and young Bob. c.1932

Jack, Hilton, Vic and Bob Mason, with their mother, Priscilla (Smith) Mason
Late 1960s. No Eric.

Will's niece **Dorothy (Mason) Loveridge,** daughter of **Will's** young brother **Arthur,** recalls him as a quiet, sensitive man, moustached all his adult life, overpowered perhaps by his very strong wife **Priscilla.** She also said he made marvellous scones! One insight from niece **Dorothy** may be relevant: there has always, in **Priscilla**'s grandchildren's generation, been an acceptance of what has been known as 'the Mason look', from those six boys. From photos of **Arthur Edmund, Will**'s brother, it would appear that 'the Mason look' was confined to **Will**'s sons. Was it therefore rather a 'Smith' look, from **Priscilla**'s family?

Birth and death records for Ethel Mason

Ref / Year	Name	First Name	Father	Mother	Location
BC 18966/1900	Mason	Ethel R	William	Priscilla	Tamworth
DC 7357/1902	Mason	Ethel	William	Priscilla	

William and **Priscilla** married in Tamworth in 1898, where their children **Arthur** and **Ethel** were born. They lived at 15 Victoria Street Redfern, from the Electoral Rolls, in 1903-1915, and Erelton, West Terrace, Bankstown, before Prairie Vale Road, Bankstown in August 1923 at youngest son Bob's birth. **Will** was then 53 and **Priscilla** 45. Finally they moved to what their grandchildren see as 'the family home' at 206 Chapel Road Bankstown in about 1931, as the family grew up. The details of **Will**'s land ownership show details of his financial success in his early marital life. They show property in less than ¼-acre blocks. Thus his income from the Railway Department was respectable.

Will was, according to family lore, supported during the depression (after his retirement) by his son **Vic**, the only one who had a good job in an apprenticeship at Garden Island. No record has been found of **Will**'s military service during WWI, which suggests that the railways work saved him from needing to enlist. His wife **Priscilla** outlived him by 33 years.

Birth and death records for Will Mason

Ref / Year	Name	First Name	Father	Mother	Location
BC 15494/1870	Mason	William	John	Maria Maher	Patrick's Plains, Tamworth
DC 18870/1936	Mason	William	John	Maria	Burwood

Addresses for William and Priscilla Mason

Years	Names	Address	William's Occupation	Land details: properties owned by William Mason.
1909-1915	William and Priscilla Mason	15 Victoria Street, Redfern	Railway Guard	35¼ perches, Lots 6&7, Section I Dep Plan 2271, **Rockdale** Parish, St George, County Cumberland. Acquired between 1896-1900. Land Titles Office Record 298498, Register Book 1299
1916-1920	William and Priscilla Mason	Erelton, West Terrace, Central Bankstown	Railway Guard	32½ Perches, Lots 1&2, Section 3, DP4207, **Bexley**, Acquired between 1911 and 1915. Land Titles Office Ref. A82201, Register book 2440, Folio 100.
1921-1922	William and Priscilla Mason	Melford, Chapel Road, Bankstown	Railway Guard	
1925-1926	William and Priscilla Mason, Plus sons Victor Oliver and Arthur William Mason	Prairie Vale Rd, Bankstown	Railway Guard Electrical engineer Wool Classer	1r 8¼ perches, Lot 15 Section 3, DP 5626 **Bankstown**. Acquired between 1911 and 1915. Land Titles Office Reg A216886, Register 2549, Folio 133

Priscilla and William Mason and their children Arthur and Ethel. At Redfern about 1903, when Priscilla was 25.

Almost illegible, this stone records the death of William and Priscilla Mason. Together.

Priscilla Ann (Smith) Mason: b. 24 Aug 1878 d. 23 Dec 1968

DAUGHTER OF WILLIAM SMITH AND ANN (CARMODY, CALLINAN) SMITH
SISTER OF MARY ETHELINE SMITH, 1881-1951
M. WILLIAM MASON 25 APR 1898 B.1870 D. 11 JAN 1935
MOTHER OF ARTHUR, SHORT-LIVED ETHEL, VIC, JACK, ERIC, HILTON AND BOB

Priscilla Smith was born to **William Smith** and his wife **Ann (Carmody, Callinan) Smith** on 24 Aug 1878, at Bullawa Creek, 20km east of Narrabri. **Priscilla**'s birth certificate, registered on 21 Oct 1878, BC 1878 17519, at Narrabri, wrongly spells her name as *Precilla*. Her first born, **Arthur** was born only three months later — their marriage was hurried!

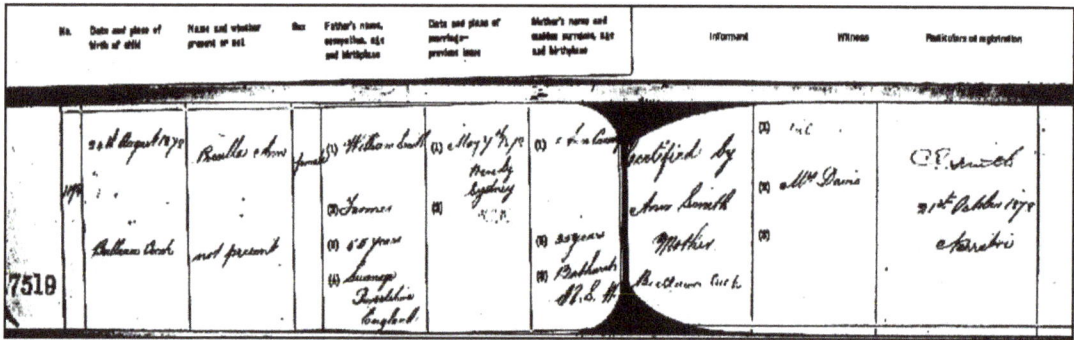

Priscilla's birth certificate, wrongly spelled Precilla

Priscilla was only 19 when she married 26 year old **William Mason**, in Singleton, NSW — ie away from the family in Tamworth, though we don't know the reason for this. There is a myth in the family that the doughty **Priscilla** rode a bullock dray from Bullawa Creek to Tamworth, which is a great story, but impossible to prove or disprove. **Dorothy (Mason) Loveridge** saw her as having her priorities firmly set as family first and house and other 'unimportant' things last. Certainly her six boys were the centre of her existence, and the (five, at least) daughters-in-law were largely considered not good enough for her sons.

Priscilla and **William Mason** had one daughter, **Ethel**, who died at less then two years old, and five sons, **Arthur**, **Victor**, **Jack**, **Eric** and **Hilton**, by 1913. Ten years later another son, **Bob**, arrived in August 1923, when **Priscilla** was 45 years old.

Priscilla, or **Prissi** as she was sometimes called in her early days, became **Grandma Mason** to her many grandchildren. She tried to keep all her sons, but particularly the 'baby' **Bob** out of the forces during World War II, but his big brother **Vic** encouraged him into the RAAF. An extremely strong character, she lived for her boys, but never did quite approve of the daughters-in-law, though in later years she was fascinated with the lives, loves, births, and travels of the series of girls who lived with her — whom she looked after to the extent of not going out at night and leaving *them*.

Dorothy (Mason) Loveridge recalls her **Aunt Priscilla**'s afternoon teas. As a mother of six, **Grandma Mason** tended to stay at home and be visited, rather than to visit, and **Dorothy**'s mother **Maude (Bailey) Mason**, wife of **Arthur Mason**, called many Sunday

Priscilla (Smith) Mason (right) and Maude (Bailey) Mason, wife of Arthur Mason — sisters-in-law

afternoons during the very busy period of owning their milk bar. Very few things changed at the **Mason** household from week to week — jelly and custard were invariably served (though others recollect it as trifle, with yesterday's cake); tea was made only once, in a large aluminium teapot having pride of place on the dining room table, and throughout what could frequently be a very long afternoon, only water was added. **Maude**, liking strong tea, chose to call early! Surviving the afternoon tea made her head feel 'as though she'd been on a long train ride'. The afternoon teas and the teapot survived into **Vic's** daughters **Jan** and **Helen's** recollection just before and during the period of their living with **Grandma Mason** during 1946/7. It was even recalled that entertainment was provided by teacup reading, provided by Mrs Hyland, a neighbour, wife of the owner of the produce store next door.

Priscilla outlived her husband **William** by 33 years. He died in 1935, just before his granddaughter, **Vic's** second daughter **Helen**, was born. **Priscilla** reached the age of 90 (of which she was inordinately proud), dying on 23 Dec 1968.

Priscilla had a younger sister, **Mary Etheline Smith**, born in 1881 in Narrabri, NSW. **Mary** married the confusingly-named **Ralph Smith**, and they lived in New Guinea together for a while, then as a widow she settled with her daughter **Irene** and Irene's husband **Robert Ward** at 79 Clarence St, Bankstown, not far from her sister **Priscilla**, dying at the age of 70 in 1951.

Children of Will and Priscilla Mason

1 **William John Mason** b. 7 Aug 1870 Hannahton (now Wittingham), reg. Singleton (BC Patricks Plains 15494/1870) d. 11 Jan 1935 Bankstown, m. **Priscilla Ann Smith** 25 Apr 1898 Tamworth, BC 4209 b. 24 Aug 1878 Bullawa Creek (Narrabri) NSW (BC 'Precilla') BC. 17519 in Narrabri. DC says Tamworth. d. 23 Dec 1968 Bankstown, NSW DC 12482/1969 [daughter of William Smith and Ann Carmody]

  2 **Arthur William Mason** b. 29 Jul 1898 Tamworth d. c.1968 England? US?

  2 **Ethel Mason** b. 1900 d. 1902 Diphtheria?

  2 **Victor Oliver (Vic) Mason** b. 3 Oct 1902 d. 6 Apr 1985 Tugun, Qld m. **Catherine Florence Hogan** 31 Oct 1931 Sydney. MC 14624. b. 6 Apr 1905 Brewarrina, NSW d. 30 Nov 1983 Tugun, Qld [daughter of John Bernard Hogan and Jessie Maude Douglass]

  2 **John Edward (Jack) Mason** b. 21 Oct 1905 Waterloo, NSW BC 1940/191390 d. 17 Jun 1976 Sydney. m. **Carmela (Mella) Macare** 2 Dec 1930 Bankstown NSW, Witnesses V Macare, WE Bell b. 11 Oct 1908 High St, Loanhead, Scotland. Reg in Lasswade Parish Scotland. d. 7 Mar 1981 [daughter of Rocco Macaro and Giacontina (Jean) Coia]

  2 **Eric Francis Donald Mason** b. 12 Jun 1910 BC 31220 at Waterloo d. 31 Jul 1968 6 Thurston Cres, Corrimal m. **Thelma Mary Davies** 6 Feb 1937 Punchbowl, NSW. Witness: brother Hilton Mason b. 17 Dec 1912. d. 25 Jul 1999 Killarney Vale Nursing Home [daughter of William John (James) Davies and Alice Gertrude Bullivant]

  2 **Hilton Matthew Mason** b. 24 Aug 1913 Redfern, NSW d. 16 Sep 1981 m. **Thelma Denny** 5 Oct 1940 St Saviors Church, Punchbowl b. 1 Dec 1912 Thelma says connections with Richard Howe, on mutiny ship Bounty. d. 23 Sep 1988 Hurstville, Sydney [daughter of Frederick and Lillian Denny]

  2 **Robert Joseph (Bob) Mason** b. 19 Aug 1923 Rickard Road, Bankstown NSW d. 10 Jun 1979 BC 13570 m. **Audrey Patricia Parker** 14 Feb 1948 b. 17 Oct 1925 d. 10 Oct 2014 [daughter of Lachlan Oswald Parker and Ivy Edith Morris]

William Smith: b. 1815 d. 29 Jul 1891
Father of Priscilla (Smith) Mason

SON OF JOHN AND ELIZABETH SMITH
BORN 1815 IN SWANAGE, DORSET, ENGLAND
M. LOUISA WHITE 1838 IN SWANAGE. 7 CHILDREN. B. 1819 D. 1882
M2. ANN CARMODY CALLINAN 1877 IN WAVERLEY, NSW B. 1841 D. 1916
HAD 2 CHILDREN, PRISCILLA AND MARY SMITH, WITH ANN CARMODY
DIED 29 JUL 1891 AT 75

By Robyn Mason

Robyn Mason has unearthed, researched and written some older history for **William Smith**, father of **Priscilla Smith**. Before he married **Ann Carmody Callinan** in 1877 and fathered two daughters, **William Smith** had a quite separate life in Dorset, England, with *another wife*. He had claimed to be a widower, but what he had in fact, was a living wife, **Louisa (White) Smith**, and seven children!

William was the son of **Elizabeth** and **John Smith**, was baptised on 6 Aug 1815 (we had believed his birth date to be 1823) in Swanage Dorset, England, and is listed as a 'dairyman' in the *Swanage Parish Records*. According to his death certificate **William** married **Louisa White** in Jersey, English Channel, in 1838, when he was 26. The 1841 census shows his parents, both 65, living at North Market Court, in Swanage, Dorset.

Louisa White was born on 26 Sep 1819 in Swanage (*Parish Records Swanage*), to **Lt. Colonel William Grove White** (a Companion of the Bath, CB) and his wife **Elizabeth Chinchen**, born in Cork, Ireland, in 1765. He won his CB award in 1799, in the war with Napoleon. At the time of **Colonel White's** death in 1844, his Will tells us that he and his wife **Elizabeth** were living at Newton Cottage, Sandwich, Swanage. (Sandwich changed its name to Swanage at about this time.)

By the 1851 Census **William Smith**, his wife, **Louisa** and their then four children were living in Swanage at their own residence. Their children are:

William aged 9, b. 1842
Francis F aged 6, b. 1845
Thomas aged 4, b 26 Apr 1846, d. 1 Jan 1926
Elizabeth W. aged 2 b. 1849
Frederick C. aged 10 months b. 1850
Twins George and Louisa Ann both b. & d. 1853
Rosalie L born 13 Nov 1858

These children's names also appear on **William Smith**'s death certificate. **Louisa**, her sisters **Elizabeth** and **Ann** as well as their brother **William** all appear in the 1843 Will of their father, **William Grove White**, which also mentions our **William** as his son-in-law.

By the 1861 census, **Louisa** was not living with **William** and was residing in Hyde Street, Winchester, Hampshire. She was financially self-sufficient and was shown as a 'Fund Holder', aged 38, living with her first son, **William** aged 19, whose profession was a photographic designer, and her daughter, **Rosalie L.** aged 2, born on 13 Nov 1858 at Alfred Place, Winchester, Hampshire. The name of the father was left blank on the Birth Certificate, as was his profession, so **William Smith** is not necessarily the father of **Rosalie**.

The split between **William** and **Louisa** probably happened just after the birth of **Rosalie**, since **William** and his three other sons and one daughter, presumably **Francis, Thomas, Elizabeth** and **Frederick** went to New Zealand in, we believe, 1859. They transferred to Quirindi NSW in 1875. He married **Ann Carmody Callinan** in Quirindi in 1877, when he was 62 and she 36, and produced **Priscilla** and **Mary Smith**. Certainly **Lt. Col. White** made his Will so that it was impossible for **William Smith** to access any of the quite-considerable inheritance he made available to his daughter **Louisa**.

By the 1871 census **Louisa Smith** was aged 50, claiming to be a widow and living in New Road, No.5 'Rose Cottage' Portsea, Portsmouth, with her daughter, **Rosalie L.** aged 12. It also stated that she was living from 'income from houses'. Her 1882 death certificate also states she was the 'wife of **William Smith**' at time of death, adding to the confusion.

William's death certificate in 1891 acknowledges one more child to **William** and **Louisa** — **Frederick Charles**, 41 at the time of the father's death, so born in 1850. He is not acknowledged anywhere else, though it is noticed that brother **Thomas** called one of his sons **Frederick**, suggesting a precursor carrying the name. Some scattered information seems to indicate that the existence of his first family is NOT a secret **William** kept all his life.

One of **William's** previous family made a successful business for himself in Australia. **Thomas,** his third son, began a mail and courier business on horseback centred on Narrabri. This developed into a respected heavier duty carriage service with big dray carts, and his death was written up in the *North Western Courier* of Narrabri. The press story after his death in January 1926 appears below.

THOMAS SMITH

At the age of 79 years Thomas Smith, one of the few remaining pioneers of the Narrabri district passed away in the private hospital on Friday, January 1st. Deceased was a well-known personage of the town and district, and was a most respected resident of the town. He was held in high esteem by the many people that knew him, and everyone regretted his death. His old associates have said that he was a good friend and was ever willing to assist anyone who needed help. In business he was courteous, and could be relied upn to carry out any business entrusted to him.

Deceased was born in Devonshire on April 6th., 1846, and while only a young lad left with his father and brothers and sisters for New Zealand, where they lived for a few years. At that time the Maori wars were in progress. He followed various occupations whilst in that country, and after a few years residence there the whole family came to Sydney in the year 1875, settling down for a time in Quirindi. They lived there for over five years, deceased marrying the daughter of the late John Foote, of Castle Mountain. In 1880 they settled in Narrabri, Mr. Smith taking a farm on Deep Creek. When the railway line was opened to Narrabri he opened up in business as a carrier and general forwarding agent, and for a number of years used to carry the mails from Narrabri West to Narrabri on horseback. The business grew, and he was given contract work for Wright Heaton and Co., Piggot and Martin, and other business places. With the assistance of his sons he conducted the business right up to the time of his death. A severe illness of a few months ago brought on an attack of bronchitis, and he was removed to the hospital where he died.

Two daughters and five sons are left to mourn the loss of a good father. They are Mrs. Foote (Narrabri), Mrs. Spice (Waratah) Thomas (Narrabri), Frederick (Sydney) William, George, and Arthur (Narrabri), and 16 grandchildren. His wife predeceased him by four years.

The remains were conveyed from the hospital to the residence, and then to the Church of England later proceeding to the cemetery. The funeral was largely attended, the burial service being conducted by Rev. Miller. Logan and Co conducted the funeral arangements.

We believe this is Thomas Smith (with the reins in his hands), and his father William Smith (leaning on a walking stick), both extracted to the left, on Thomas Smith's carrying dray in Narrabri. It would be the late 1880s. The kids (who may well be Thomas' own) seem to be making a holiday of it.

Descendants of William Smith

1 **William Smith** b. 1823 d. 29 Jul 1891 m1. **Louisa White**, b. 1819 d. 1882 m2. 7 May 1877 **Ann Carmody** b. 8 Nov 1841 d. 9 Nov 1916
[Children of William Smith and Louisa White]
   2 **William Smith** b. 1841
   2 **Francis Smith** b. 1844
   2 **Thomas Smith** b. 26 Apr 1846 d. 1 Jan 1926
   2 **Elizabeth W Smith** b. 1849
   2 **Frederick C Smith** b.1850
   2 **George Henry Smith** b. 1853 d. 1853
   2 **Louisa Ann Smith** b. 1853 d. 1853
   2 **Rosalie L Smith** b 13 Nov 1858
[Children of William Smith and Ann Carmody]
   2 **Priscilla Smith** b. 24 Aug 1878 d. 23 Dec 1968 m. **William John Mason** 25 Apr 1898 b. 1870 d. 11 Jan 1935.
      3 **Arthur Mason** b. 1898
      3 **Ethel Mason** b. 1900
      3 **Vic Mason** b. 1902
      3 **Jack Mason** b. 1905
      3 **Eric Mason** b. 1910
      3 **Hilton Mason** b. 1913
      3 **Bob Mason** b. 1923.
   2 **Mary Smith** b. 1881 m. Ralph Smith
      3 **Irene Smith** m. Bob Ward 1930

Descendants of Lt. Colonel William Grove White, father of William Smith's first wife Louisa White

1 **Colonel William Grove White** b.1765 d. 1844 Newton Cottage, Sandwich, Swanage, Isle of Purbeck, Dorset, England. Companion of the Bath (BC) m. **Elizabeth Chinchen** 1799 b. 1780 d. 1846. [Son of James White and Sarah Grove]
   2 **Louisa White** b. 26 Sep 1819 Swanage, Dorset, England (Swanage Parish Records) d. 1882 New Road, 5 Rose Cottage, Portsea, Portsmouth, England m. **William Smith** c1838 Jersey, English channel [son of John Smith and Elizabeth Smith], b. 1815, d. 29 Jul 1891
      3 **William Smith** b. 1841 Swanage, Dorset
      3 **Francis F Smith** b. 1844
      3 **Thomas Smith** b. 26 Apr 1846 d. 1926
      3 **Elizabeth White Smith** b. 1849
      3 **Frederick C Smith**, b. 1850
      3 **George Henry Smith** b & d. 1853
      3 **Louisa Ann Smith** b.& d. 28 Mar 1853 Swanage, Dorset (Swanage parish records)
      3 **Rosalie Louisa Smith** b. 13 Nov 1858 Alfreds Place, Winchester, Hampshire, England
   2 **William White**
   2 **Francis Fane White** b.? d. 1840 from an accident

Ann (Carmody, Callinan) Smith: b. 8 Nov 1841 d. 1916

MOTHER OF PRISCILLA (SMITH) MASON
DAUGHTER OF PATRICK CARMODY AND BRIDGET DOUGHAM
WIFE AND WIDOW OF THOMAS CALLINAN M. 1862 D. 1862
M. WILLIAM SMITH 7 MAY 1877 B. 1841 D. 1935

Information, background and certificates gathered by Robyn Mason, granddaughter of Priscilla Mason, great-granddaughter of Ann (Carmody, Callinan) Smith

Birth and Death records of Ann (Carmody, Callinan) Smith

Ref / Year	Name	First Name	Father	Mother
2362/1841	Carmody	Ann	Patrick	Bridget
16015/1916	Smith	Ann	Patrick	Bridget

Ann Carmody was born on 8 November 1841 in Bathurst, (baptised there 15 Dec 1841), to **Patrick Carmody** and **Bridget Dougham,** both from Kilmurry, in County Clare, Ireland, who had arrived here on the *Magistrate* on 21 July 1838, with no children with them upon arrival.

Ann, at 21, married her first husband, **Thomas Callinan**, on 5 Jan 1862, at Haydonton, Murrurundi. MC. 1862/2479. The marriage certificate shows **Thomas** was 28 and a farmer, living at Scotts Creek, Murrurundi. She was a servant living at Bloomfield, Murrurundi.

Immigration records show that **Thomas Callinan** came out on the *Vocalist* at age 21, arriving here on 9 Oct 1856, with brothers **Cornelius**, 35, **James**, 23, and **Patrick**, 18. They came from Borrisoleigh, Tipperary, between Thurles and Nenagh, and north of Cashel — now a quite large and prosperous-looking township — with grandparents listed as **James** and **Nancy Callinan**, both dead. They were four of 285 adults and 90 children under 14 on the 1020-ton vessel for many months.

It would seem that they partly paid their way, £5 each, and were thus assisted immigrants. **James** also claims a sister **Mary** in the colony, but identifying her has not been possible.

Name	First Name	Age	Ship
Callinan	Cornelius	35	*Vocalist*
Callinan	James	23	*Vocalist*
Callinan	Patrick	18	*Vocalist*
Callinan	Thomas	21	*Vocalist*

Vocalist Immigration records 1856 include Callinans

Thomas Callinan was accidentally killed only months after marrying **Ann Carmody.** His death certificate shows that he died on 18 Sep 1862, thrown off a horse and killed on the spot. **Thomas** had been to the courthouse with his father, relative to some land he had selected and was on his way home to his wife. And while **Ann**, heavily pregnant, rushed off to her husband when the accident occurred, their house and all its contents burnt to the ground. The baby miscarried, presumably because of the trauma — an awful experience for a young girl! She was only 21 at the time. **Thomas'** body was taken to the nearest public house to await an inquest, which brought in a verdict of accidental death. He had been only six years in the colony. He was buried on 20 Sep 1862 at Haydonton, Murrurundi. No birth or death record of the (girl) baby is recorded except as '1 female deceased' on **Ann Carmody Callinan Smith's** death certificate.

Death Record Thomas Callinan

Ref/Date	Name	First Name	Father	Mother	Location
4869/1862	Callinan	Thomas	Cornelius	Sarah	Murrurundi

Notices of Thomas Callanan (sic) in the Sydney Morning Herald

MURRURUNDI.
[FROM A CORRESPONDENT.]

FATAL ACCIDENT.—Yesterday afternoon, a young man, named Thomas Callanan, residing at Bloomfield, four miles from this township, was thrown from the horse he was riding and killed on the spot. Deceased had been to the court-house with his father relative to some land he had selected, and was on his way home to his young wife, to whom he had been married only a few months. An inquest was, this day, held upon the body by Captain Wheeler, coroner for the district, and a verdict of accidental death returned.

SMH dated 22 Sep 1862, p 2

MURRURUNDI.
[FROM OUR CORRESPONDENT.]

THE LATE LAMENTABLE DEATH OF YOUNG CALLANAN. —The accident to Callanan happened some five miles from his residence, and as the body was taken to the nearest public-house to await an inquest, a messenger was sent to his poor young wife, who shut up her house and forthwith went to the place where her dead husband was. The next day some neighbours called at the residence to see if all was correct, when they were horrified to find the house and its contents all in ashes. How or by what means this occurred at present is a mystery.

SMH dated 23 Sep 1862, p 5

Not surprisingly, it took **Ann** 15 years before she again contemplated marriage. On 7 May, 1877 **Ann** married **William Smith** at St. Charles Church, Waverley. A notice of her second marriage appeared in the Sydney Morning Herald, Friday, 1 Jun 1877 page 9 Ref 1877/1729. **William** had recently arrived from New Zealand and was 62. **Ann**'s parents were recorded as **Patrick** and **Bridget Carmody** (*church register 775*), that she was then 36, a widowed housekeeper residing in Waverley, and that new *English* husband **William Smith**, living at Murrurundi, son of **John** and **Elizabeth Smith**, was (said to be) a 55 year old Catholic farmer, born in Swanage, Dorset, England, also previously married, and with seven children from that marriage.

The birth certificate for their daughter **Priscilla Ann Smith** shows that she was born on 24 Aug 1878, and confirms that her parents were married on 7 May 1877, mistakenly recorded as 1878.

Ann had two daughters to **William, Priscilla** and **Mary**, born in 1878 and 1881, and lived another 40 years to the age of 75, dying at her home at 77 Raglan St. Waterloo in 1916, of 'malignant disease of colon; pneumonia and cellulitis'. She was buried at RC Rookwood Mortuary 2, Section Q, Grave 11 with her baby granddaughter, **Ethel Mason**, the only daughter of **Priscilla Smith Mason**. The informant for her death certificate was her son-in-law, **William Mason**, of 'Erelton' West Terrace, Bankstown

SMITH—CALLINAN—May 7, at St. Charles's Church, Waverley, by the Rev. Father Garavel, William Smith, of Quirindi, to Ann Callinan, of Quirindi.

Marriage notice of William Smith and Ann Callinan in the Sydney Morning Herald

SMITH.—In loving memory of Ann Smith, who died November 2, 1916. Gone, but not forgotten. Inserted by her loving daughters, Priss and Mary.

Memorial Notice of Ann Smith in the Sydney Morning Herald, Friday 2 Nov 1917, page 6

Mary Ethel Smith: b. 1881 d. 31 Oct 1951

Sister of Priscilla (Smith) Mason
2nd daughter of William Smith and Ann (Carmody, Callinan) Smith
m. Ralph Smith
Mother of Ethel Irene (Irene) (Smith) Ward, m. 1930

Priscilla's sister, **Mary Ethel Smith**, born at Murrurundi, married **Ralph Smith** and resided at 79 Clarence St, Bankstown. The family believes that at some stage **Mary** went to New Guinea. **Mary** and **Ralph**'s daughter **Ethel Irene** (known as **Irene**) was born in Redfern around 1907. When **Mary** died in 1951, the Informant was their daughter, **Irene Ward** who is recorded on the death certificate as aged 44.

Mary died 31 Oct 1951, aged 70, from cerebral haemorrhage and hypertension at Clarence St Bankstown. She was cremated at Rookwood, Church of England. Her parents were **William Smith** and **Ann (Carmody, Callinan) Smith**.

Death record of Mary Ethel Smith:

Ref / Year	Name	First Name	Father's Name	First Name	Mother's Name	Place
29365/1951	Smith	Mary Ethel	Smith	William	Ann	Bankstown

On 26 Apr 1930, aged 22, **Irene** married **Robert Ward**, a motor mechanic born in Hendon, England, at St Pauls Church, Sydney (Church of England). She was living at 79 Clarence St, Bankstown. He was 29, and resided at Cooma, son of baker Frederick Joseph Ward and Ethel Haymorn. Her father was listed as plumber **Ralph Smith** (deceased), mother **Mary Ethel Smith**.

Wedding record of Irene (Ward) Smith:

Ref / Year	Name	First Name	Name	First Name	Place
5099/1930	Ward	Robert	Smith	Ethel Irene	Sydney

Arthur William Mason: b. 29 Jul 1898 d. c.1968

BORN 29 JUL 1898
ELDEST SON OF WILLIAM AND PRISCILLA (SMITH) MASON, WITH SIBLINGS ETHEL VIC, JACK, ERIC, HILTON AND BOB
LIVED AT ERELTON, WEST TERRACE, BANKSTOWN
SERVED IN WWI FROM OCTOBER 1917
QUALIFIED AS A WOOL CLASSER IN 1923
TRAVELLED TO THE US AND BRITAIN IN THE 1920S AND EARLY 30S

This article is much indebted to Robyn Mason, who has provided the research.

The Mason family (at 206 Chapel Rd, Bankstown) gathered around Arthur, in his WWI Corporal uniform. (L – R) Jack, mother Priscilla, small Hilton, Arthur, a very proud Vic in long pants, standing with his hand proprietorially on his brother's chair, small Eric, and father William. The year, from his military record, would have been 1919 on his return.

Birth Record of Arthur Mason

BC / Year	Name	First Names	Father	Mother	Place
5885/1898	Mason	Arthur William	William J	Priscilla	Tamworth

Arthur was the first-born son of **William Mason** and **Priscilla (Smith) Mason,** who married on 25 Apr 1898. Arthur arrived on 25 Sep 1898, so their marriage was somewhat hurried. He was involved in WWI, enlisting on 19 Oct 1917 when he was 19, at a rate of 6/- (6 shillings) per day.

His 'Application To Enlist in the War' is dated 29 Oct 1917 and confirms his address and parentage — both **William** and **Priscilla Mason** counter-signed his Application. He was 5ft 7inches tall, 19¼ years of age, and resided at *Erelton*, West Terrace, Bankstown, with his parents.

The WWI records from the National Archives of Australia show his military record. Having signed his 'attestation paper' (presumably giving his agreement to be sent overseas) on 20 Oct 1917, supported by his mother's signature, he was enlisted in the AIF (Australian Imperial Force) 35th battalion (Service No. 54707) on 20 May 1918, as a Private. He was appointed Corporal (VO/Cpl) on 19 Jun 1918 on embarkation on HMA D60, disembarking in London on 26 August 1918. He was still a Private when on 26 Sep 1918 he was accidentally shot in the right arm by another Private in the rear rank of his training unit who found that his rifle was cocked, so shot it into the ground to clear it. **Private Arthur Mason** acquired two metal pieces in his arm, was extensively examined in hospital, and cleared for service.

In and out of hospital, he was transferred to No.2 group, clearing hospital at Weymouth on 3 Jan 1919. No disciplinary action was taken against the shooter, though a Court of Enquiry was held and many witnesses gave evidence. **Arthur** was promoted to Acting Corporal, as the photo shows on his uniform, but it does not appear to be confirmed by the records a few weeks after the incident. He was 'allotted' to 9th Training Battalion, 35th battalion on 26 or 30 Sep 1918 and was, on 5 Jan 1919 (after the war had ended) in Weymouth, marked to return to Australia on the *Margha* with 'gsw R.arm' (Gunshot wound Right arm), back to Australia on 18 Jan 1919.

A letter from Arthur's father **William** (well written, with good handwriting) on 28 Nov 1918 (ie after peace was declared) asked the Army about his welfare and whereabouts. The response of 8 Dec 1918 about '**A/Cpl AW Mason**, 8th (NSW) reinforcements', was that 'no report has been received', asking for documentary evidence. The response also claimed no advice that **A/Cpl Mason** has been transferred to the 35th battalion (in which he had enrolled when he joined). A Regimental report of 20 Sep 1918 on his forearm was marked 'no further treatment necessary' and the patient was required to do remedial gymnastics (7 Jan 1919) on a ladder. By 3 Feb 1919 the necessary extension of his arm was nearly complete.

Arthur's Will, organised by the military, left all his goods to his mother, **Priscilla Mason**.

Having not seen active service, but having been shot on parade, **Arthur** was awarded the 14/15 Star medal (for before he joined), the British War Medal, and the Victory Medal. Thus, though he would have been seen as a returned serviceman, having been overseas, it would appear that he saw no actual war service, since the war ended on 11 Nov 1918. Was he a slacker? Was he just lucky?

Family lore has him variously in the UK and/or the US, and coming home 'after the war' drawling 'Hi Mom' with an American accent to the family home at 206 Chapel Road, Bankstown. This 'after the war' sews doubts — he could only have got an American accent, one presumes, in America, and that by all accounts happened much later.

Recently he has been found in the Electoral Rolls as a 'Clerk' in 1921-1922 and as a Wool Classer at Chapel Road with his parents in 1925, but not in 1926. He qualified as a Wool Classer in the examinations of 1922 and 1923 with Honours, after a course in the Sheep and Wool Dept, Sydney Technical College. One wonders what future he planned for himself with that. No actual evidence of him, or of any family or occupation, has been found, though family stories proliferate.

Bob Mason's son-in-law **Bill Davies'** research, however, has made some finds. **Bill** has this to say, presumably from recollections within the family: *Arthur became a Wool Classer... and travelled to the USA either to teach or learn more himself — later he moved back to the States and met a woman leader of a famous religious group, becoming her secretary and later marrying her. Arthur believed in this movement and was upset when it proved to be a fraud. He then travelled to England where he died.*

Shipping records show him travelling between Sydney and the US a couple of times. **Arthur** travelled on ms *Ventura*, in 9 Jul 1924, soon after his Wool Classing course. He was 26, with his mother (living at Prairie Vale Road, Bankstown) noted as 'nearest relative' for this 'alien', arriving in San Francisco on 29 Jul 1924. He was also recorded in the 1930 US Census as being a boarder at the Bible Institute in South Hope Street, Los Angeles, California, his age being correct at 31.

Before 1931 he must have returned to Australia, as on 22 Jan 1931 he sailed from Sydney, arriving back in Los Angeles on 13 Feb 1931 on the *Monowai*, requiring a permit (No. 654366, issued 6 Oct 1930) to re-enter the USA.

Arthur also left Sydney on the *Largs Bay* in early 1934, arriving at the Port of Hull in England on 22 May 1934, defining himself as an Evangelist, his address being the YWCA building on Tottenham Court Road in London.

He does seem to have foregone the pleasures of wool-classing for Evangelism!

These dates and facts tell us **Arthur's** movements, but little of his life. We have no record of his marrying, though the stories around his marrying a woman in a religious movement continue. His death date appears to be 1968, perhaps in the UK, but we have no proof of that.

The documents below and on the following page show:

Below:	Passenger on the *Largs Bay*, giving his occupation as *Evangelist*, at 34, and country of permanent residence as California, going to the YWCA in Tottenham Court Road, London from Brisbane.
Next page:	
Left	Passenger on the *Ventura* in 1924, leaving Sydney for San Francisco
Centre	Living at the Bible Institute in Los Angeles at 31, in 1930.
Right	Passenger on the *Monowai* in 1931 from Sydney to Los Angeles

These however don't clear up much of the details of his life.

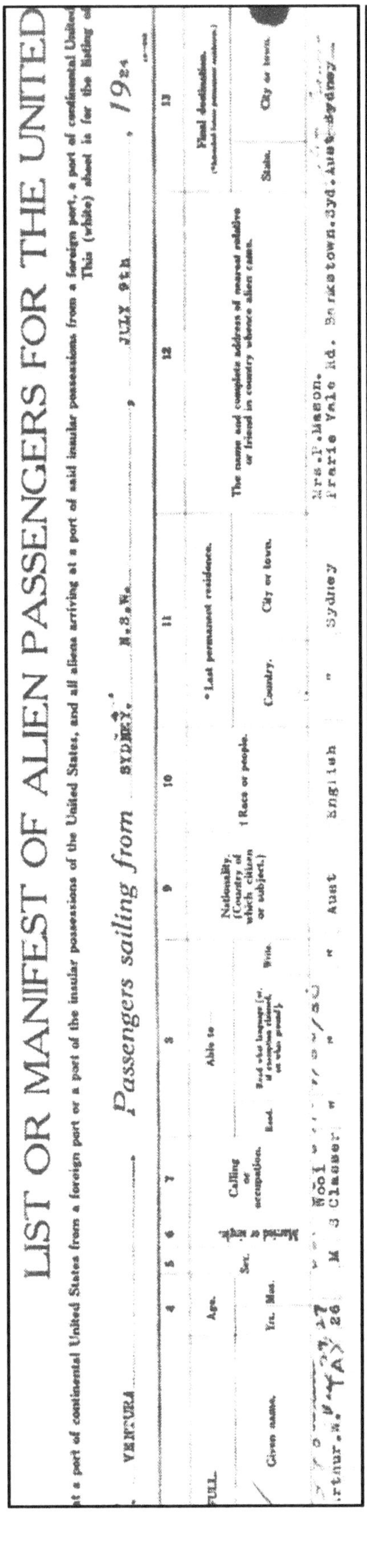

LIST OR MANIFEST OF ALIEN PASSENGERS FOR THE UNITED

VENTURA Passengers sailing from SYDNEY, N.S.W., JULY 9th, 1924

Arthur W. 26 M S Wool Classer Aust English Sydney Mrs. P. Mason. Prarie Vale Rd. Bankstown. Syd. Aust. Sydney

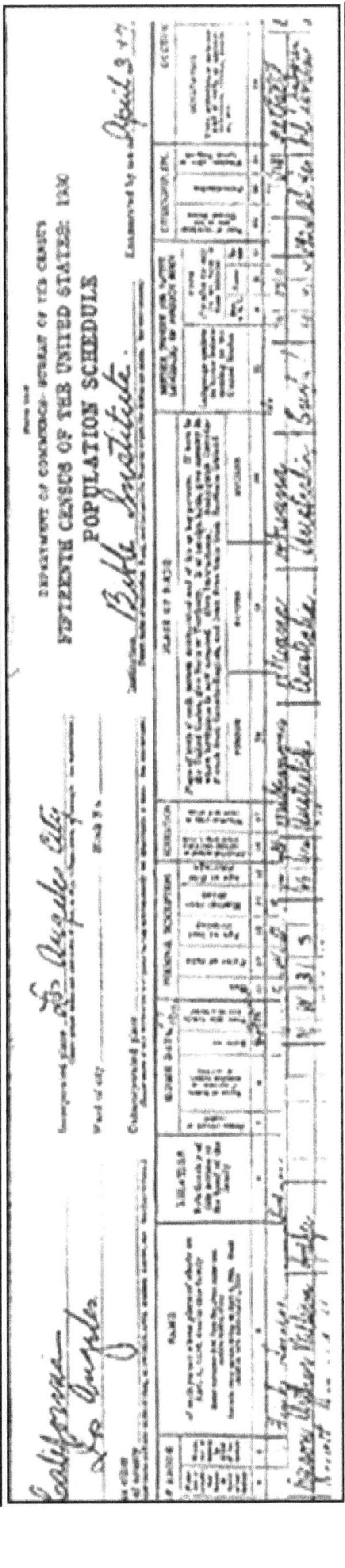

DEPARTMENT OF COMMERCE—BUREAU OF THE CENSUS

FIFTEENTH CENSUS OF THE UNITED STATES: 1930

POPULATION SCHEDULE

California

Los Angeles

Los Angeles City

Bible Institute

April 3

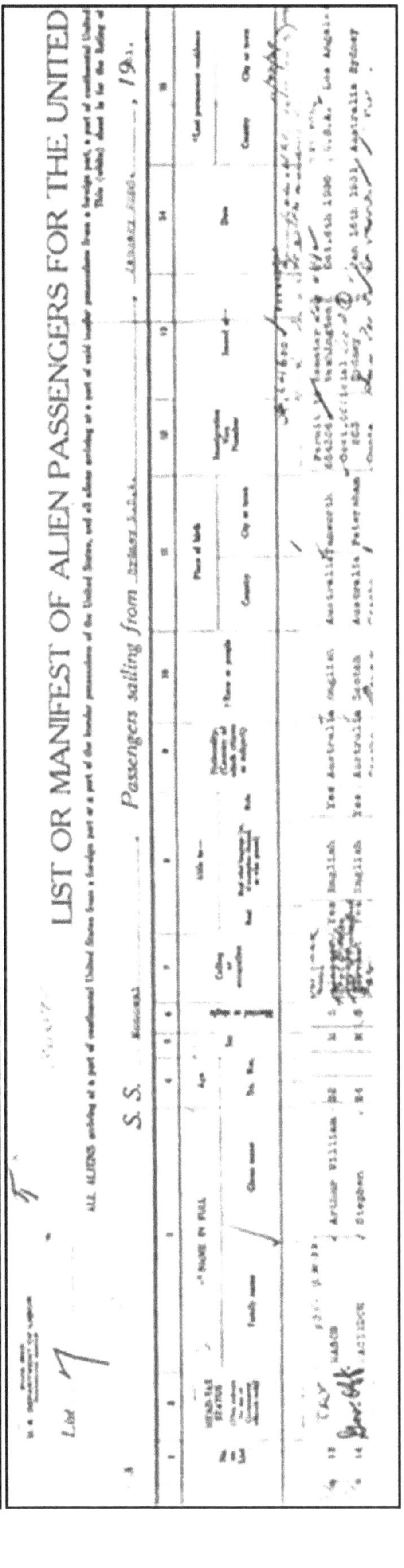

LIST OR MANIFEST OF ALIEN PASSENGERS FOR THE UNITED

List 7

S.S. Passengers sailing from Sydney, 1931.

MASON Arthur William 32 M S Yes English Yes Australia English Australia Tamworth

Stephen 24 M S Yes English Yes Australia Scotch Australia Petersham

Victor Oliver (Vic) Mason, Lt.Cmdr, RAN: b. 3 Oct 1902 d. 6 Apr 1985

2ND SON OF WILLIAM AND PRISCILLA (SMITH) MASON
BROTHER OF ARTHUR, SHORT-LIVED ETHEL, JACK, ERIC, HILTON AND BOB
M. CATHERINE (HOGAN) MASON 1931 B. 1905 D. 1983
FATHER OF JAN (MASON, FAGAN) O'DONNELL AND HELEN (MASON) MALCHER

Written by his daughter Helen Malcher, largely from the recollection of his older daughter Jan O'Donnell

Vic Mason was a man of wry and gentle humour, and one of whom the cliché 'honest to the core' was completely true. He lived with some panache in his 20s, racing motor bikes, exploring new technology in sound, cars and, by the late 1920s, even planes. He was born in October 1902, prematurely, so the family story goes, because of the death of his almost two-year-old sister Ethel, from diphtheria in that year, which must have been dreadful for their mother, **Priscilla.**

The family was living in Redfern at the time, having moved there from Tamworth. **Vic** attended school locally, was made (it is believed) 'dux' of that local school, which helped him win a scholarship to Sydney High, a great achievement at the time.

Vic Mason as we remember him — at his daughter Helen's wedding on 8 April 1961

Vic Mason, Lifesaver (standing, at back) Tamarama Beach between 1925 & 1930, aged about 25

However, straitened circumstances in the family meant his education finished either at or just before his Intermediate Certificate. His parents **Will** and **Priscilla,** according to Lands Dept. records, had property progressively at Rockdale, Bexley and Bankstown, but since (his Railways employment record tells us) his father was employed by the Railways all his working life until his retirement in 1935, and there were eight people in the house, money was always a little scarce. Family photos show what became the family home at 206 Chapel Road. Bankstown, still without adjacent houses and without the landmark wholesale feed merchant on the corner nearby.

Vic had an apprenticeship at Garden Island, as an electrical fitter, to about 1922. His 'indenture' labels him so, and paid him 10/6 (ten shillings and sixpence) for the 1st year, 18/6 for the second, 26/5 for the third year, 36/3 for the fourth and 52/6 for the 5th year. Thereafter he was employed by Western Electric, which was just getting into the exciting world of sound for films. He was thrown into an intriguing and at first confusing new world, and fairly quickly became the sound specialist, visiting Sydney, Melbourne,

Vic in what became known as the 'honeymoon Austin' — 1931

Adelaide and Perth to install sound equipment into the new cinema theatres. He was blazing new trails in this country in this field, and loved every minute of it. He stayed with Western Electric until the outbreak of WWII in 1939.

His life as a young man seems exciting: employed in a quite glamorous new industry, racing Norton motorbikes, owning cars at a period when few people did (which he drove like a motorbike anyway), joining the Air Force for a short time, being a lifesaver at Tamarama 1928/9, crossing the Nullarbor in a little Austin Wasp, and travelling quite extensively within Australia installing new cinemas.

Vic and Cath's wedding, with his brother Jack Mason and her sister

Vic met his future wife, **Cath Hogan**, at the 21st birthday of a mutual friend, **John Linton**, in 1926 and the Lintons and **Masons** stayed friends all their lives. **John** and **Vic** had probably met through **Vic**'s electrical apprenticeship at Garden Island, the Sydney Naval base, or perhaps through Western Electric. **Cath** was then living at Tamarama, and had trained at Chartres in Sydney, who had obtained for her a prestigious job as a Hansard reporter in Canberra. She had been engaged to a friend of her brother, **John Hogan**. But **Vic**'s turning up put an end to that, though they waited some time before they got married – probably **Vic**'s high sense of what was 'right'. They were married on 31st October 1931, nearly five years later.

At that stage **Vic** was seen to be supporting his parents and his youngest brother **Bob** in the near depression from about 1925, and the full depression from the October crash in 1929. The other brothers had at that time largely married and were fending for themselves. His father was 60 years old in 1930, and was to retire in 1932, without superannuation.

Before World War II broke out — married, now with two children — with his advanced sound background from Western Electric, **Vic** joined the **RANVR** (the voluntary reserve of the Navy) as a SubLieutenant (Electrical), lowering his age two years to 35 to achieve it. His war story follows.

Vic Mason's WWII War Experiences

Drawn considerably from the works on Naval history for World War II, by Official Naval Historian G H Gill.

In Apr 1939, Vic was selected for the new RANVR Anti-Submarine school at HMAS *Rushcutter*, the shore training establishment at Rushcutters Bay, Sydney, under Commanding Officer **Captain H M Newcomb**, RN. Only 8-12 of 56 applicants for this school were selected, so **Vic**'s sound background was obviously valued. On 3rd Aug 1939 he was accepted for the 'F' course within the school, and was mobilised (after declaration of war) on 15 Nov 1939.

Vic was never on a ship which 'fired in anger'. His specialty was new in that war — RADAR — radio detection of ships, submarines and planes, which meant mostly shore postings and training establishments. His posting to London under the auspices of the British Navy was to increase and use his knowledge in this area.

Australia was understandably keen to have, and to have control over, her own Navy. But during World War II, Britain still saw undivided naval control in war as essential to her *own* conduct of the war. Australia's isolation, and

Cath Mason's WWII "To the Women of Australia" badge, as wife of Vic Mason

thus vulnerability by sea, had been a perceived problem. Australia's concern was that in time of war the British ships so frequently and comfortably seen off her shores in peacetime would, undoubtedly, be sent to areas closer to Europe to care for Britain's own interests, leaving Australia undefended.

So the Australian Navy, the RAN, was born (officially, in 1911), with Australia's Regulations necessarily resembling the British RN's, as well as a *'readiness on the part of the Australian Government'*, Australia accepting the theory that in time of war *'the indivisibility of the seas demanded, as far as possible, an undivided naval control'*. Historian Gill sees this unity as a 'concomitant of victory' in World War II.

Japanese expansion between the wars was seen as a problem, and Singapore the only ray of hope for Australia that British shipping would be in the Pacific, increasingly seen as a new theatre in any forthcoming war. But Britain repeated her previous mistake in Singapore — using land forces to defend against an invasion by forces having sea control. So Australia was forced into a much increased expenditure on its OWN shipping. Yet Britain had stated her position clearly and firmly – *'local defence was the primary responsibility of each portion of the Empire'*.

From 1929 the abolition of compulsory military training and growing dictatorships in Europe — Italy, Japan, and Germany — all meant the necessity of rearmament, resulting in the construction (in Britain) amongst other things, of two cruisers, the *Australia* and the *Sydney*, over the next few years, further increasing naval expenditure in Australia.

Despite the problems, however, Naval Historian Gill argues that Australia's Navy entered the war adequately equipped, *'wholly manned by Australians, well-trained, keen, and soon to prove themselves efficient. While the status quo in the Pacific was maintained this force was, even without a British fleet at Singapore, equal to the task for which it had been designed.'*

At outbreak of war, the RAN had 5040 officers and men, inflated immediately to 10259 by reserves. By 30 Jun 1940, an additional 2914 had joined. The RANVR, according to Gill, were *'persons who had followed the sea as a profession, followed the sea in recreation and desired sea service in time of war, were ex-members of the RANR who had completed their compulsory training, or possessed some special qualifications'*. It is probably to this last group that **Vic**, with his background in sound — so central to RADAR — belonged, joining as a 'Subbie' (Sub-Lieutenant) before the outbreak of the war.

Anti-Submarine School.

That **Captain Newcomb** (**Vic**'s mentor throughout the war), Commanding Officer of the A/S (anti-submarine) and RDF (radio detection finder) schools was British Navy (RN) rather than Australian Navy (RAN) gives an indication of the purpose of this A/S school — it was set up to meet the British demands. It had been established to 'provide facilities for training officers of the A/S Branch of the RANVR, and for the training of ratings of the A/S Branch', 'for service with the RN'. The majority were destined for posting direct to the RN, in a proportion of 6-RN:1-RAN: that is, it was producing for British Naval requirements rather than for the needs of the Australian forces. The school took recruits from the RAN, RANVR and RANR, but numbers were not high at first. RANR officers and men were reluctant to transfer to the RANVR for acceptance into the A/S school, and did in fact see those who did transfer being slow to be posted overseas as war broke out. Patriotism was high in Australia at the time, and most young men (and particularly those in the Defence Forces) were impatient for overseas postings. By 31 Oct 1940 (**Vic** having left for overseas on 3 Oct 1940), the ratio of graduates to those who 'proceeded overseas for service with the RN' was still high — 94% of officers and 41% of ratings from the A/S school being transferred to the British Navy.

The British requested *'Officers recruited from civil life, viz pilots for the Fleet Air Arm, ex-Mercantile Marine Officers* (in neither of which category the RAN could send men), *and Yachtsmen'*, of which 259 officers and 250 ratings were sent by October 1942. The last categories required by the RN were ratings (non officers) - *'telegraphists and signalmen, artificers, electrical and W/T scientists for Signal School, and skilled electrical workmen'*, shortages of whom were equally acute in Australia, so no men could be sent. **Captain Newcomb**, in his reports to the British Secretary of the Royal Navy, was also proposing the entrance of officers 'with electrical qualifications' (such as those held by **Vic Mason**), and the increase by 100% of the length of course for the ratings within the school to raise the standard of its graduates, including the training of personnel, for 'production and repair of Anti-Submarine equipment'.

RADAR

Astonishingly however, these exhaustive reports (and even **Captain Newcomb**'s comprehensive history of the A/S school, all studied by this writer), make no mention whatever of the immensely-secret anti-submarine technique and equipment RADAR, the core of it all. Indeed, that important development, in the early to middle stages of the war, is left almost untouched by general naval histories, and it was in this area that **Vic** was most involved. Since the reports quoted here were being written under extremely secure conditions, addressed from the CO of the establishment to the British Secretary of the Navy, this omission could hardly have been a matter of security, and is hard to explain. RADAR was however the 'edge' that Britain (and Australia) had over the ubiquitous German submarines during the first years of the war, and security around it was very high indeed. Even with the 30-year rule freeing almost all war records for research, and with computerised databases facilitating 'topic' searches, very little accumulated information surfaces on the subject, and log books of anti-submarine ships carrying RADAR are often missing for crucial periods. In fact it was only in June 1941 that, with the US cruiser *Chicago* off Sydney and Brisbane for a flag-waving exercise, *'those in the RAN who had not been off the Australia station'* had their first view of RADAR equipment, in *'the massive and cumbersome square framework she carried on her mast'*.

Though this Anti-Submarine school stayed high in **Vic**'s consciousness and background throughout the war and beyond, the dates supplied by the Department of Navy do not seem to indicate that he was at any stage an instructor there, though he was certainly lecturing in RADAR by 1942, despite a stutter that completely disappeared when he was lecturing.

By the second half of 1940, Britain was preoccupied with thwarting Hitler's attempted invasion plans in the Battle of Britain, and there were German mines off the coast of Australia. Coastal ships were travelling without lights, *Niagara* was lost, and the P&O troop-carrying *Strathmore* needed a minesweeping escort for its 439 troops enroute to Britain. Coastal patrols in Anti-Submarine vessels were another major part of the RAN's responsibility. It was to one of these, the HMAS *Bingera*, that Vic was posted on 3 Oct 1940, using and training others in the anti-submarine RADAR skills acquired at *Rushcutter*. He stayed on the *Bingera* till 30 Jun 1941, leaving her in Fremantle. *Bingera* was later escort to coastal convoys after the Japanese midget submarine attack in Sydney Harbour on 31 May 1942.

His next posting, on 1 Jul 1941, was to the auxiliary ship HMAS *Wyrallah*, patrolling on the west coast of Australia, staying till September. Two months later, on 24 Nov 1941, *Wyrallah* was part of the search group 120 miles off Carnarvon, WA which picked up a raft of 25 German survivors (eventually 315) from the German ship *Kormoran*, sunk on 19 Nov 1941 after action with the Australian cruiser HMAS *Sydney*. At that stage, the *Sydney* had been missing for two days. Her whole complement of 603 men and 42 officers was lost. Handling by Navy Office of media, and notification to families, was the subject of controversy and criticism at the time. Eight days after the action, HMAS *Heros* picked up the only material evidence from *Sydney* — a gun-raked life-float with two naval lifebelts, 160 miles north-west of Carnarvon, now kept in the Australian War Memorial in Canberra. This ship was Australia's major naval loss of the war.

In the meantime, **Vic** was posted to London, to the RN, (as a high percentage of the Anti-Submarine school officer graduates were), travelling on the *SS Ceramic* as 'OIC Draft' (Officer in charge of Draft) in October and November of 1941. Navy Correspondence files disclose the fascinating titbit that for this not-too-onerous task of taking charge of the non-crew ratings enroute to Britain on this non-Navy ship, he was refunded a massive £10 for expenses. *Ceramic* sank on its next voyage, in December. Till May of 1941 **Vic** was listed by the Navy as being at London Depot, a major post for him, training and learning, and on the Gunnery and Communications shore base that was *HMS Mercury* at Portsmouth, the big naval centre on the south coast of England. No other details are forthcoming from the Navy for this period, and it may be indeed that this was a function of the security surrounding RADAR. Further research through the British Naval Historian failed to bridge the gap. However, **Vic**'s own report was that he was then – in what was the most important stage of the war for him — in convoy in the bitter North Atlantic escorting merchant supply ships into Murmansk to victual the Russians, and he had a much-loved Arctic jersey lasting in the family for some years to prove it. Even his medals reinforce the gap: there is no 'area' medal covering the North Atlantic amongst those carefully kept and framed by the family. Shared remembrances with the Austrian **Malcher** family reveal that **Ober Leutnant Franz Malcher**, father of **Harry Malcher**, who married **Vic's** daughter **Helen**, was shooting at those supply convoys during 1942 from German placements in Kirkenes, Norway, at the top of the Scandinavian peninsula, to protect nearby Murmansk, the supply centre for allied Russia. In one story out of this period, told with **Vic**'s usual gentle sense of humour, he admitted to being scared out of his wits during air raid alarms, but being quite unable to admit it, or leave for the air-raid shelters whilst the stoic Brits stayed where they were. This doesn't help with placing him geographically, since both Portsmouth and London were being subjected to considerable bombing during this period.

Kirkenes, Norway, with nearby Murmansk, Russia, the supply port for the allied Russians.

1942 – The Pacific War

Vic was at this time still a Lieutenant. In 1942 the focus of the war for Australia turned to the Pacific – Pearl Harbour in December 1941, British might at Singapore failing and 15,000 Australian troops being taken prisoner, Australia's coast being broached by the Japanese bombing of Darwin (with 240 Australians killed), Japanese strength so evident in the Pacific, and the US/Japanese Coral Sea battle so central to Australia's security.

... comes to Sydney

On 31 May 1942, with Japanese war fortunes at an all-time high, and after a remarkable and unchallenged reconnaissance flight by Japanese small aircraft over Sydney, three Japanese midget submarines entered Sydney Harbour. They managed to blow up the ferry *Kuttabul* (missing the USS *Chicago* at which their torpedoes were aimed) and killing 21 people, before the search-and-destroy actions of the USS *Chicago*, HMAS *Kanimbla* and *Yandra*, plus other ships, managed to sink one of the subs. The boom net strung across the harbour entrance entangled another, which its men subsequently destroyed. The third sub was not found until 2006. In the very bad year of 1942, after Singapore, the bombing of Darwin had seen for the first time Australians killed in war action on Australian soil, and the fear of Japanese invasion was tangible. Now with these Japanese vessels inside Sydney Heads, killing civilians, 'frantic' is not too strong a word to describe civilian reaction.

At the time, **Vic's** whereabouts are hazy. Navy records show him as having just returned from London, and *perhaps* embarked on the *Port Darwin* enroute to *Cerberus* in Melbourne. His family, however, was at Watson's Bay, within a few hundred yards of the harbour boom nets where the action against the Japanese subs took place, and **Vic**'s daughter **Jan** recalls her mother, fearfully awake, soothing her back to sleep during the clamour of the action. On a personal level, the war had come far too close to his family for **Vic**, and he hurriedly organised (from a distance) their move away from Sydney and perceived danger, some of his Navy colleagues on the spot assisting **Cath** with 9-year-old **Jan** and 6-year-old **Helen** to Condobolin, in the midwest of NSW, where they stayed for about 18 months.

Vic's whereabouts however remained vague – to the extent that in October 1942 **Cath** overcame her considerable lifelong awe of the Navy to enquire from them **Vic**'s 'whereabouts and welfare', and was assured he was not in danger.

Australia's Allegiance changes from Britain to the US

With the war coming so suddenly and powerfully to her doorstep, Australia's eyes (in the person of her then Prime Minister, John Curtin), turned for protection to the US rather than Britain (herself so stretched in European affairs), and to the necessity of local defence. Curtin thus rejected Churchill's call on 20 Feb 1942 for Australian troops into Burma on the grounds that it was not 'a reasonable part of [Australia's] war', and by 19 Mar 1942 *accepted the US General Douglas Macarthur as Supreme Commander of Allied Forces in the South West Pacific.*

By September 1942, the RAN's position was not dire, recording in the War Diaries. They had ships, minesweepers, A/S vessels, destroyers, 90 troop carriers, the A/S school, and close cooperation between the Australian Defence Services, RN, USN, NZN, and units of the Royal Netherlands Navy, as well as over 17000 personnel. *'A number of [Australian] Reserve Officers and men with Anti-Submarine qualifications were also offered to and accepted by the Admiralty. Up to October 1942, the following had left Australia: Officers — 148: Ratings — 352'.* **Vic Mason** was one of these.

By the April 1943 report to the British Secretary of Defence, the Australian Naval Chiefs felt secure enough to say *'In view of the increased local requirements, the supply of Anti-Submarine personnel to the Royal Navy has been suspended'* – a total turnaround from the completely British RN-oriented position at the beginning of war.

1943 to the end of the war

The last couple of years of the war, from July 1943, **Vic** spent as Port RADAR Officer on HMAS *Moreton*, the shore establishment in Brisbane, chafing at being in a 'safe' posting. His family, however, was able to move from Condobolin to join him in this posting. **Vic** and **Cath** began some lifelong (mainly Navy) friendships during this period, including some of the many US Navy officers in Australia by then (Brisbane being Allied Naval Headquarters). Australia was finally dependent on her own resources, whether she allied herself with Britain or with the US. Her naval concentration remained in the Pacific until the end of the war.

At war's end, the RAN being unable to conform to his request of guaranteeing him employment to the age of 55 (ie some 12 years), **Vic** was demobilised with the rank of **Lt. Commander (Electrical), RANVR** (the RAN Voluntary Reserve), and re-entered civilian employment in sound.

Post-war

After demobilisation at the end of the war, **Vic** had a time with Tasman Electrics back in his old area of sound. In retrospect, he admitted to a US Navy friend in the 1970s that leaving the Navy was 'the greatest mistake he ever made'. This period saw his finances considerably reduced when a builder contracted to build a home for the family in Dover Heights overlooking the sea, went broke. The family then lived with **Vic**'s very strong widowed mother **Priscilla** for a couple of years — 1946/1947 — before building a family home in Gallipoli Street, Bankstown, where they stayed for a quite unprecedented 3-4 years. **Vic** and **Cath** then took on a 'mixed business' in Arden Street, Waverley, demonstrating a considerable versatility in both of them. **Vic**'s daughters' (**Jan** and **Helen**) impression is that until this time, with navy postings, their childhood was never spent in any place longer than two years.

By January 1951, at the age of 49, under the auspices of his mentor Captain Newcomb, **Vic** rejoined his beloved Navy, finally being granted transfer to the RANR, rather than the RANVR, which promised him some little more security on retirement. The period out of the Navy had, however, ensured that promotion to full Commander would never be possible, a fact he regretted considerably. This 'swing' in the Navy saw him posted from 1954 to 1956 to HMAS *Tarangau*, on Manus Island, New Guinea, a shore post on which **Cath** joined him. This period made a big impression on both of them, being so distinctly different from their previous experience. Their daughter **Helen** joined them for a couple of months for her 21st birthday. It also saw **Vic** on HMAS *Watson* at Watson's Bay for two periods, so that the family could live close to (and in fact for the first period ON) the base, from 1952 to 1954, and from 1959 to 1964, when they lived 100 metres away from the entrance to the Watson shore base. **Vic** was demobilised at the age of 62. He returned to sound (a much changed industry), working with AWA for 3-4 years before he retired.

His later years were much coloured by the good fortune of winning the Lottery in about 1960. **Vic** and **Cath** bought income-producing property at Kirra on the Gold Coast of Queensland, and eventually retired to live in Tugun in the same area. His loyalty to the Navy, and his interests in new developments never wavered. In the later 60s he developed a technique in the then-unknown area of lasers, and being **Vic** offered it to the RAN for their use. It was extremely unfortunate that (in the way of science), a similar technique was developed overseas at the same time, and the Navy therefore had to decline **Vic**'s offer. He found it difficult to overcome this disappointment, but this did not stop him ensuring he was up to date in technological developments, taking some training in computers in the Northern Territory (during an extended visit to his daughter **Jan**, then living in Darwin), in the period of the 1970s before PCs, when such training was painful, complex, and highly mathematically based, and he was himself in his 70s.

His later life was surrounded by the wife and family so central to him. He died 16 months after **Cath**, on 6th April 1985, at the age of 83, and is much missed.

Plaque dedicated to the memory Vic and Cath Mason

Descendants of Victor Oliver (Vic) Mason

1 **Victor Oliver Mason** b. 3 Oct 1902 d. 6 Apr 1985 Tugun, Qld m. **Catherine Florence (Cath) Hogan** 31 Oct 1931 Sydney. MC 14624 b. 6 Apr 1905 Brewarrina, NSW d. 30 Nov 1983 Tugun, Qld [daughter of John Bernard Hogan and Jessie Maude Douglass]
    2 **Janet Claire (Jan) (Mason, Fagan) O'Donnell** b. 14 Oct 1932 Windermere Private Hospital, Melbourne m1. **Arthur Fagan** 8 May 1955 Rose Bay, Sydney b. 24 Jul 1930 Divorced d. <1970 m2. **Cyril Francis (Cy) O'Donnell** 12 Dec 1968 Lae, New Guinea b. 27 Jul 1922 New Zealand d. 11 Jun 2006 Macleay Island, Qld [son of Francis Leonard O'Donnell and Lilla Cecilia (Dot) Brewer]
    2 **Helen Marie (Mason) Malcher** b. 24 Sep 1935 Rose Bay Hospital m. **Heinrich Carl (Harry) Malcher** 8 Apr 1961 Sydney b. 1Apr 1925 an Austrian, born in Turramurra, NSW [son of Franz Xaver Ernst Malcher and Hedwig Barbara Malik]
        3 **Victoria Frances (Vicki) Malcher** b. 16 Aug 1964 Sydney m1. **Timothy Martin Brown** 28 Nov 1992 div. Apr 1997 Sydney b. 31 Oct 1961 Middlesborough, England m2.(df) **Scott William Richardson** 28 Jul 1999-30 Sep 2013 b. 11 Sep 1963 Helensburgh, Scotland
        3 **Alexandra Jane Louise (Sandy, Alex) (Malcher, Mitchell) Fullerton** b. 18 Sep 1966 Sydney m1. **Graeme Paul Mitchell** 14 Jan 1989 div. 3 Nov 2004 Sydney b. 22 Sep 1964 Maidenhead, England [son of Gary Donald Mitchell and Ann Camille Fowler] m2. **Ian Neil Fullerton** 20 Nov 2014 Maleny, Qld b. 10 Jun 1956 Nambour, Qld [son of Hector Fullerton and Daisy Lillian Cross]
        [Children of Sandy Malcher and Graeme Paul Mitchell]
            4 **Flynn Oliver Gary Mitchell** b. 13 Jan 1998 Buderim, Qld
            4 **Elouise Victoria (Ella) Mitchell** b. 18 Nov 2000 Nambour, Qld
        [Children of Ian Neil Fullerton]
            4 **Kate Daisy Fullerton** b. 2 Mar 1989, identical twin
            4 **Sarah Jill Fullerton** b. 2 Mar 1989, identical twin
            4 **Laura Rose Fullerton** b. 15 Nov 1990
            4 **Ellen Amelia Fullerton** b. 12 Nov 1992
            4 **James Ian Fullerton** b. 4 Nov 1995
        3 **Christopher Charles (Chris) Malcher** b. 14 Nov 1968 Sydney m. **Giang Le Truong** 5 Dec 2009 Sydney b. 24 Nov 1972 Hung Yen, Vietnam [daughter of Truong Viet Hung and Le Thuy Dau]
            4 **Oliver Truong Malcher** b. 24 Jun 2012 Canberra
            4 **Emily Le Malcher** b. 2 July 2014 Canberra

Catherine Florence (Cath) (Hogan) Mason: b. 6 Apr 1905 d. 30 Nov 1983

DAUGHTER OF JOHN HOGAN AND JESSE DOUGLASS
M. LT CDR (L) VICTOR MASON RAN 31 OCT 1931
MOTHER OF JAN (MASON, FAGAN) O'DONNELL AND HELEN (MASON) MALCHER
SISTER OF MAY, NORM, AND JOHN HOGAN

Cath Hogan lived at the family home in Tamarama, and had trained at Chartres in Sydney, who obtained for her a prestigious job as as a Hansard reporter in Canberra. She and **Vic Mason** were married at St. Anne's North Bondi in 1931. She was always intensely proud of **Vic**'s career with the Australian Navy, and accepting of the many changes of home address that that entailed. Their marriage lasted a very comfortable 52 years until her death in 1983.

What records we have found of **Cath**'s father's ancestors show that they are from Bree, County Wexford, Ireland, that her father **John Hogan**'s father was **Peter Hogan**, and his father was **John Hogan** also. **John Hogan I** married **Catherine Regan** in Ireland. They were in Australia in 1845, when their son **Peter Hogan** was born. In 1869, Peter married **Catherine (Kate) Hannan**, born on the *Inchinnan* enroute to this country, in 1849. Her parents, shepherd **Owen** (then aged 27) and **Bridget Hannan** (then 23), were also on board. He was from Lower Ormond, Tipperary, she from Athy, Queens County (now Leix). Both were Catholic, and could read and write.

Vic and Cath Mason

Records from the *Inchinnan*

One of **Peter** and **Kate Hogan**'s ten children was **John Bernard Hogan** (1874-1935), father and grandfather to the Sydney Hogans. **John Bernard** married **Jesse Douglass** (1874-1956), of Scottish stock, born in Dungog. The first of their four children, **May**, and the youngest, **John Peter**, were born in Bourke, the middle two, **Norbert Leo (Norm)**, and **Cath**, were born in 1903 and 1905 in Brewarrina. **John Bernard** kept a diary from when he was 20, intent on detail: he shows his page of expenses for his father's (**Peter Hogan**) funeral in May 1915, for a grand total of £27.19.6 including coffin, hearse, three coaches, a Chaplain and interment! His salary when he first started work was £39/year and six months later £52/year, or £1 per week. When he left that firm six years later in 1899, he was receiving £2.5.0 per week, or £117/year.

Little is known of **John Bernard** and **Jesse Hogan**'s life together. After **John Bernard**'s death in 1935, 'Gran Hogan'(Jesse) lived for another 21 years, first with her daughter **May** in Kings Cross, then at 10 Bon Accord Avenue in Bondi Junction, where in a beautiful large fan chair she would sit on her balcony and preside serenely over visitors, including her daughter **Cath** and her grandchildren **Jan** and **Helen**. She reached the grand old age of 82.

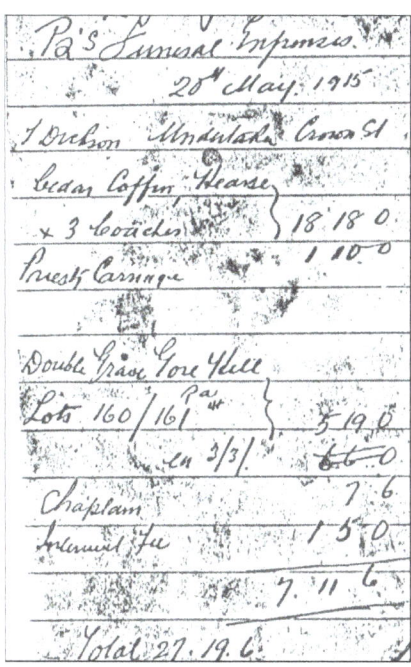

This very battered page of John Bernard Hogan's leather diary shows the level of detail he chose for his father's funeral in 1915.

John Bernard and Jesse Hogan's children

BC / Year	Name	First Name	Father	Mother	Place	DC / Year
20377/1901	Hogan	Lucy M	John B	Jesse M	Bourke	22387/1944
19654/1903	Hogan	Norbert L	John B	Jesse M	Brewarrina	28013/1960
11454/1905	Hogan	Catherine F	John B	Jesse M	Brewarrina	30 Nov 1983
11462/1906	Hogan	John P	John B	Jesse M	Bourke	103861/1979

> **John Bernard and Jesse (Douglass) Hogan's children**
>
> 5 **Lucie May (May) Hogan** (1901-1944) exuberant and much-loved, **May** married **Ron Robinson**, a plantation manager for Burns Philp, and lived with him (somewhat unhappily) in New Guinea for some years.
>
> 5 **Norbert Leo (Norm) Hogan** (1903-1960) lived in Tamarama until his marriage to **Ralda Burns** in 1930, then in the Manly area for the rest of his life. Their children were **Leonie** and **Ken**, born in 1931 and 1934. Norm served in the 6th Division of the Australian Army during WWII, and was imprisoned by the Japanese in the *hell* that was **Changi** prisoner of war camp from 1941 to 1945. He came home looking like a skeleton in late 1945, and his health never quite recovered. He died in 1960.
>
> 5 **Catherine Florence (Cath) Hogan** (1905-1983) married **Vic Mason** in 1931 (1903-1985) and produced two children, **Jan** (1932-) and **Helen** (1935-), the present biographer, who has three children.
>
> 5 **John Peter Hogan** (1906-1979) DC 103861/1979 had something of a larrikin character, which served him ill when he joined the Army in WWII. **John** and his wife **Nora** had one daughter, **Pat**, who married **Kevin Slattery** and lived in the Ettalong area on the Central Coast of NSW for many years.

John Hogan, Cath (Hogan) Mason's brother in WWII

Norm Hogan, Cath (Hogan) Mason's brother, with her husband Vic on an ANZAC march

Jesse (Douglass) Hogan, Cath (Hogan) Mason's mother

Chapter 3: John Mason II and III and their descendants

Ancestry and descendants of Cath (Hogan) Mason

1 **John Hogan** b. 1808 Bree, Co Wexford, IRL d. 2 Jun 1878 DC 3328/1878, Australia. Irish Civil Registers say died in IRL 1878 m. **Catherine Regan** Ireland b. 1810 Bree, Co Wexford, Ireland d. 19 Feb 1878 Randwick. DC 3315/1878 [daughter of John Regan and Johannah Quinlin]
  2 **Peter John Hogan** b. 16 Apr 1845 BC. 1919 134 & 308 62 d. 19 May 1915 Double Bay. Buried Gore Hill, Lot 160/161 m. **Catherine (Kate) Hannan** 8 Oct 1869 MC 5101 b. 9 Nov 1848 on board *Inchinnan* in Bay of Biscay, enroute to NSW d. 18 Nov 1928 DC 20262 at Randwick [Had 10 children, 4 of whom are mentioned below] [daughter of Eugene (Owen) Hannan and Bridget Hennessy]
    3 **Kate C Hogan** b. 5 Nov 1870 Randwick NSW d. 21 Jul 1906 Mosman, pneumonia m. **Arthur Richards** 30 May 1900 MC. 2966/1900 b. 18 Sep 1872 BC 951/1872 d. 19 Jul 1921. BuriedGore Hill Lot 160/161
      4 **Eugenie Clare (Genie) Richards** b. 13 Aug 1905 m. **Charles Edmondson** 14 Oct 1933 b.1900
        5 **Charles Edmondson** b. 9 Aug 1944 m. **Ann Cummins** May 1979
      4 **Marie Richards** m. **Rupert Sheldon** m. 1930 b. 1901 d. 1975
        5 **Pollyanna Sheldon** b. 15 Aug 1935
    3 **Elizabeth Lea Hogan** b. 15 Nov 1872 Hill End NSW d. Apr 1964 Bondi NSW.
    3 **John Bernard Hogan** b. 21 Aug 1874 BC 4768/1874 Randwick d. 30 May 1935 St Ignatius, RC Rose Bay, of throat cancer m. **Jessie Maude Douglass** 28 Nov 1900 Bourke, NSW MC 8342/1900 b. 9 Feb 1874 Dungog NSW d. 28 Oct 1956 DC 27540/1956 [daughter of James Rodger Douglass and May Jane (Jean) Davis, died 7 Jan 1924 Buried CTE cemetery Lot 555)]
      4 **Lucie May (May) Hogan** b. 18 May 1901 Bourke NSW BC 20377 d. 9 Dec 1944 Sydney, DC 22387/1944 (JBH diary says 1946) m. **Ron Robinson** 25 Jun 1932 d. 4 Oct 1948
      4 **Norbert Leo (Norm) Hogan** b. 29 Apr 1903 Brewarrina, NSW BC 19654 Lived 43 Sunshine St, Manly Vale. d. 18 Sep 1960 Manly NSW DC 28013/1960 m. **Ralda Marjorie Burns** 5 Jun 1930 d. 1951 DC 17152/1951 buried French Forest
        5 **Leone Hogan** b. 2 Jun 1931 m. **George Alexander White** 1952 Manly
        5 **Ken Hogan** b. c 1934
      4 **Catherine Florence (Cath) Hogan** b. 6 Apr 1905 Brewarrina, NSW d. 30 Nov 1983 Tugun, Qld m. **Victor Oliver (Vic) Mason** 31 Oct 1931 Sydney. Ref 14624. b. 3 Oct 1902 d. 6 Apr 1985 Tugun, Qld [son of **William John Mason** and **Priscilla Ann Smith**]
        5 **Janet Claire (Jan) (Mason, Fagan) O'Donnell** b. 14 Oct 1932 Windermere Pte Hospital, Melbourne m1. **Arthur Fagan** 8 May 1955 Rose Bay, Sydney b. 24 Jul 1930 Divorced. m2. **Cyril Francis (Cy) O'Donnell** 12 Dec 1968 Lae, New Guinea b. 27 Jul 1922 New Zealand d. 11 Jun 2006 Macleay Island, Qld [son of Francis Leonard O'Donnell and Lilla Cecilia (Dot) Brewer]
        5 **Helen Marie (Mason) Malcher** b. 24 Sep 1935 Sydney m. **Heinrich Carl (Harry) Malcher** 8 Apr 1961 Sydney b. 1 Apr 1925 Turramurra, Sydney, an Austrian [son of Franz Xaver Ernst Malcher and Hedwig Malik]
          6 **Victoria Frances (Vicki) Malcher** b. 16 Aug 1964 Sydney m1. **Timothy Martin Brown** 28 Nov 1992 div. Apr 1997 Sydney b. 31 Oct 1961 Middlesborough, England m2.(df) **Scott William Richardson** 28 Jul 1999-30 Sep 2013 b. 11 Sep 1963 Helensburgh, Scotland
          6 **Alexandra Jane Louise (Sandy, Alex) (Malcher, Mitchell) Fullerton** b. 18 Sep 1966 Sydney m1. **Graeme Paul Mitchell** 14 Jan 1989 div. 3 Nov 2004 Sydney b. 22 Sep 1964 Maidenhead, England [son of Gary Donald Mitchell and Ann Camille Fowler] m2. **Ian Neil Fullerton** 20 Nov 2014 Maleny, Qld b. 10 Jun 1956 Nambour, Qld [son of Hector Fullerton and Daisy Lillian Cross]
          [Children of Sandy Malcher and Graeme Paul Mitchell]
            7 **Flynn Oliver Gary Mitchell** b. 13 Jan 1998 Buderim, Qld
            7 **Elouise Victoria (Ella) Mitchell** b. 18 Nov 2000 Nambour, Qld
          [Children of Ian Neil Fullerton]
            7 **Kate Daisy Fullerton** b. 2 Mar 1989, identical twin
            7 **Sarah Jill Fullerton** b. 2 Mar 1989, identical twin
            7 **Laura Rose Fullerton** b. 15 Nov 1990
            7 **Ellen Amelia Fullerton** b. 12 Nov 1992
            7 **James Ian Fullerton** b. 4 Nov 1995
          6 **Christopher Charles (Chris) Malcher** b. 14 Nov 1968 Sydney m. **Giang Le Truong** 5 Dec 2009 Sydney b. 24 Nov 1972 Hung Yen, Vietnam [daughter of Truong Viet Hung and Le Thuy Dau]
            7 **Oliver Truong Malcher** b. 24 Jun 2012 Canberra
            7 **Emily Le Malcher** b. 2 July 2014 Canberra
      4 **John Peter Hogan** b. 3 May 1906 Bourke, NSW BC 11462 d. 1979 Ref 103861 m. **Norah Hogan** 1936
        5 **Patricia Hogan** b. c 1936-1937 m. **Kevin Slattery**

Norbert Leo (Norm) Hogan: b. 29 Apr 1903 d. 18 Sep 1960

Son of John Bernard Hogan and Jessie (Douglass) Hogan
Brother of Catherine Hogan (Cath) Mason
Married Ralda Burns 5 Jun 1930
Father of Leone Hogan White, b. 2 Jun 1931 and Ken Hogan, b. c1934

Norm was married, 37, and the father of two teenagers when he joined the 2/20 Battalion of the Australian Imperial Forces on 1 Jul 1940, number NX57364. His war experience was not long, since he was captured in Singapore at its fall on 15 February 1942, and for 3½ dreadful years he was a prisoner of war in the *hell* that was Changi, which must have been the lowest period of his existence.

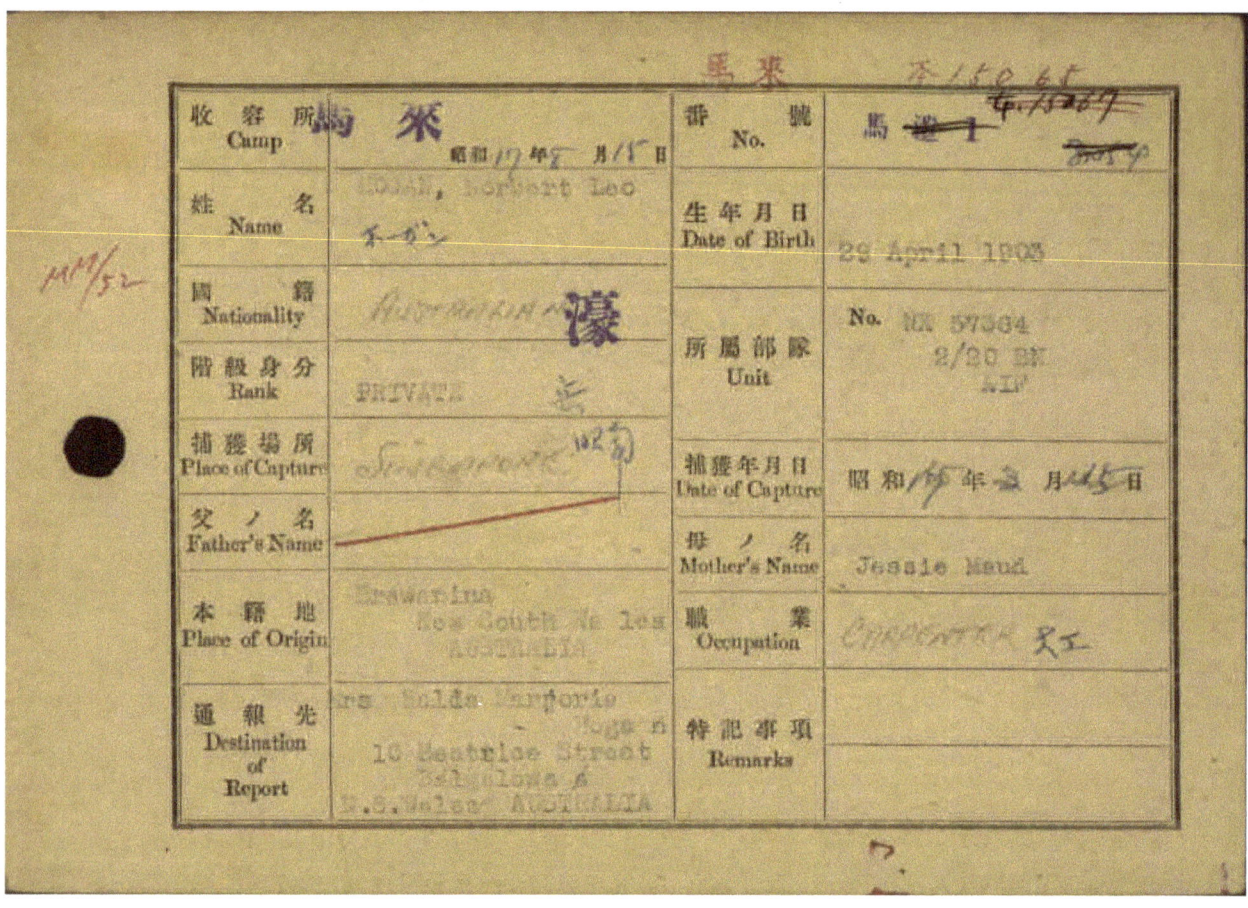

This nearly illegible Prisoner of War record is from Singapore / Changi for Norm Hogan

He came back to Australia, however, and his sister **Cath Mason** and family met his hospital ship when it arrived in Brisbane after the war. **Vic** took his family downriver in a Fairmile boat to meet the ship, and had to wait for hours while the hospital ship was made 'legal' to come up the river. **Cath** and **Norm** were very emotional but **Norm** found his way down to a porthole so he could hold Mum's hand. He was however, much emaciated, and never did recover his health, dying in 1960.

John Hogan: b. 1808 d. 2 Jun 1878

GREAT-GRANDFATHER OF CATH (HOGAN) MASON
FROM BREE, BALLYHOGUE, COUNTY WEXFORD, IRELAND
HUSBAND OF CATHERINE REGAN
GREAT-GREAT-GRANDFATHER OF JAN (MASON) O'DONNELL AND HELEN (MASON) MALCHER

John Hogan arrived on the *Ayrshire* on 25 Oct 1841 with his wife **Catherine Regan**, of the same Parish. They left Ireland with their three children, however two died on 11 Oct 1841 during the voyage.
    Richard, aged 9, who died on the voyage of an illegible disease
    Margaret, aged 3
    Ellen, aged 2, also died on the voyage of marasmus, or malnutrition

Despite the positive note in the Surgeon's records for the trip (below), it must have been hell. An outbreak of typhoid, and two of their three children dying on the same day, a large number of small children, with a death rate of 21%, and an area of only 19 square feet (just over a single bed size) for each person to live, eat, exercise, sleep, and perform their toilet operations. This does not take into account the 80 under-7 children who further crowded the passenger deck.

The ship's records show that **John Hogan** was a farm servant, as was his wife, he aged 27 in 1841 (ie born 1814 – compared with the death certificate by his son, which says born 1808). His wife **Catherine** is shown as a year younger than her husband (ie born 1815 compared with the death certificate which suggests a birth date of 1810). They give the 'health, strength and probable usefulness' of both as 'very good'. With no complaints against them, and show **John** as being able to read, while **Catherine** is said to be able neither to read nor write. One source gives **John Hogan's** father as **Peter Hogan**, mother **Ellen Doyle**, now dead. **Catherine's** father is given as **John Regan**, mother **Joanna Quinlin**, also now dead.

The **Hogans** (or at least **John**) were brought out, as were many on their ship, by AB Smith & Co. who were recorded as *'introduced into the colony of NSW on government bounty by Messrs AB Smith & Co. in pursuance of the Colonial Secretary's Authority to them dated 20 Apr 1839'*. The entire shipload were assisted migrants. Agents list No. R2135. The bounty appears to have amounted to £19 each for **John** and **Catherine**, and £5 for the 3 year old **Margaret**. This appears to be the right range in view of the comment in Reid & Johnson that *'overall an adult assisted emigrant from Ireland to Sydney in the 1850s probably had to find a sum of money somewhere between £6 and £10'*. This can be compared to the 1950s contribution from British assisted migrants of £10.

The *Ayrshire*, a ship of 873 registered tons, left Liverpool on 10 Jul 1841, and spent 106 days on the voyage, during which time, according to the Surgeon's report, it called at NO ports. It carried 212 adults on board (the total permissible), and had a passenger deck of 150' x 33' to carry them and their several children. It was quarantined on arrival with Typhus Fever, from which there were a number of deaths on the voyage.

Surgeon's Report from the *Ayrshire*

	Adults		Children 7-14 Years		Children Under 7 Years		Totals	
	M	F	M	F	M	F	M	F
Embarked	100	102	23	25	34	45	167	172
Death on voyage	2	3	1		11	5		
Total deaths	2	4	1	0	12	5	15	9
Total landed	108	98	22	25	24	40	154	163

This does not include the seven births where death occurred almost immediately. The maths of the statistics don't appear to work, but are verbatim.

- Only the Hogans came from Wexford (of 63 Protestant, 125 Catholic Irish).
- There were 8 Scots.
- Most were physical workers – 55 Agricultural labourers, 16 carpenters, 9 blacksmiths, 3 shepherds (of 94 males)
- Of the 34 females, 5 were house servants, 9 farm servants, 8 housemaids. Married women's occupations were not listed.
- The ship suffered typhus fever, infantile fever, dysentery and diarrhoea. One poor woman, Elizabeth Ritson, at the age of 31, having given birth to a son on the 13 Aug, died of 'chronic diarrhoea' on 27 Oct after the ship arrived, during the quarantine period, followed shortly after by her 11-week-old son who died of convulsions.
- Several of the reported deaths were from Typhus, several from Marasmus, particularly in young children, about which the surgeon makes an (almost illegible) comment that this is hardly surprising given the absence of the milk supply necessary for the preservation of young children. The outbreak of Typhus seemed to have been late in the voyage, most of the deaths occurring from mid-to-late October (arrival date being 25 Oct), and it took even the young adults — two sisters, aged 22 and 25, a young man of 26, and a woman of 36, all of whom died on 19 and 21 Oct.

Sections of the Surgeon's report are reproduced verbatim.

During voyage.
   The adults came, generally, in good health. The children suffered diarrhoea, from the difficulties of the voyage [on arrival]. *With the exception of those in hospital the immigrants were all in good health on arrival.*

Did the vessel prove to be of a desirable description for the conveyance of passengers?
   In every respect.

Any defects in the nature and quality of the accommodations for the fitting up of the vessel?
   In the absence of a proper supply of milk on board a ship, having so many children of an age where attention and proper diet is absolutely mandatory for their preservation.

Medical supplies.
   [Illegible] *Seem OK.*

Were the provisions of good quality?
   Without exception.

General condition and character of the immigrants?
   General condition and character of the immigrants my opinion is good. Many of them, particularly those from the manufacturing districts of England ... [Illegible]

Divine Service?
   On 10 Sundays, which was all that weather permitted. [ie on the open deck]

School on Board?
   Yes, attended by 90 children and 14 adults. [a need demonstrated by first the fact that literacy or the lack of it was part of the recorded information for each individual and second by the number who could neither read nor write, or could only read – or when, as succinctly put on one case who 'read poorly and wrote worse']

Janet Claire (Jan) (Mason, Fagan) O'Donnell: b. 14 Oct 1932

FIRST DAUGHTER OF VIC AND CATH (HOGAN) MASON
SISTER OF HELEN (MASON) MALCHER
MARRIED ARTHUR FAGAN, M1. 8 MAY 1955-1960 B. 24 JUL 1930 D. C1970
MARRIED CY O'DONNELL M2. 12 DEC 1968 B. 27 JUL 1922 D. 11 JUN 2006

By Jan O'Donnell

Jan was born at Windermere Private Hospital in Prahan, Victoria on 14 Oct 1932. **Vic** was obviously a little excited as on the Birth Certificate he registered the mother as **Kathleen Florence** instead of **Catherine**.

Dad, employed by Westrex (Western Electric), installed sound in theatres in Melbourne, was transferred back to Sydney in 1933 and travelled back with **Cath,** with **Jan** in a washing clothes basket in his very tiny open Austin Wasp to a new house in Palmer Street, Dover Heights.

Helen was born at Minto Hospital in Rose Bay. I certainly remember being taken by **May** (**Mum**'s sister) to visit **Mum** and the new

Jan and one of her many beloved poodles, Kelly, 2008

sister. I can remember walking the stairs and the flowers on the landing. I was given a celluloid doll bigger than **Helen** with a complete outfit knitted by **Mum**.

On my fifth birthday in 1937, **Dad** organised on-screen cartoons, with Mickey Mouse etc at the party. Very new and of course very special. All so different from today.

I walked to school at Mary Magdelene Rose Bay, then to St. Anne's later in year. One outstanding memory about this time is that **Mum** and her sister **Auntie May** met me after school one day down at Rose Bay and **May** bought ice creams for us all. We were walking back across the street to **Mum** and **Helen** and I dropped one of the two ice creams I was carrying. I said immediately 'Oh I've dropped **Helen**'s'. Got a healthy smack on my bottom for my trouble. I can't remember though if ice cream was replaced!

Aunty May was a very special person in **Helen**'s and my life. She was the relative we saw the most of. She apparently did not have a particularly happy life herself and had no children of her own. She lived on plantations in New Guinea with her husband Ron Robinson 1932-1937. One of our very special treats was to be dressed to the nines, warned in no uncertain terms how we would conduct ourselves and be taken to the 6th floor of David Jones for afternoon tea with **Gran Hogan** and **Aunty May**. She sadly died around Christmas 1944.

I remember **Mum** coming in one day wearing dark glasses, about 1938. Huge drama as I had apparently been home at lunchtime and may not have closed the door, and **Mum**'s engagement ring had been stolen from our place. **Mum** always said she knew which woman had taken it. It was a beautiful two diamond ring but was never replaced.

We moved to No.1 Gap Road Watsons Bay, and my sister **Helen** and I both went to the nearby Star of the Sea school. **Mum** and **Dad** had lots of friends visiting, and there was much laughter at home. But **Dad** was away at the war (in the North Atlantic, we believe) on the night in May 1942 when the Japanese submarines came into the Harbour through the Boom, very close to the harbourside Watsons Bay. Mum stayed close to both **Helen** and I, and we were the only kids at school who had not been up throughout all the fuss and excitement of sirens and searchlights. We were *not* allowed to be upset.

With **Dad** and the Navy organising us, we were then very swiftly transferred to Condobolin out of the danger zone, with **Mum's** friend **Mona** and her daughter Barbara McMinn, whose home at Warners Avenue we visited so often. In Condobolin I remember the most fearsome dust storm: we watched it coming in and then completely enveloping the town and making everything very dark. After it passed by — it had been in the daytime and we were all at home — everything was covered in red dirt. Extraordinary, but not damaging, and it certainly made for lots of heavy housework. We also had an extraordinary little cotton dilly bag which hung from the shoulder. I would think it was for a gas mask but don't remember having to cope with one of those, but it did have a little 'school' rubber which had to be bitten very strongly between the front teeth as we practised jumping into trenches built inside the school yard. It just does not bear thinking about the shape the country would have been in if the war had gotten through to Condobolin, so I think the jumping into trenches was a waste of time!

In July 1943 after our affiliation with the UK was changed to the US, **Dad** was posted to HMAS *Moreton* in Brisbane, where the US Navy personnel were much evident. So we all moved again, to Lothian Street, Annerley, a big Queenslander with a wrap-around verandah and a large loquat tree in the front yard to be climbed, sat in and explored. We were there from mid-1943 to the end of 1945.

1944 was the Christmas that **Dad** took himself off to Maryborough in 'the hearse' (our family car) and decided to treat the family to a small, very live suckling pig and some live chooks, installing them under the house and making plans for a huge Christmas dinner. With all his American servicemen friends, rationing was not a problem we had had to cope with, but all that extra meat really was going to be quite something. **Mum's** young brother **John Hogan** was there on Army leave (on his way back to the Middle East) and **Dad** and **John** decided they had to slaughter the pig. They hung the poor thing by his back feet on the washing line and poked a carving knife at its throat umpteen times. The pig squealed, **Dad** and **John** were fearfully upset and had lots of drinks to settle them, and the bloke next door had to come in and do the murdering. The whole time that both the pig and chooks resided under the house **Mum** was threatening to leave 'permanently'.

I can remember VP (Victory in the Pacific) day very clearly in 1945. The noise created by people celebrating was horrific! **Dad** and **Mum** took us into Brisbane in the back of 'the hearse' to see everything, but apparently the celebrations got a little too boisterous for our very protected eyes and we were brought home.

Another big memory was being taken down the Brisbane River in late 1945 to welcome **Mum's** older brother **Norm Hogan** home. **Dad** took us down in a Fairmile boat, and we had to 'hove to' for hours while the hospital ship was made 'legal' to come up the river. **Mum** and **Norm** were very emotional (he had been in Changi prison camp for 3½ dreadful years), but Norm found his way down to a porthole so he could hold **Mum's** hand.

We left Brisbane in February 1946, and very shortly after discovered that **Dad** had been 'gypped' by the builder of what was to have been our own new home at Dover Heights, overlooking the ocean. Recovery was difficult, but it meant that all four of us had to live at **Grandma (Priscilla) Mason's** for a while. The school chosen for the two of us, extraordinarily, since **Grandma** lived at Bankstown, was Holy Cross College at Woollahra, near Bondi Junction. I had to go straight to 2nd year and was thus unable to take any subjects which had had to be started in 1st year i.e. languages, chemistry, maths. I'd been shattered at the interview to join the school as **Mum** had snuck in the question 'Would they take boarders'? – a subject that had definitely never been discussed at home. Fortunately they didn't – we would have had to go to OLMC Parramatta. So we had to commute daily from Bankstown to Woollahra by train and bus – about 1½ hours each way.

Living with **Grandma Mason** was hard for **Mum** and **Dad**. Grandma did not like any of her daughters-in-law and as **Mum** was the senior one she was particularly unpopular. So the house had **Grandma**, **Dad's** young brother **Bob**, **Mum** and **Dad** and **Helen and I**, in a two-bedroomed house and one fearful outside toilet. Dad filled in the front verandah a bit and **Helen and I** shared it as a bedroom. The back verandah was filled in at one end so **Bob** could have a bedroom. But everything we owned as a family was in the front bedroom as well as **Mum** and **Dad**. Quite a snug fit.

During this year **Mum** had a complete break-down. She collapsed in **Grandma's** dining room and was hospitalised, but she did all her recuperating at the house of her long-term friend **Mona McMinn's**.

By 1948, though, we were able to move into our own new home at 12 Gallipoli Street Bankstown, still travelling to Holy Cross. **Helen** transferred to Santa Sabina for 3rd year, and

Chartres Business College for us both, one after the other — **Helen** did shorthand and **I** was taught the eccentricities of accounting machines, which I'm still convinced should never have been allowed to be used in office procedure. My first job was with Sargood Gardiners, then Hoffnungs for a couple of years, and I was usheretting part time at Bankstown Cinema during those years.

To improve the family income, in 1950 our parents bought and moved into a dwelling/mixed business shop combination in Arden Street, Waverley. At one stage **Gran Hogan** came to live with us in the top front room. She can't have been there for very long because I really only remember her in her one bedroom and front verandah flat at Bon Accord Avenue, Bondi Junction forever knitting baby clothes to make some sort of income. Pensions as such were certainly not available in those days.

Dad at this stage wanted to go back into the Navy, regretting his resignation at the end of the war. There were many conversations between **Mum** and **Dad** about how the shop 'would be seen as a conflict of interest' when he was back in the Navy. **Mum** had to 'let every one know it was only hers'. When it was sold, we moved to the Captain's cottage on HMAS *Watson* navy base. **Helen** and I were often in trouble for rushing down to the bus through the 'gangway' at the same time as 'Colours', and not showing the necessary amount of respect (there should be *no* movement or other sound during 'Colours'!). A glorious spot on the southern headland of Sydney Harbour, with the highlight each year being the luncheon party organised by **Mum** and **Dad** for their friends for the start of the Sydney-Hobart Yacht Race. I had my 21st there — a delight.

In 1954 I went to Melbourne to hostessing school with Australian National Airways (ANA) — the best 18 months of my life. I still have friends from ANA. I married **Arthur Fagan** in May 1955 at St Mary Magdelene Rose Bay. **Dad** was posted up to the Navy base on Manus Island, New Guinea. **Mum** went up to join him, followed later by **Helen**, for her 21st in 1956.

I lost my first child in 1956. **Dad** talked to me from Manus on a pedal radio. Me shouting from a hospital ward so he could hear was not a big success. Two more children were lost by 1958. No valid or acceptable medical cause was ever given. **Arthur** was unfortunately institutionalised in 1959 and we divorced in 1960. I retained the Holden **Mrs Fagan** had bought for us — the only thing I kept from the marriage — and went to work for Simon Carves.

Jan's wedding to Arthur Fagan 1955. Sister Helen in attendance

Gran Hogan died in October, 1956, a month after **Mum** came home from Manus.

The greatest memory from 1960 was decidedly the holiday **Mum** and **Dad** organised at Sussex Inlet. **Helen** remembers the holiday as a horrendous introduction to our family *en masse* for **Harry,** her prospective husband. The most glorious day was when we went out in the boat (I suppose primarily to go fishing), **Dad** was happily playing Captain, threw the anchor overboard and firmly attached us to the submarine cable. **Helen** had to dive in (a few times) to unhook it. Not a happy afternoon and certainly not helped by laughter from all of us. But **Helen** and **Harry** were married in April 1961 anyway.

That year I went to U.K. on the *Himalaya* for twelve months to work for the Australian High Commissioner (Sir Eric Harrison), driving around England in my supplied Mini Minor van with a map of Australia painted on the door and a matching one on my light blue pleated suit uniform, promoting Australian canned fruit. The 14-week promotions boosted the bank account while giving a wonderful opportunity to mix with the locals. The classic was the Poms' reaction to passionfruit being in cans of fruit salad. The promotions were in the local supermarkets and I stayed in local small hotels. The job kept paying the rent on a flat in Swiss Cottage, a London suburb, while I was away and subsidised extended trips to Europe between promotions. As the little van was mine seven days a week and they were quite happy to fill it with petrol on Fridays and Mondays it certainly was a wonderful way to travel cheaply through the UK each and every weekend staying primarily in Youth Hostels, or whatever was cheapest.

Vicki was born to **Harry** and **Helen** on 16 Aug 1964. I got the telegram (via *Post Restante*) in Salzburg. I would have preferred to have been at home with family to celebrate, but within weeks I met **Harry's** family in Innsbruck, stayed with them overnight and *really* enjoyed them.

In February **1964** I had a wonderful weekend in New York with Neil Falconer staying at the Plaza. I shared the flight from Heathrow to Idlewild (which later was renamed JFK) later that year with the Beatles, so it took a *long* time to disembark while they had their photos taken on their first trip to the States.

I came back to Australia and returned to work with Norman & Addicoat but was not happy, the Neil affair was not working. Met a lass who suggested I join her on the *Malekula* to Port Moresby in May. She lived and worked up there. I decided to join her on the cruise and loved the whole New Guinea Territory atmosphere. In March 1965 I flew home after a month, resigned, got rid of my flat, packed my bits and pieces and went back. I stayed until late 1973 and loved every minute. Worked with the Electricity Commission for a short time but then Carpenters asked me to join New Guinea travel with a view to opening a new branch in Lae in '66. I jumped at it.

Sandy was born 18 Sep 1966, and **Mum/Cath** came up with **Vicki** to Moresby to stay with me. The poor little mite, such a delight on her first holiday away from her mother, fitted in everywhere but then got Chicken Pox. It wasn't very comfortable for her with the three of us, **Mum, Vicki** and **me,** sharing a bedroom.

My Holden and I were transferred to Lae on *Bulolo* and I was given a two-bedroomed house. Life was once again shining.

Chris — first son, third child for **Harry** and **Helen** — was born 14 Nov 1968. **Cy** and I married in December in Lae, New Guinea. **Cy** had been working at the TAA club in Lae but had accepted the job at Rabaul Golf Club as Secretary/Manager from New Year's Eve. I'd always enjoyed Rabaul with its volcanoes and its permanent sulphur smell. We came to Sydney to meet **Chris** and introduce **Cy** to the family.

Unfortunately **Grandma (Priscilla) Mason** died a couple of days before Christmas (23 Dec 1968) and we were unable to stay to be with **Dad. Cy** and I had been out to the home where she was staying and she proved she had not changed at all. She suggested I let down the hem of my dress which was not a lot above my knee. **Cy** was very amused that *anyone* was prepared to tell me what length to wear *anything!*

1969 and 1970 were the Rabaul golf club and the Kieta hotel for **Cy**, and early 1971 it was Konedobu Club Port Moresby. **Helen** visited with **Chris**. She enjoyed diving in Port Moresby harbour and included a visit to Mt Hagen, and we enjoyed looking after **Chris.**

I went to work with Ansett in Port Moresby and wore long mumus, much admired in Sydney so **Helen** and **Mum** wore them too. Our tiny house on the harbour was delightful and a perfect spot for breakfasts out on the lawn with Yabi dancing attendance.

1971-73 were the Kieta Club on Bougainville for **Cy** and for me Ansett in Kieta. During these past years on Bougainville, I'd sat in the same chair and worked for umpteen airlines — Ansett Airlines of Australia, Ansett Airlines of Papua New Guinea, TAA and Air New Guinea, as they all sorted out who and what would be able to cope after Independence. Air New Guinea became the name when Michael Somare took over as Prime Minister at Independence in 1975. As he decreed that we would all have to have PNG passports after independence, both **Cy** and I decided very sadly that we would have to leave New Guinea, in October 1973.

Vicki, Sandy and **Chris** came to Kieta for three months in 1973 while **Helen** and **Harry** travelled to Europe. **Chris** started school here. The children and I all enjoyed every minute of their visit. And so did Yabi my 'house boi' who sat at the table with them every afternoon learning from them as they did their homework. **Sandy's** tooth fairy story was glorious. The tiny tooth came out at school and of all places she tucked it into her bikini knickers. As was normal we had a swim in the harbour on the way home from school and of course the wretched tooth washed out. It's quite exciting trying to write to Tooth Fairies and explain how tooth was lost and have to stick it on the outside of the wire door because 'herself' had of course worked out that that door was locked at night and so how could the tooth fairy get in to do her trick with the money in the glass?

I can only remember one slight hiccup. I suppose the three children had been in Kieta for a few days and had suddenly realised they were missing **Mum** and **Dad**, so a few tears and they had gone to bed a bit unhappy. **Sandy** eventually said '**Auntie Jan** you just don't *understand*! It's all SO different.'

The three of them thoroughly enjoyed their weekends out on plantations and/or on our boat going out to the small islands in the harbour with the Dale family, Tiffany and Donna being at school with **Vicki** and **Sandy**. We always took a 'boi' or two either to dive for lobsters or to help gather the glorious wild orchids out on the island. Another story. **Sandy** had big problems from birth with eating bread (being gluten intolerant) so she had to take her 'special biscuits' as her lunch each day. Eventually heard from Trish Dale the story of how **Sandy** was trading her biscuits for Tiffany's sandwiches each day — and there had obviously been no adverse reactions. I decided to introduce bread at home. I'll never forget talking to **Dad** (on my happy phone at work) and telling him how I was coping. 'Not fair, not fair' claimed he. Decisions which could have an effect on the child's health MUST be discussed with **Helen** before I changed the life style. Bit late. But thank heavens it was a success. Maybe it was because that was the year **Sandy** would have been seven (the old-wive's tale says children's ailments will disappear on their 7th birthday).

Probably one of the most memorable flights of my New Guinea life was the final DC3 flight from Bougainville (Buin) in 1973. The flight had been operating from Rabaul to Bougainville for many years and was almost as important as the coastal ships that plied their way down through the plantations. I'd been working for Ansett for so long I was given the opportunity to crew the final flight with a TAA guy who had been around as long as I had. He did the ditching bit — 'suppose this pella balus him e go buggarup pinnis…' (spelt so it can be read), and brought the invited passenger list to their *knees*. Our friend Paul Mason (no relation) of Innus plantation had filled the cargo hold with orchids and the night we were down in Buin the local 'bois' and 'meris' (New Guinea men and women) made huge leis for the nose cone of the aircraft and as we took off from Buin the skipper waved and dipped the wings until the leis came off… Absolutely spectacular!!

We left Bougainville in 1973, visited Sydney then to Melbourne for a 'Down to Earth' gathering (ANA ex hostesses), with multiple tickets written in Kieta. We saw a great deal of wonderful Australia together, and in Perth we opted for Darwin to live, and rented a brick house in Pott St there. (It blew apart in Cyclone Tracy).

In 1974, **Cy** was appointed to Darwin Community College (now NT Uni), and I worked with Ross Hallam travel. We moved to Trower Road in July, paid for it on 3 Dec while Cyclone Sabrina was hovering around, so our Solicitor ensured that our insurance was valid at that date. **Cyclone Tracy** demolished it on 24 Dec 1974. Floorboards of the 2nd story were left, so we lived underneath those for the next 18 months, but were luckily given a fairly large caravan from the College which helped. Our beautiful nine-month-old Rotary Cappela was drowned at Brisbane wharves on its way from PNG in Brisbane's floods that year. The car had been packed solidly with all our artifacts from all parts of the Territory and the boot was stuffed with all our diving and snorkeling gear. A huge loss, and Acts of God are a bit hard to have reimbursed. Ross Hallam Travel were wiped out, so I went back to Ansett in Darwin.

Helen, Harry and kids came to visit for Christmas 1975 and have a holiday in Alice Springs on the way home. Friend Gerry Isiker played Santa for **Chris** in the front yard, having arrived on back of **Cy**'s ute. We all went down to Adelaide River, and I can't believe we swam there. These days it is absolutely alive with very large crocodiles.

We bought 31 Hamilton Parade, Macleay Island, landwards of Stradbroke Island off the south Queensland coast, in November 1982 while down South on a driving holiday. Early in 1983 we drove down from Darwin to Macleay in a Toyota van with two poodles (Madam and Mischa) and settled into our new home 28 Feb 1983. The population was then well under 200, no town power or water, so we had a huge generator, gas lights and a gas/electric fridge and a gas stove. Marvellous! We were able to have quite some exchange visits with **Mum** and **Dad** at Tugun and on the Island which they both loved. **Dad** was nursing **Mum** and was often very tired so every so often we would bring him to Macleay for a break with **Cy** and I'd go down and stay with Mum.

This seemed to give them both an enjoyable rest. **Mum** passed away in Nov 1983 at Southport Hospital after a fearful year fighting cancer which she had decided none of us should be told about. Even **Dad** didn't know!

In 1984 we were able to have our last Family Christmas. **Helen, Harry, Dad, Punti** (Harry's uncle) and **Vicki, Sandy** and **Chris** all came to visit for Christmas dinner. We'd been able to borrow a huge tent for the overflow of people in the back yard. **Dad** and **Punti** had always enjoyed each other's company so it was quite a happy gathering. **Helen** and **Harry** went off to Stradbroke afterwards and enjoyed more of Moreton Bay for a few days.

Dad passed away on **Mum**'s birthday (Saturday 6 Apr 1985) at Greenslopes hospital – quite a shock to us all. He had spent quite some time in and out of the Private Hospital at Currumbin, had come to stay with us on Macleay and was coping reasonably well. We drove him to hospital and were promised 'it was definitely not a one way trip'. **Helen** visited him on the Thursday on her way up to Byron Bay to locate **Sandy**, and thought he was well, and we visited on the Friday. **Cy and I** were shocked when they called on Saturday to say we had lost him. We then had the problem of trying to find **Helen** and **Sandy** in Byron over the Easter weekend.

Cy started to build his golf course in 1987, which kept both of us much involved for the next nine or ten years. In fact it remained **Cy**'s main interest until his death in 2006. Although a lot of work, it certainly was a lot of fun and of course gave us the opportunity to meet a huge number of wonderful people who each in his or her own way helped **Cy** to build his dream.

Cy was diagnosed with both bowel and prostate cancer in Aug 1996. He had just had his 84th birthday. He was operated on at Logan Hospital within 30 hours, as at that time QEII hospital (where he was diagnosed) did not have an Intensive Care ward. In Dec 1996 he had his first surgery on his prostate, and chemo and radiation were nominated as definitely necessary. So from January to June '97 we stayed in a motel near the Mater from Monday to Friday each week. We came home each weekend to stay at our home and of course to see our poodle Para Port who was being baby-sat by a particularly good friend, Carol. **Cy**'s greatest argument against having chemo had been leaving Para but Carol fixed that. The treatment did however give him another ten years living on his Island. He passed away peacefully at Redlands Hospital on 11 Jun 2006. I was with him.

The Mason family congregates in 1989 for the 150th anniversary of the landing of the first Masons in Australia in 1839, at the home of Harry and Helen (Mason) Malcher
L-R: Bob Mason, Helen (Mason) Malcher, Jack Loveridge, Dorothy (Mason) Loveridge, Amanda Lillington, her mother Lyn Mason, Lillington Newman, Robyn Mason, Jan (Mason) O'Donnell and Chris Malcher.

Helen Marie (Mason) Malcher: b. 24 Sep 1935

DAUGHTER OF VIC AND CATH (HOGAN) MASON
SISTER OF JAN (MASON, FAGAN) O'DONNELL
MARRIED HEINRICH CARL (HARRY) MALCHER 8 APR 1961 B. 1 APR 1925
MOTHER TO VICTORIA FRANCES (VICKI) B. 16 AUG 1964
ALEXANDRA JANE (ALEX, SANDY) B. 18 SEP 1966
CHRISTOPHER CHARLES (CHRIS) B. 14 NOV 1968

Childhood memories are few — perhaps being the 'little sister' left it up to **Jan** to remember everything. The shop at Arden St Waverley where we lived during my high school years gave me the opportunity to walk the 2km down Arden Street to Coogee Beach fairly frequently, for a swim. Later our home at Watsons Bay, Fort Southern, was also close to the Watsons Bay baths, so I could continue my love of swimming. It was here I met **John Lyons**, a close friend and excellent swimming coach.

The family stayed in the Captain's cottage on the Navy base at Watsons Bay in our late teens, and it was memorable if only because my sister **Jan** and I running for a bus to work *always* clashed with the essential short silence for 'Colours' at 8am, to the considerable enjoyment of the ratings.

After leaving school at 15, I first worked on the Navy switchboard at Watson, then at 18 joined the Army, stationed at Victoria Barracks and training as a truck driver. I also attended Chartres Business College then the Scottish Union Insurance Group, which taught me a great deal.

For my 21st birthday my parents gifted me a trip to the Navy base on Manus Island, where **Dad** was stationed. I spent three months here and put my truck driving skills to use racing jeeps up and down the airstrip with the sailors.

In my early 20s I worked as private secretary to the charismatic **Charles Anton**, insurance broker and president of the Ski Tourers Association of Australia, now the Australian Alpine Club. I accompanied him on trips to the NSW snow fields and learned to ski, a skill I would use more than I realised. **Harry Malcher** was much involved in opening up the snow fields with **Charles**. I met **Harry** a few times when he came in to the office in the late 50s. Neither of us took much notice of the other until the long weekend of October 1960, when we were all at the original Roslyn Lodge at Thredbo. We hit it off so well that we married in April 1961, in the Holy Family church in Lindfield.

With **Harry** as a builder it took more time to plan than to build, but our house in East Lindfield, completed by **Harry** in 1963, has been marvellous for us both for over 50 years.

Our three children, **Victoria Frances (Vicki)**, born 1964, **Alexandra Jane (Sandy, Alex)**, born 1966 and **Christopher Charles (Chris)**, born 1968, were all christened at the Star of the Sea church at Watsons Bay, which **Jan** and I attended as a teenager.

When the children started school I enrolled in university, completing high school then majoring in history while working full time as an executive secretary. I was a History Mistress at Benilde Senior Boys High School Bankstown, then went on to start a small computer company, Micro Business Services in the late 1980s.

In retirement I have volunteered extensively, in a gardening group as well as history and literary societies, including, particularly, the Jane Austen Society of Australia. For 22 years I edited and published their bi-annual publications and some books— almost always a real pleasure.

Helen and Harry Malcher at their wedding on 8 Apr 1961

Sunday Sun and Guardian, 21 Nov 1937. Helen at 2, modelling Glare Glasses

Before starting this family history I published a history of **Harry's** family, *The Story of the Von Kronenfeldt and Malcher Families* (2007), *50 Years of The Austrian Club Sydney* (2011) and the DVD *Charles Anton, the Main Range, and Thredbo, 1952-66.* We enjoyed many trips to the Thredbo area with our children and continue to do so — skiing in the winter and bushwalking in summer.

Travel to **Harry**'s homeland and family in Austria, to the UK and Europe has always been a joy. We've been fortunate to visit most areas in Australia, plus Czechoslovakia, Germany, the UK and Ireland, Finland and Russia.

But after over 50 years of marriage, our greatest achievement is our children: **Vicki,** a travel executive; **Sandy**, an editor and publisher with two children, **Flynn** and **Ella** and recently married to **Ian Fullerton**; and **Chris**, a Senior Business Analyst with two children, **Oliver** and **Emily** with his wife **Giang.**

Four Mason women at Jan's 80th birthday, Landsborough, Qld
October 2012. Vicki, Helen, Jan, Sandy

Sandy, Harry Malcher — still the best skier of us all even now at 90 —
Sandy's daughter Ella and Vicki. Thredbo, NSW, September 2012

> **Descendants of Helen Mason and Harry Malcher**
>
> **1 Helen Marie (Mason) Malcher** b. 24 Sep 1935 Rose Bay Hospital m. **Heinrich Carl (Harry) Malcher** 8 Apr 1961 Sydney b. 1Apr 1925 an Austrian, born in Turramurra, NSW [son of Franz Xaver Ernst Malcher and Hedwig Barbara Malik]
>   **2 Victoria Frances (Vicki) Malcher** b. 16 Aug 1964 Sydney m1. **Timothy Martin Brown** 28 Nov 1992 div. Apr 1997 Sydney b. 31 Oct 1961 Middlesborough, England m2.(df) **Scott William Richardson** 28 Jul 1999-30 Sep 2013 b. 11 Sep 1963 Helensburgh, Scotland
>   **2 Alexandra Jane Louise (Sandy, Alex) (Malcher, Mitchell) Fullerton** b. 18 Sep 1966 Sydney m1. **Graeme Paul Mitchell** 14 Jan 1989 div. 3 Nov 2004 Sydney b. 22 Sep 1964 Maidenhead, England. m2. **Ian Neil Fullerton** 20 Nov 2014 Maleny, Qld b. 10 Jun 1956 Nambour, Qld
>   [Children of Sandy Malcher and Graeme Paul Mitchell]
>   **3 Flynn Oliver Gary Mitchell** b. 13 Jan 1998 Buderim, Qld
>   **3 Elouise Victoria (Ella) Mitchell** b. 18 Nov 2000 Nambour, Qld
>   [Children of Ian Fullerton]
>   **3 Kate Daisy Fullerton** b. 2 Mar 1989, twin
>   **3 Sarah Jill Fullerton** b. 2 Mar 1989, twin
>   **3 Laura Rose Fullerton** b. 15 Nov 1990
>   **3 Ellen Amelia Fullerton** b. 12 Nov 1992
>   **3 James Ian Fullerton** b. 4 Nov 1995
>   **2 Christopher Charles (Chris) Malcher** b. 14 Nov 1968 Sydney m. **Giang Le Truong** 5 Dec 2009 Sydney b. 24 Nov 1972 Hung Yen, Vietnam [daughter of Truong Viet Hung and Le Thuy Dau]
>   **3 Oliver Truong Malcher** b. 24 Jun 2012 Canberra
>   **3 Emily Le Malcher** b. 2 July 2014 Canberra

Victoria Frances (Vicki) Malcher: b. 16 Aug 1964

Born 16 Aug 1964
m1.Timothy Martin Brown 28 Nov 1992 – Apr 1997
m2. (df) Scott William Richardson Jul 1999 – Sep 2013

Vicki has travelled extensively throughout Australia and UK/Europe and has lived in Sydney, Maidenhead, Cairns, Glasgow and now calls St Kilda, Melbourne, home. She works in management in the travel industry, has a fascination with purple, music, Formula 1 and photography. **Vicki** is a proud aunty to two nieces and two nephews.

Vicki's editing and formatting skills have been invaluable to this publication, for which I'm extremely grateful.

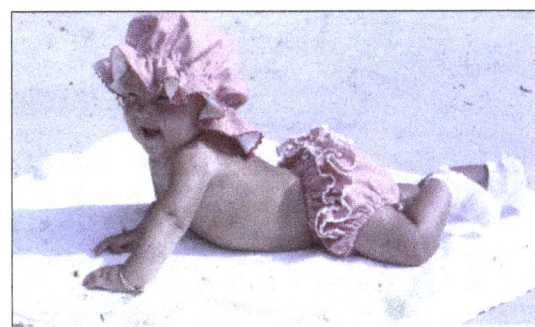
Vicki as a baby, 1964

Vicki in 2007

Alexandra Jane Louise (Sandy, Alex) (Malcher, Mitchell) Fullerton; b. 18 Sep 1966

M1. Graeme Paul Mitchell 14 Jan 1989-4 Dec 2004 b.22 Sep 1964
M2. Ian Neil Fullerton 20 Nov 2014 b.10 Jun 1956
Mother of Flynn Oliver Gary Mitchell b. 13 Jan 1998
Elouise Victoria (Ella) Mitchell b. 18 Nov 2000
Stepmother to Kate Daisy Fullerton b. 2 Mar 1989
Sarah Jill Fullerton b. 2 Mar 1989
Laura Rose Fullerton b. 15 Nov 1990
Ellen Amelia Fullerton b. 12 Nov 1992
James Ian Fullerton b. 4 Nov 1995

Sandy (also known as **Alex**) travelled to over 26 countries as a young woman and met her first husband, **Graeme Mitchell** in England in 1986, marrying him in 1989. After their separation, she raised their children, **Flynn** and **Ella,** as a single parent and travels extensively with them. The children were four and six when they were lucky enough to survive the tsunami on Boxing Day 2004 while on a remote island in Rangong Province, Thailand with their mother. **Sandy** spent many years in administration and supplements her income through real estate investment. Since 2008 she has run a successful business as a non-fiction book coach and editor, as well as leading a not-for-profit organisation educating Sunshine Coast business women. **Sandy** met **Ian Fullerton**, a father of five, in 2010, and they married in Maleny Qld on 20 Nov 2014. They live on **Ian**'s 240-acre pineapple farm in Beerwah, Queensland.

The Fullerton-Mitchell clan, at Sandy and Ian's wedding, Maleny, Qld, 20 Nov 2014
L-R Sarah, Ellen, James, Ian, Sandy, Ella, Flynn, Laura, Kate

Christopher Charles (Chris) Malcher: b. 14 Nov 1968

BORN 14 NOV 1968
M. GIANG LE TRUONG 5 DEC 2009 B. 24 NOV 1972
FATHER OF OLIVER TRUONG MALCHER, B. 24 JUN 2012,
EMILY LE MALCHER B. 2 JULY 2014

Chris was born in St Leonards, Sydney, grew up in his parent's home in East Lindfield and now lives in Canberra. His working life has been in Information Technology and Knowledge Management, focusing on business analysis. He completed a Master of Business at the University of Newcastle in 2004 and married **Giang Truong** in 2009. **Giang** arrived in Australia from Vietnam in 2004, and earned a PhD in economics at the University of Sydney in 2007. They have two children **Oliver Truong Malcher**, b. 24 Jun 2012 and **Emily Le Malcher** b. 2 Jul 2014.

Giang and Chris Malcher, with Emily at 2 months, and Oliver at 2¼. Canberra, Sep 2014

Sandy and Chris's families scrambled together in August 2014
L-R: James Fullerton, his father Ian Fullerton, Sandy nursing Emily Malcher, Ella Mitchell holding Oliver Malcher, Ba Truong (Giang's mother), Flynn Mitchell, Giang and Chris Malcher, at their house in Chifley, Canberra

John Edward (Jack) Mason: b. 21 Oct 1905 d. 17 Jun 1976

3RD SON OF WILLIAM MASON AND PRISCILLA (SMITH) MASON
MARRIED TO MELLA (MACARE) MASON 1930 B. 1908 D. 1981
FATHER OF CLARICE MARGARET (MASON) REID

Born the third son of **William** and **Priscilla Mason** in Waterloo, **Jack Mason's** early work was as a carpenter on the railways (which also employed his father **William Mason**, and his cousin **Oliver Alphonsus Mason** and others), then worked as a builder. **Jack** had a series of successful car sales and caravan sales yards during his life. He commenced building caravans, trading as Advance Caravans, which was, his daughter **Clarice** understands, the first commercial enterprise of caravans in Australia. In this venture he proved to have a flair for buying well and selling extremely well. He also operated a used car sales yard for many years, on the Pacific Highway at Yagoona, NSW, and at one stage owned a local paper which was taken over by his brother **Hilton Mason**.

Jack and **Carmella (Mella)** met and married in Bankstown, where his parents were living, in 1930, and as the economic depression tightened, they had their only child, daughter **Clarice**, born in October 1931. **Mella Macare** was the daughter of **Rocco** and **Giacontina (Jean) (Coia) Macaro** (the earlier spelling the family used). Italians, they had married in 1912 in Glasgow, Scotland, where **Jean** was born, and arrived in Sydney on 12 Sept 1912. Little is known of ancestors in Italy, but they seem to have come from Martale, now Monforte, in southern Italy. **Rocco** and **Jean's** eight children, including **Mella**, were later born in Scotland. **Mella**, with an Italian background, met with considerable disapproval from **Grandma Mason**, who referred to **Mella** throughout her entire long life as 'that Italian woman'.

Finances were extremely tight, and **Jack** made the decision to take the huge step of asking his uncle, **Dan Mason**, a successful gentleman's outfitter in Lismore, to give him a loan, for the welfare of their new daughter and to establish his business. Literally all his life he treasured in his wallet the graceful, positive letter from **Dan Mason**, granting his request and expressing his interest in the whole family of **Jack's** father **William Mason**. **Dan** died only a few months after this exchange.

Descendants of John Edward (Jack) Mason

1 **John Edward (Jack) Mason** b. 21 Oct 1905 d. 17 Jun 1976 m. **Carmella (Mella) Macare** m. 2 Dec 1930 b. 11 Oct 1908 d. 7 Mar 1981
  2 **Clarice Margaret (Mason) Reid** b. 12 Oct 1931 m. **John Arthur (Blade) Reid** 1 Oct 1954 b. 24 Mar 1932
    3 **Ross James Reid** b. 5 Jul 1956 m1. **Christine Helen Street** 4 Dec 1980 b. 20 Aug 1959 m2. **Fariba Soltani** m. 26 Jun 1993
    [Children of Ross James Reid and Christine Helen Street]
      4 **Melanie Jane Reid** b. 9 Aug 1984
      4 **Caroline Michelle Reid** b. 27 Feb 1987
      4 **Nicholas James Reid** b. 10 Aug 1990
    [Children of Ross James Reid and Fariba Soltani]
      4 **Sam Reid** b. 26 Aug 1998
    3 **Glenn John Reid** b. 19 Apr 1958 m. **Jennifer Stanley** 1 Dec 1984 b. 17 Mar 1962
      4 **Jessica Nicole Reid** b. 23 Feb 1989
      4 **Kate Elizabeth Reid** b. 23 Feb 1989
      4 **Eliza Margaret Reid** b. 16 Apr 1993
    3 **Brett Mathew Reid** b. 2 Oct 1960 m. **Judith (Jude) Bowen Triemer** 8 May 1982 b. 4 Apr 1963
      4 **Michael John Reid** b. 26 Apr 1996
      4 **Andrew Jules** b. 17 Oct 1997

Angelantonio Macaro and **Maria Macaro** were the grandparents, and **Rocco Macaro** and **Giacontina (Jean) Coia** the parents of **Mella Macare**. For the first four years of **Clarice's** life, by economic necessity, the three members of this family lived in the pleasant home of **Mella's** parents, at 291 Canterbury Road, Bankstown. Also living there, for the same reasons, were **Mella's** brothers **Tony**, his wife **Alice** and son **Tony**; and **Joe**, his wife **Vie** and son **Joseph**. **Clarice** was delighted to have company her own age.

Jack and his family moved over to Perth, and there, in 1954, **Clarice** married **John Reid** and produced two of their three sons, **Ross, Glenn** and **Brett Reid**.

About 1958-1959, when television was in its infancy. **Jack** had the initiative to open Mason's Television, a TV sales and service business in Attadale, WA , near Perth which was just coming into the TV age – a very successful venture. His brother **Eric Mason** was, coincidentally, initiating a similar successful venture in Wollongong at about the same time. There is no evidence that they assisted each other, but both were breaking new ground, and doing it well.

In 1932 **William's brother Dan** bequeathed £250 (in 1932!!) to each of **William's** six sons, and to each of their brother **Arthur's** four children. That has never been mentioned in Helen's recollection: one wonders if it actually happened. Certainly it appears in **Dan's** Will, which was probated.

Clarice sees herself as having had a happy and carefree childhood, making friends with her cousin **Tony**, and another cousin **Billy Bell** in the Bankstown area.

Jack died in 1976. His wife of many years, **Mella** lived till the age of 72, in 1981. They are survived by their daughter **Clarice** and grandchildren.

Clarice Margaret (Mason) Reid: b. 12 Oct 1931

DAUGHTER OF JACK MASON AND MELLA MACARE
M. JOHN REID 1 OCT 1954-1997
MOTHER TO ROSS, GLENN AND BRETT
GRANDMOTHER TO MELANIE, CARLINE, NICOLAS, SAM, JESSICA, KATE, ELIZA, MICHAEL AND ANDREW

by Clarice Mason herself

For the first four years of my life, my mother, father and I lived in our grandparents' house, together with my mother's brother **Tony Macare**, his wife **Alice** and their son **Tony**, as well as, sometimes, his brother **Joe**, wife **Vie** and son **Joseph**. My grandparents had the main front bedroom; **Mum, Dad** and myself had the other front bedroom; and **Tony, Alice** and little **Tony** had the middle bedroom. There was the sleepout at the back for anyone to stay if needed – **Joe** and his family lived in Narrabri and came down to stay in Sydney from time to time.

That house was in Chapel Road, Bankstown. Further along from the house was a small tuck shop opposite Revesby School which my grandmother ran as a business. I remember ice blocks on sticks made from soft drinks. She also cooked chips, scallops and sold lollies and ice creams.

Grandfather Macare worked on the Railway, but also made fantastic ice cream the Italian way. I remember watching him make it in the garage — dry ice was an important component. It was yummy ice cream. Somehow, I remember, he attached the container in which it was made to a pushbike and pedalled around the streets selling the ice cream.

There was a large bushland area at the side of the house, and a large backyard where **Tony** (some time later) ran a pipe-making business — lots of machinery and a very large kiln. Once my cousin **Billy Bell** got caught in the conveyor belt when he was working there. It was horrific, and caused great distress. **Joe** and his family at some stage returned to Sydney were he ran a successful dredging business around Botany.

My first memory was when I was about four, and the cat killed my pet rabbit. I slept in a cot next to my parents' bed, and remember hearing a lot of talk when they came in and told me what had happened. I was heartbroken. As I write this I realise that it may have been the root of my intense dislike of cats.

All the families got along well. **Mum** and **Alice** remained close, and **Tony** was like a brother to me. **Billy, Etta** and **Bill's** son, visited often; **Tony, Billy** and I were great playmates. We used to roam the bush, pitch tents in the backyard in searing heat and read comics and drink bottled water — and climbed the fruit trees which surrounded the house. We were close, and only children. It is sad that contact was lost in later years.

The reason we lived with the Italian grandparents was because of the Great Depression. My parents married in December 1930, and I was born in October 1931. Work was hard to find — my father was a builder by trade. For some time he worked on the Railways as a carpenter. His request to his uncle **Dan Mason** for assistance was at this time, and **Uncle Dan's** letter in response was kept by my father throughout his life — indicative of what it meant to him.

I must have been around four when we moved to the home my father built with the help of **Bill Bell** and a friend, at 165 Northam Ave Bankstown. Whenever I had mumps, measles or chicken pox **Billy** and **Tony** would come and visit me. When I was five I acquired a two-wheel bike, and **Dad** took me to Glorianna, the site on which the Bankstown hospital now stands. The roads were gravel and I fell off — more bandaged legs. I mastered the art of riding and every Sunday I rode my bike to church at Revesby — about 2-3 miles. **Tony** was still living there and I think must have continued to live there throughout his life. There always seemed to be in that house the aroma of spaghetti which grandfather cooked.

Clarice, left, 4 years old, with her cousin Jan Mason, 3.

In Northam Avenue, I made friends with the Jordan family next door, the the Wilsons across the road. A band of 11 children. I became close to June Wilson and Frank Jordan — in fact I decided I would marry him. That came to an end when one day he pushed me into a murky gutter and I gave him a bleeding nose in return. There was much wailing all round. Come bonfire night we would spend weeks collecting firewood and building the bonfire. When all the fireworks were spent, we'd run around the street putting crackers in people's letter boxes. There was much ado about that, but I think we only got in strife once.

A block away from our homes was the brickworks, which were out of bounds, thus being more enticing for us to pick the wild blackberries which grew around the grounds. During the berry season we did this often – always with bated breath. In those days we roamed free for hours on end and we knew we had to be home at a certain time and we did abide by that. There was never a thought that anyone or anything would harm us.

I remember hot nights when families got together on the verandah sharing ice creams and trying to cope with the heat, and going to bed leaving the doors open.

During all this period of growing up, we actually went to school. Vivid in my mind is my first day at school. Mum took me and we met the headmistress (Mum in later years told me the headmistress said it was a shame I had to start school as I would get all sorts of illnesses). When we arrived at the school I decided I did not wish to go. Apparently I was very definite so my mother said she would take me home, but I was to stay in my bedroom for the whole day. This I did. Luckily my father's banjo was behind the door and I amused myself with that. Come the next morning I was ready to go to school, realising it was not much good staying in one's bedroom. From that day on I loved school and hardly missed a day thereafter. My school years were happy, and I did enjoy learning. In later years I discovered learning is a lifelong process – there is no end to learning, about the world, the people and ourselves, forever evolving.

During my school years World War II was raging. We had to build an air raid shelter, black out windows, use ration cards for food and clothing. Survival kits were at school, and air raid drill was on a regular basis.

At Northam Avenue I remember we all grew our own produce. Potatoes, spinach, carrots, sweet potatoes, cabbage, beetroot, rhubarb, banana passionfruit, tomatoes, pumpkin, chokos, watermelon, peas and beans. We raised chickens, which provided eggs, and come Easter my mother would have to take one of the chooks and prepare it for a special feast. There was no such thing as buying a cooked chicken.

At one stage there were ducks, but not for long because they attracted rats. We had an aviary with canaries, and very large fish ponds in the fern house. To me it seemed we had a big backyard, but in retrospect it wasn't so very big.

We had a gramophone with George Formby records, and used to sit on the back step to play them. Radio was the only source of news and entertainment. Every night we would sit around the radio, as though it was a TV set, to listen to the evening news on the BBC, then our favourite shows, such as *Dad and Dave* etc. They went on forever, like *Days of our Lives*. It was 1958 when we were in Perth before we saw TV, and of course it was black and white.

The growing years included wonderful holidays – first in tents, then in caravans along the south coast of NSW. Lake Illawarra, Lake Tabourie, Kiama, Batemans Bay, Moruya, Jervis Bay were all familiar places. Lake Illawarra and Tabourie were the places we mostly camped

By the time I reached the end of primary school, I decided I wanted to be a teacher, but that was not to be. I continued through to high school and studied a Commercial Science course which included Business Principles, Typing and Shorthand. In these years women were being accepted as doctors, and apart from that our choices were teaching, teaching home science, nursing or secretarial work.

On leaving school I joined the staff of a large Insurance company in Martin Place, Sydney. After a short while I resigned and took up the position of secretary to the accountant at the large warehouse of Robert Reid & Co Ltd in York Street, Sydney. These were the days of stenographers. The manager would dictate his mail and the stenographer would take it down in shorthand (Pittmans) then type it in the form of letters. There was no white-out or back-spacing and deleting. One had to be accurate and able to touch type. Here I worked with friends and enjoyed with them the activities of the company Social Club. Today there is still a group of six to eight people who meet together every three months.

The Social Club of Robert Reid's included a girl's softball team, which competed in the district competitions. We would also play against the Melbourne team of the firm, who flew us down there, then the Melbourne team would come to Sydney to challenge. My memory is that the visiting team never won, but we had lots of fun.

Grandfather (Rocco) Macare died in 1951. His last words to me as I visited him in his home just a few hours before he died were – it was but a whisper – "Clarice, be a good daughter for your mother." How important and powerful words are – they can encourage or destroy.

It was after his death that I began to search for the meaning of life. What was it about? What was the purpose? I never doubted the truth of God – Mother and Auntie wanted God's love and even though they never attended church they encouraged me to do so. As I was growing up I rode two miles on my bike to attend mass at the Catholic church in Revesby. The mass was in Latin, and I had to go to confession every Sunday. After mass we had to have tuition on the

Clarice Mason and her parents, Jack and Mella Mason, on her wedding day, 1 October 1954

catechism, the tenets of the Catholic Church. I can remember during the mass just gazing out the window or looking at the statues, but understanding nothing of what was being said. It was all ... bells and incense. By the time I was 14 or 15 I ceased to go to church. I reached the point where I asked myself how can another person forgive my sins — for me it did not add up.

It was not until I met **John** and he asked me to be his wife that things changed. John changed his surname from **Blade** to **Reid** after his father's death in 1936, when his mother re-married. He did not want to marry in the Catholic Church, but in the Church of England. Therefore we agreed to decide which church we wanted to be married in, and having done that began attending church and also attending classes to understand the church's teaching. This was important, as we wanted the children we would have to attend Sunday school, and we wanted to be able to support and guide them.

This was a major turning point in our lives. As we attended classes we were encouraged to read the Bible — the first time I had ever seen or read one. I could not put it down, for every page I read answered the questions I had been seeking answers to for some time, and I realised that so it is with the spirit of God. From that moment the support of his spirit has never left me, nor has his promise to be with me ever been withdrawn. His promise to me was revealed and sealed. *Do not be afraid ......*

That was the wonderful beginning as we entered into marriage, and then came the marvellous years of bringing into life three splendid sons. These years we lived in Perth were *wonderful* years of growth in so many ways. John had been moved to Perth to manage the Perth office of Columbia Pictures. It was the first step of his career in the movie industry.

John and Clarice Reid, with sons Ross, Glenn and Brett. Feb 1961

In 1961 we returned to Sydney, living at first West Lindfield. Then with the help of my parents we were able to build a house in Avalon. Christmas holidays then developed in Blackheath, in the Blue Mountains. This was a means of attending the Katoomba convention and having lots of fun for six weeks in the mountains. This we had to do to increase our income.

Together after much deliberation we decided to book the boys into Barker College, which we considered to be a high standard education. When the decision was made we moved from Avalon to Gordon where for the first three years we rented a lovely home, with wonderful holidays up in Queensland. Then eventually we moved in to our own home in 29 Baldwin St. Gordon.

In 1971 I underwent major surgery, and was critically ill. The recovery was slow – very slow. My prayer at that time was that God would allow me to see my children grow to maturity. He granted me that request. At this time **John** was at the peak of his career, and began overseas travel, which continued through our marriage. After I recovered I had the opportunity to have a part-time position as secretary to the Minister, Rugby Foord. I was in that position for ten years, and it was a period of great personal growth and satisfaction, feeling I was giving some support to many.

On 16 Jun 1976, my father wanted to be with the Lord. He was a kind and tender-hearted man, and a wonderful father. As a child I spent many hours working in his garage and watching him build caravans. He built the first caravan — Advance Caravans. The market had just opened up. After the difficult years of depression, he did very well in the building trade, then moved to building caravans, then to a car sales yard. He built a shop at Yagoona and leased it out, first to Franklin's, then over the years to other leaseholders. He had a passion for spear-fishing, growing orchids, hypnotism and photography.

I was deeply saddened and missed him so much when he died. I never once heard him speak an unkind word to my mother. **Mum** used to help him build caravans — holding timber in place and making curtains. If **Mum** thought something was not right, she would give it the silent treatment and then eventually he did whatever had to be done. He took great care of my mother.

How they loved their three grandsons!

After my father's death, my mother came to live with us. We had five years together, and she was a great help to us as a family. They were busy years, and she contributed to **John** and I being able to keep up a busy schedule during the teenage years.

In 1981 after a 13-month illness, **Mum** wanted to be with the Lord. She was a great witness to the grace of God at work in her life. She suffered a lot, but never complained. Her heart was at peace and her kindness and gentleness were there right to the end. I thank God for those years together and that we were able to keep her at home almost to the end.

Ross and **Christine** were to be married in Dec 1980, and **Mum** was determined to see that wedding. She even made the bridesmaids' dresses. She made it to the wedding, collapsed at the church, and from that point she was confined to bed permanently. She died on 7 March 1981. **Mum** knew for certain that around her were the everlasting arms of the Lord.

The Macare family of Mella, Clarice's mother.

In 1984, **John**'s parents **Mum** and **Dad Reid** moved into a unit attached to a new house we had bought in Sutton St, St Ives. There were difficulties, but they were mixed with high times as well. **Mum** and **Dad Reid** had never been so well off, and it was good for them to have the comforts they enjoyed in living there. Despite the difficulties, I do not regret it having been able to support them as we did.

Brett and **Jude** married in 1982. **Mum** knew they were engaged, and was happy for them. 'They will be able to grow up together', she said.

In 1984 **Glenn** and **Jen** married.

Now we moved into the period of the coming of grandchildren, and what a delight they all turned out to be! I got so much pleasure out of seeing them grow through the stages of their lives.

At this point in our life we had acquired a lovely unit in Ballina, to which we retreated often, and where the family and grandchildren used to come out of school to join with us.

After mum died, **John** started up his own business with Rod Pushar. They each worked from home, and I was **John**'s secretary for 15 years. During these years we had an opportunity to travel together once a year, and there are many wonderful albums covering these journeys.

Then came August 1997. John left me, my world fell apart, and my heart was truly broken. Words cannot describe a broken heart — it encompasses the whole of one's being. You discover someone you love does not, and probably never has loved you. No road can be harder to travel.

Eric Mason: b. 12 June 1910 d. 31 Jul 1968

4TH SON OF WILLIAM AND PRISCILLA (SMITH) MASON
HUSBAND OF THELMA DAVIES, 6 FEB 1937 B. 17 DEC 1912 D. 25 JUL 1999
FATHER OF BILL, JOHN, DENNIS AND ERIC MASON
BROTHER OF ARTHUR, ETHEL, VIC, JACK, HILTON, BOB

By Eric's first son, Bill Mason

Eric Mason, born in Redfern, lived most of his early life at 206 Chapel Rd Bankstown. On leaving school he became a salesman, later some said the best on south coast of NSW. At an early age he was involved in a motor bike accident and suffered a fractured skull. He lost most of his hair, and on professional advice shaved the rest off, believing it would all grow back. It didn't. He lived with only a small amount of hair for the rest of his life. This had a marked effect on him and he always wore a hat. He would arrive late for a movie screening and leave before the lights came back on.

During the Great Depression, **Eric** rode a horse with his friend around the northern districts of NSW, camping wherever at night and working on farms during the day for meals. On his return to Bankstown in 1937, he managed after a fairly long courtship to get **Thelma Davies** pregnant. For family reasons, they had to leave town, leaving for a place three hours' drive from where they had grown up, but with no friends or family. They married on 6 Dec 1937.

During the next 4 years they moved 21 times whilst trying to get work and find a permanent home. In the middle of this war broke out and **Eric** went to work for AWA in their ammunitions factory. He finally moved back to the South Coast after the war and managed to get work with Herb Palmer, a local electrical retailer, and then with Ron Lavis, also an electrical retailer.

Eric and **Thelma** had four sons, **Bill, John, Dennis** and **Eric**. They also fostered a young girl called **Rhonda** for a year or so, until the mother reclaimed her.

Initially on their return to the south coast the family lived in tents at Lake Illawarra and then Stuart Park (near Wollongong). The tenants who occupied the home which he and Thelma had built in Corrimal just before war broke out, refused to vacate the home.

Eventually after two years in tents, the family moved back in and lived at 299 Princes Highway Corrimal NSW. **Eric** later started his own business in electrical retailing in Woonona on the south coat of NSW and was very successful. His two sons **Bill** and **John** joined him in the business while it was getting established. He retired when he was 56 leaving the business to the sons to run. However after a short time he decided it was too boring and went back to work.

Eric suffered a heart attack and died on 31 July 1968. His wife **Thelma** survived him 32 years until 25 July 1999. She married Richard Hogan in 1972.

'Grandma' (Priscilla) Mason, with Thelma Mason and Thelma's and Eric's first son, Bill. Outside the Sydney GPO, about 1943.

William Eric (Bill) Mason: b. 2 Sep 1937

GRANDSON OF WILLIAM AND PRISCILLA (SMITH) MASON
1ST SON OF ERIC MASON AND THELMA (DAVIES) MASON
BROTHER OF JOHN, DENNIS, ERIC
M. ANNE BENJAMIN 1960, B.1940
FATHER OF SHARON (MASON) SALATNAY AND GLENN MASON

Written by Bill Mason

Bill went to Bankstown public school at first, and it didn't go well. He 'fell in love with' his teacher Mrs Brown, at 7, and she was instrumental in helping him transfer to the Catholic school in the area till he was 9. That was a one hour walk each way.

His first job was with an electrical wholesaler. The pioneer of radio 2WL (Alan Yeldon) became his patron in moving to radio 2WL, with a very steep learning curve. **Bill** became Producer there, and spent three to four years producing AIS documentaries.

He worked in his father **Eric Mason**'s radio shop, 'fixing things'. **Eric** began to stock amongst other appliances, the Elna sewing machine — first and only in Australia, sole agent, no maintenance. Self taught, **Bill** began servicing these sewing machines.

Bill Mason

Eric employed a part time TV mechanic, and **Bill** 'carried his bag around' for a while, picking up enough to start a TV service department for **Eric**. They offered clients — service being in its infancy, and not easily available or competent — a contract of sale and service (parts and labour) for the first year, which was most successful, returning failed parts to the insurance company HGPoland. The head of that company eventually turned up and asked for assistance organising the mountain of parts they had thus acquired. **Bill** took this on, had it catalogued and disposed of.

Next was WIN Channel 4 in Wollongong, just starting up. After several calls to the head of the organisation, **Bill** was invited to join them, and was told when he started that the other four Audio bods who should have been there, chose not to join the organisation. There was only a box of parts! So **Bill** was it, and was promoted on the spot to 'training engineer'. First programmes were due to air in eight weeks, and **Bill** had to get them up and running. He was promoted soon after to Director — and so was much better paid.

He later went to BTQ7 in Brisbane as producer/director, and stayed there for four to five years, also becoming Sports Director / News Director / Current Affairs Director / Producer of Network Children's Program.

Then in 1969 Reg Grundy, his organisation well known and respected in the industry, offered **Bill** a job managing the production segment of his organisation in Brisbane. He was with Grundy from 1969 to 1995, eventually becoming Joint Managing Director of the organisation, despite some ups and downs in the relationship with Reg Grundy. His first task was to produce two panel shows in Brisbane, as well as sorting out production problems in Adelaide, Melbourne and Sydney. By 1974 he was producing such successes as *Family Feud*, *Wheel of Fortune*, and *The Price is Right*, etc — producing 40 hours airtime per week.

In 1975 however, proving the dangers of a volatile head of company, **Bill** was put 'on ice' for eight long months. Finally Grundy realised what he was missing, and brought him back into the fold. Airtime had reduced to five half-hours per week, and Bill had to get in and sell formats, quickly recovering it to 25 half-hours a week. He went on to produce *Blankety Blanks* and *It's A Knockout*.

In 1980 *Sale of the Century* (formerly *Temptation*) was returned to air. It had an (unheard of) unlimited budget, and achieved 80% of the market — also unheard of.

By 1982 **Bill** had itchy feet, so went to Asia and Europe and the US to initiate/produce similar shows in Hong Kong, USA, UK, France, Germany, Italy, Spain, etc — a mammoth task that consumed some 12 years of his life. He discovered many discrepancies — the history of each area differed from our own version; the nature of presentation had to be changed from 'chatty' to direct and unembellished; communication with people of many languages had to be managed; to-air presentations obviously had to be in the language of the area; contracts and their language had to be understood and utilised; accounting had to be understood to achieve realistic quotes for production of programmes.

In the US he worked with NBC, CBS, ABC, producing, teaching, and making deals for his firm. He also worked with computer programmers to take over many of the minor, time-consuming production tasks — timing, graphs, graphics to the screen, insertion of elements. This was a massive task, but very much reduced the necessity for onsite production personnel — to the station's delight.

In budgeting, care had to be taken with estimating giveaways. Part of the *Sale of the Century* and many other quiz/game formats was to give away cars, appliances and massive amounts of money. The risk of this happening too often had to be insured against. One Australian client chose, when asked, to allow **Bill** (ie the Grundy organisation) to take that risk, and the quote obviously reflected that. **Bill** was proved competent in that budgeting aspect when that same client came back a few years later and said they would carry the risk — and thus have Grundy's charge to them adjusted.

In the US, the production of *Sale*, *Scrabble*, *Hotstreak* and *Time Machine* eventually consumed 100+ staff. The production was putting out five half hour shows weekly of each.

For *Sale*, and other quiz-based programs, one major problem was to get questions, their grading, and their content, right. Given different histories and different cultures, this proved to be quite a task, and a separate one for each region. Academics, translators and researchers were committed to the task.

Margaret Thatcher, when she was British Prime Minister, decreed that the BBC had to reduce their internal production expenditure by 15 per cent, with extra work to be done by external organisations. This meant retrenching a large number of staff. **Bill** was 'fortunate' — he was the first external contractor to BBC and had to trail-blaze through many difficulties.

At that time, **Bill** was training production personnel. Over 16 weeks he had 16 teams to train — all of them being less than happy with reductions in BBC staff. But at that time the BBC's facility at Elstree was empty: the BBC wanted to move the show because of the problems experienced during its infancy, but **Bill** suggested to the BBC chief that this Elstree studio could be used instead of the one in London. All 16 teams applied to continue to work on the show, so his position with staff and his ability to train good teams was recognised by staff as well as management. Out of all that, Elstree became the game show centre!

Personally, his life was very mobile. He was always abroad, and his wife **Anne** had to choose to stay in Australia with the two young children **Sharon** and **Glenn**, visiting her husband when she could. Later they lived in Monaco (for Grundy's tax advantage) for a while, and in a villa in the south of France as well as in the UK, Paris and Munich.

The formats, having been so successful, were drying up, and it became necessary for Grundy to sell his company. Its had become the leading production company in the world, with which **Bill** had had much to do. Now new formats were necessary. Several deals later, it was most successfully sold (by a few intervening steps) to Fremantle Media for $300m — a pretty profit.

Finally it all came to an end, and **Bill** retired in 1995 at the age of 58. This was quite a shock to him — from a peripatetic lifestyle to a much more leisurely one. His occupations however are still many: he did a three-year TAFE course on computers and the then-upcoming relationship between TVs and PCs, teaches at Computer Pals, took a three-year IT course at an online university, runs his son's business in development of intercoms, and still does computer programs to ease processes.

In their marriage, he and his ever-patient wife **Anne** have moved an unbelievable 27 times, still developing, extending, selling their current home. Recently they made another move — integrating the whole family. Their daughter **Sharon (Mason) Salatnay** has produced two grandchildren, **Zachary** and **Zoe**, born in 1998 and 1999, and now, having divorced, lives in the same residential complex as her parents.

Glenn Mason: b. 18 Feb 1962

Son of Bill Mason and Sally Anne (Benjamin) Mason
Brother of Sharon (Mason) Salatnay

Written by Bill Mason

Born in Bulli (on the south coast of NSW), at 18 months **Glenn** developed German measles and nearly died as a result of a brain infection (encephalitis). We were told he would not recover and if he did would be mentally affected. However, he did make a full recovery.

On leaving school he worked at various jobs including Combat Team Leader for *It's a Knockout*, a TV program made in Sydney for the Ten Network. Shortly after that, **Glenn** went to America and enrolled at the UCLA college for Television and Film Production. After completing the course he became a Water Ski instructor at Corsica and then a Snow Ski instructor in the French Alps. He spent some time in various jobs in many European countries(eg deck hand for some very wealthy owners and large ships in the Mediterranean).

Glenn Mason

On his return to Australia, he joined two other partners in an intercom venture. Unfortunately the partners absconded with his funds, owing many people a lot of money. **Glenn** took out loans to keep the company afloat and repay the debts. He then went on to run this successful intercom company for the next 15 years.

He has always been an inventor and many of his inventions were years before their time. He is currently working with a venture capitalist on an international concept which has a very promising future.

Descendants of Eric Francis Donald Mason

1 **Eric Francis Donald Mason** b. 12 Jun 1910 at Waterloo BC 31220 d. 31 Jul 1968, 6 Thurston Cres, Corrimal m. **Thelma Mary Davies** 6 Feb 1937 Punchbowl, NSW. b. 17 Dec 1912 Says descended from 1st Fleet, Co. Cork, IRL. No Irishmen recorded in the First Fleet. d. 25 July 1999 in Killarney Vale Nursing Home. Thelma married Dick Hogan after Eric died.
  2 **William Eric (Bill) Mason** b. 2 Sep 1937 Wollongong, NSW m. **Sally Anne (Anne) Benjamin** 18 Apr 1960. b. 21 Dec 1940 Wollongong
    3 **Sharon Narelle Mason** b. 6 Feb 1961 Bulli NSW m. **James Richard Salatnay** 9 Sept 1998 Bahai Temple, Ingleside, NSW b. 15 Sep 1965
      4 **Zachary Salatnay** b. 4 May 1998 Mona Vale, NSW
      4 **Zoe Salatnay** b. 28 Nov 1999 Mona Vale, NSW
    3 **Glenn Anthony Mason** b. 18 Feb 1962 Bulli, NSW
  2 **John Robert Mason** b. 14 Sep 1941 Corrimal m1. **Dorothy Callahor** Wollongong m2. **Robyn Grant**, m3. **Sue Ballard** 1994 Perth WA, m4. **Lorraine Donaldson**
[Children of John Robert Mason and Dorothy Callahor]
    3 **Debbie Mason** b. 13 Nov 1962 Wollongong
    3 **Mark Mason** b. 29 Jan 1965 Wollongong
[Children of John Robert Mason and Sue Ballard]
    3 **Joshua Mason** b. 1994
  2 **Rhonda Mason** b. c 1944 Fostered. Returned to her mother
  2 **Dennis James Mason** b. 25 Sep 1948 Corrimal, NSW m. **Marilyn Sweeney** b. 22 Sep 1949
    3 **Kylie Mason** b. 16 Nov 1974 Wollongong m. **Scott Osborne** 19 Feb 2000 Moorooduc, Vic
      4 **Ella Louise Osborne** b. 19 Jan 2003 Melbourne, Vic
      4 **Abby Georgia Osborne** b. 28 Sep 2005 Melbourne Cabrini Hospital, Brighton, Vic
    3 **Bradley Mason** b. 15 Jun 1977 Wollongong m. **Katie Hewitt** 28 Feb 2009 Eltham, Vic
    3 **Grant Mason** b. 5 Apr 1979 Frankston Vic m. **Sarah Cannon** m. 30 Aug 2009 Sydney,
  2 **Eric John Mason** b. 22 Feb 1950 Corrimal, NSW m. **Linda Giles** 1970 Wollongong
    3 **Adam Mason** b. 2 Jan 1971 d. 1994 Wollongong NSW
    3 **Chantel Mason** b. 17 Aug 1972
    3 **Heath Mason** b 15 Aug 1973

Eric Mason's Descendants

Bill and Anne Mason's daughter Sharon (Mason) Salatnay and her children Zack and Zoe

Bill Mason's brother Dennis and his wife Marilyn (Sweeney) Mason

Offspring of Dennis and Marilyn Mason:
L-R: Kylie (Mason) and Scott Osborne (parents of Abby & Ella), Brad Mason and Katie (Hewitt), Grant Mason and Sarah (Cannon).

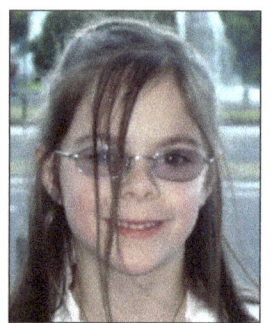

Abby and Ella Mason, daughters of Kylie and Scott Mason

John Robert Mason, son of Eric and Thelma Mason, his son Mark Mason and daughter Debbie Mason

Hilton Matthew Mason: b. 24 Feb 1913 d. 16 Sep 1981

5TH SON OF WILLIAM MASON AND PRISCILLA (SMITH) MASON
M. THELMA (DENNY) MASON 1940 B. 1 DEC 1912 D. 23 SEP 1988
PARENTS OF SHORT-LIVED PAMELA MASON, LYNETTE (LYN) (MASON, LILLINGTON) NEWMAN AND ROBYN MASON

Written by his daughter Robyn Mason

Hilton was born in Redfern, the second youngest of six. The family moved to 206 Chapel Road, Bankstown before or during the Depression. His father, **William Mason** worked on the railways, and also, it would seem, invested in property. **Hilton** attended Bankstown High School, where he obtained his Intermediate Certificate. During the Depression, work was hard to find so **Hilton** drove a horse and cart delivering bread and also as a butcher in Bankstown for several years. Later **Thelma** also worked casually there. In between jobs **Hilton** played cricket with best mate Jack Fitzpatrick, on the oval opposite their house.

Hilton Mason in his younger days outside the Baker for whom he made deliveries.

Hilton met **Thelma Denny** when she was only 16, possibly through their mothers, and (the family say) courted for 11 years till 1940 — probably waiting so long because of the disapproval of Hilton's mother, **Priscilla (Smith) Mason**. **Thelma** was the second child of **Lillian** and **Frederick Denny**, whose firstborn, **Sonny (Dennis)** died of pneumonia in England at only a year old, on 30 May 1913. The Dennys emigrated from Walthamstow, London, England arriving in Australia on 22 Mar 1914 on an assisted passage of £10, on the *Norseman*.

Hilton with his then-fiancée Thelma Denny at Taronga Zoo.

The passenger ship was converted from a cattle ship and the journey was long, with basic accommodation. The cabins were rough, with the rings still intact where the cattle were tied prior to its conversion to a passenger ship. **Lillian** was pregnant with **Thelma** during the trip. She told me about enduring morning sickness and rough seas along the way. Some passengers didn't survive the journey and there were burials at sea.

After **Thelma**'s birth when they arrived in Australia, **Fred** and **Lillian** had two more children, **Joyce** and **Raymond Erskine Denny**. They first settled in Erskineville and later moved to Bankstown. **Fred** became Head French Polisher at Bebarfalds.

Thelma was very bright but disinterested at school, leaving at 14 to get a job. She was the only family member working for much of the Depression, during which time she also lost one kidney. She worked at WD & HO Wills' cigarette factory in Sydney for about 12 years before her marriage, then settled in Bankstown in the house **Hilton** built at 29 Percy Street, Bankstown.

Hilton completed his apprenticeship as a Fitter and Turner on the NSW railways and was based for many years at the Chullora workshops, riding his bike to work. During the Second World War, he was classified as a worker in the essential industries, so did not serve in the Army, to his brother **Vic**'s disapproval. He in fact built the perspex window screens for the Canberra Jet Bombers.

In the early 1950s **Hilton** built and sold caravans from home to earn extra income. The caravans were the old style oval design, selling them for about £250, making a reasonable profit. He also sold electrical appliances. Here are two advertisements from the *Sydney Morning Herald*.

CARAVAN, streamlined, 3-berth, '46 model, beautifully fin., cream. elec. lighting, rust lounges, £275, exchange good Player Piano, cash adjust. 29 Percy Street, Bankstown.

For Sale — The Sydney Morning Herald, Friday 3 Dec 1946

REFRIGERATOR, green, Electrice. Electric Lawnmower. Both good cond. 29 Percy Street, Bankstown.

The Sydney Morning Herald, Saturday 20 Mar 1948

He also built a fibro house on land he purchased in Petunia Avenue, Bankstown, providing a few luxuries for the family. In the mid 1950s, **Hilton** was offered a job as salesman at his friend Jack Fitzpatrick's electrical store, Jay Jays at Bankstown. He later managed the store and worked there till the late 1950s when his **brother Jack**, who owned the newspaper *The North Ward Voice* offered him a position selling advertising space. When **Jack** decided to sell and return to the second-hand car business, **Hilton** purchased the newspaper, and the business slowly flourished, but his hard work wrecked his health. Each weekly edition had to meet a deadline to go to press (overnight) and be ready for delivery to the shops and homes by the Thursday morning. Due to ill health, **Hilton** sold the business in the early 1960s to *The Torch* newspaper at Bankstown, and it was then merged with another local newspaper. It later re-emerged as *The Voice* in the early 1990s and was distributed again in the Bankstown area. **Hilton** is remembered for his humility and his sense of justice. When we were in primary school, **Mum** worked in the shop across the road from the school which supplied lunches for the school children. The owner of the premises made home-made sausage rolls and pies which **Mum**, with her typical sense of humour, used to call 'Dickie Bird Pies', as the owner's name was Richard. We would sometimes go to the lunch shop before school with **mum** and have a home-made sausage roll. **Mum** later worked casually at Waltons, Bankstown Square for a short time when we girls were young teenagers and also for a while in a cake shop.

Lyn, after graduating from Sydney University, spent most of her working years as a social worker in the health field, retiring in 2002. On 25 Aug 1967 **Lyn** married **Paul Lillington** at the Punchbowl Baptist Church and have two children, **Wade** and **Amanda**. They are now divorced and have both since remarried.

Wade Lillington, born on 21 Dec 1971, now works for an international insurance company involving regular trips overseas. He and his partner **Megan Edwards** have two sons; **Aidan**, born on 30 Jan 2002 and **Rhys,** born on 24 Jul 2009. One other child, **May**, was born on 24 Apr 2007 but lived only briefly.

Amanda, born on 16 Nov 1974, married **Paul Platt** from Shropshire, England in 1999 and they had two sons, **Jamie** and **Alex**. They are now divorced. In May 2007 she graduated from the University of Wales with a Bachelor of Science Honours in Surveying and Property Management. Upon graduation she found employment with a London-based Property Development Company and now lives in Shrewsbury working in Property Management. In 2011 **Amanda** completed her Masters Degree in Real Estate.

Lyn married for the second time, to **Roger Norman** on 12 Dec 1992, and has three step-children, **David**, **Lyndell** and **Melanie**. **Lyn** and **Roger** now have ten grandchildren from their blended families. **Lyn** attended the Kogarah Art School for a number of years and now has ventured onto other pastimes, one of them being an avid traveller. She has settled at Bundeena, but after years of being unwell **Roger** passed away on 17 Mar 2014.

Robyn Mason is single and lives at Menai in the Sutherland Shire. Her hobbies include ceramics and archaeology and she has taken the challenge of researching her family tree. She retired on 24 Feb 2014 after working in the hospital industry for most of her working life and is now looking forward to travelling. She has no children. **Robyn** has happy memories of Mason family gatherings at **Nanny Mason's** place at 206 Chapel Road, Bankstown where the family met on Sunday afternoons for special occasions. These were the occasion of great family photos.

Descendants of Hilton Matthew Mason

1 **Hilton Matthew Mason** b.24 Aug 1913 Redfern, d. 16 Sep 1981 m. **Thelma Denny** 5 Oct 1940 St Saviors Church, Punchbowl b. 1 Dec 1912 d. 23 Sep 1988 Hurstville. [daughter of Frederick and Lillian Denny]
    2 **Pamela Mason** b. 26 April 1941 Royal Hospital for Women, Paddington, Sydney d. 8 June 1941
    2 **Lynette Joywyn (Lyn) (Mason, Lillington) Newman** b. 12 Sep 1945, Paddington, Sydney m. **Paul Lillington** m. 25 Aug 1967 div. 1992 b. 18 Jun 1948 m2. **Roger Newman** 12 Dec 1992 b. 20 Nov 1940 NZ d. 17 Mar 2014
    [Children of Lynette Mason and Paul Lillington]
        3 **Wade Evan Lillington** b. 21 Dec 1971 m(df) **Megan Edwards**
            4 **Aidan Manning Lillington** b. 30 Jan 2002
            4 **May Lillington** b. & d. 24 Apr 2007
            4 **Rhys Lillington** b. 24 Jul 2009
        3 **Amanda Lillington** b. 16 Nov 1974 m. **Paul Platt** Jan 1999 England div. 2006
            4 **James Paul Evan Platt**
            4 **Alexander David Platt**
    2 **Robyn Gai Mason** b. 3 April 1947 Royal Hospital for Women, Paddington, Sydney

Robert Joseph (Bob) Mason: b. 19 Aug 1923 d. 19 Jun 1979

6TH SON OF WILLIAM MASON AND PRISCILLA (SMITH) MASON
BROTHER OF ARTHUR, ETHEL, VIC, JACK, ERIC AND HILTON
HUSBAND OF AUDREY PARKER, M. 1948, D. 2014
FATHER OF BILL, SUE, LINDA AND TERECE

Bob was born ten years after his nearest sibling, Hilton, and was therefore much spoiled by his brothers, particularly Vic, 21 years older. His daughter Terece sees this as something of a compensation — his brothers were too much older to play with him, and he found it hard to socialise. A good looking man, he and his piano playing are remembered with affection by his nieces Jan and Helen (Vic's daughters). A family story has Bob calling to Vic 'catch me!' from the rooftop at Bankstown, while Vic and his soon-to-be wife Cath were cuddling, and their Mum was out, causing a mad rush. Bob must have been all of seven at the time!

Bob Mason in the 1960s

Bob was 16 when WWII broke out. His father Will had died when he was 12, but when he was old enough, and against his mother's wishes, he wanted very much to get into the forces, and managed, with the encouragement of his big brother Vic. In the RAAF, Bob saw active service as a Morse Code radio operator in Burma.

Bob and Audrey Parker married in 1948, not long after the war, and their four children were born by 1954. Working as a carpenter/builder, in 1951 Bob had a major accident at work, which virtually broke his back. He had surgery, was hospitalised for three months, wore a heavy back brace and was unable to work for another two years. The compensation payout did not happen until 1972, which made the long interim period quite difficult. They stayed with Grandma Mason (Priscilla) for nearly ten years, in that positively *elastic-sided* house, so open to residence by her sons and their families.

During this difficult period, Bob did many things — he built stereos (probably then called gramophones) in the dining room at Chapel Road, then started 'Chapel Ready Cut Garages' (beginning with renovating an old one, on the basis of a loan from his mother), which was ingenious and quite successful.

Their living standards improved greatly at this time. New clothes, eating out and family parties made a very different picture for them. Bob demonstrated entrepreneurial skills in the things he enjoyed, didn't enjoy working for others, and was a Labor voter (and perhaps even further Left) all his life.

Bob started a newspaper in the Wollongong area (that makes three of the family in this industry — Jack, Hilton and Bob working as editor, salesman, writer and distributor. The distance between their home with Priscilla in Bankstown, and Wollongong where the paper was (just over 70km), was too much eventually.

He and Audrey also ran the Hospital Kiosk at Bankstown, which ended with a considerable financial loss from the $20,000 guarantee he did NOT get from the next purchaser. It was also a great deal of work, particularly for Audrey, since Bob's back injury turned him into a drinking, physically violent man, even to his wife, rather than the gentle, laughing person he had been. It seemed to the younger generation of the family that Audrey ran the kiosk all day, and had also to be the housewife for them at night while Bob was at the RSL.

Audrey Parker, at her 1948 wedding to Bob Mason, with his nieces
(L-R) Helen and Jan, daughters of Vic Mason and Clarice Mason, daughter of Jack Mason

His son **Bill** recalls **Bob** escorting him from Bankstown to the Wahroonga blind school and back — a distance of some 30km each way — every day for some weeks or months. **Bill**'s overcoming of this impairment, particularly in his adulthood, is to his considerable credit.

When they moved to Mona Vale in 1977 **Audrey** believed things were improving, but **Bob** had his fatal stroke two years later.

Bob's widow **Audrey** survived till 10 Oct 2014, dying peacefully after coping some seven years with Alzheimers. It was her son **Bill** who cared for her and kept her involved with the family from her nursing home in those last years. Her children were with her on her last evening.

Bill married **Barbara de Sorcy** in 1985, and continues to travel widely, to be family-conscious and was particularly caring of his elderly mother **Audrey**.

Bob and **Audrey**'s oldest daughter **Sue** married Welshman **Bill Davies** on her parents' 28th wedding anniversary in 1976, at the same church in Punchbowl. **Sue** and **Bill** have two sons, and now grandchildren.

Bill's next daughter, **Linda**, married **Bruce Parr** and moved to New Zealand, producing twin girls and a son. That marriage ended and **Linda** moved back to Sydney, with the children and grandchildren living in New Zealand, Shropshire, Wales and Sydney.

Terece, **Bob** and **Aud**'s youngest, married **Sue**'s husband **Bill**'s brother **Gareth Davies**, and has a much-loved special son, **Deinyon**.

Audrey in her later years.

Descendants of Robert Joseph (Bob) Mason

1 **Robert Joseph (Bob) Mason** b. 19 Aug 1923 Rickard Road, Bankstown NSW d. 10 Jun 1979 DC 13570 m. **Audrey Patricia Parker** 14 Feb 1948 b. 17 Oct 1925 d. 10 Oct 2014
  2 **William David (Bill) Mason** b. 15 Dec 1948 Sydney m. **Barbara de Sorcy** 2 Nov 1985 Toronto, Canada b. 13 Apr 1951 Toronto, Canada
  2 **Suzanne (Sue) Marie Mason** b. 17 Aug 1950 Sydney m. **William Thomas (Bill) Davies III** 14 Feb 1976 b. 17 Nov 1951 Wales
    3 **William Thomas Davies IV** b. 3 Apr 1978 Cefn Hengood, South Wales m. **Renee** 14 Feb 2005
      4 **Jye Davies**
      4 **Luke Davies**
      4 **Jake Davies**
      4 **Ellie Davies**
    3 **Robert Gareth Davies** b. 2 Aug 1979 m. **Vanessa**
      4 **Shayla Davies**
      4 **Kyuss Davies**
  2 **Linda Louise Mason** b. 8 Aug 1952 m. **Bruce Alexander Parr** 10 Apr 1972 Sydney b. 17 Nov 1951 Wales. Divorced
    3 **Shane Alexander Parr** b. 16 Oct 1972 Sydney m. **Alison Mary Reid** 13 Jul 2002 Shropshire, UK b. 6 Dec 1969 Bangor, Anglesey, Wales
      4 **Euan Alexander Parr** b. 30 Nov 2002 Manly, NSW
      4 **Finnley Stewart Parr** b. 14 May 2004 Shropshire, UK
      4 **Daniel Parr** b. 5 Nov 1974 Upper Hutt NZ m. **Renee Lee Carton** 5 Jan 2007 Carterton
      4 **Riley George Parr** b. 10 May 2008 Lower Hutt
      4 **Mason William Parr** b. 10 May 2010 Lower Hutt NZ
    3 **Katherine Parr** b. 17 Sep 1976 NZ — twin with **Louise Parr**
    3 **Louise Parr** b. 17 Sep 1976 NZ — twin with **Katherine Parr** m.(df) **Cesar Concha de Rurange** b. 8 Mar 1981 Santiago, Chile
      4 **Emily Katherine de Rurange** b. 26 Mar 2010 Manly, NSW
      4 **Vivienne Monica de Rurange** b. 29 Sep 2011 Manly, NSW
  2 **Terece Ivy Mason** b. 28 Sep 1954 m. **Gareth Davies** 28 Oct 1990 b. 4 Sep 1954 Wales
    3 **Deinyon Davies** b. 2 Aug 1994 Sydney

Chapter 3: John Mason II and III and their descendants

Descendants of John Mason and Johanna Quigley — the 1989 Family Reunion at the home of Helen Malcher at East Lindfield, 150 years since the first Masons migrated to Australia.

Back row, L-R Vicki Malcher, granddaughter of Vic Mason; her mother Helen Malcher; Bill Mason, son of Bob Mason; Jan O'Donnell, daughter of Vic Mason.

Front row, L-R Lyn Norman, daughter of Hilton Mason; Clarice Reid, daughter of Jack Mason; Dorothy Loveridge, daughter of Arthur Mason; Robyn Mason, daughter of Hilton Mason; Audrey Mason, widow of Bob Mason; Suzanne Davies and Terece Davies, Bob Mason's daughters.

Arthur Edmund Mason: b. 29 Apr 1872 d. 9 Sep 1939

5TH SON OF THE MIGRATING JOHN MASON III AND MARIA MAHER
BROTHER OF OLIVER, PETER, PATRICK, DAN AND WILLIAM
MARRIED MAUDE, NÉE BAILEY 14 NOV 1917, B. 9 AUG 1893 D. 25 DEC 1974. PROBATE 244588
FATHER OF PEG, JOHN, BOB AND DOROTHY MASON

By his son Bob Mason

> *Conticuere omnes, intentique ora tenebant.*
> *Inde toro pater Aeneas sic orsus ab alto.....*
> *Virgil, Aeneid II*
>
> *They all fell silent, turned and fixed their gaze on him.*
> *Then from his lofty couch, in this wise*
> *Aeneas our forefather began....*

Arthur Edmund Mason was not the sort of child, or man, about whom careful records would necessarily be kept. The youngest son of a farming family at Tamworth — peasant stock, if it were admitted that Australia had any peasants in the late 19th century. Who would see the need? Records might be, and apparently were, optional. Yet, his siblings were all duly registered — but then the family *was* Irish.

Indeed Australia never had peasants in the fullest sense: families who had land for subsistence but nothing else, fixed in both location and social position for generations back, and in expectation for generations ahead, even if they should grow quite rich. That, along with recurring famine, was what many of the early free immigrants had left behind, to chance their future on what their enterprise could wring from a spacious new land. For many, this meant a succession of moves out, then further out, from their point of arrival, Sydney. Such a series of moves, over a few decades from 1840, brought **John Mason** and his burgeoning family to settle as small farmers in the still-young town of Tamworth, according to his own marriage and death certificates.

Tamworth's main street, Peel Street, in 1876 — still a growing community, but an indication of what the Masons were living with

It was hardly foreseeable that anyone would be writing about **Arthur Mason** in the 21st century. Seventy years after his death (and about 140 after his birth) he is still a cherished presence to his children, but quite unknown to almost anyone else. None of his grandchildren ever knew him. Beyond the most basic facts, the knowledge we have of his first 50 years is very sketchy, and its survival fortuitous. However from what we know of Tamworth itself, we may form a limited picture of him and his brothers: **Oliver** the housepainter who stayed all his life in Tamworth, **Dan,** on occasion Daniel or Denis, a prosperous 'mercer' and a rather public figure in Lismore, and **Will Mason.**

While they lived he did have close and happy relations with his family. When he flew (in 1932!) to Lismore for **Dan**'s impressive funeral (two bishops, young Father Gilroy who later became the Cardinal-Archbishop, sundry secular dignitaries and a cortege of 74 cars), the local press described him as the 'chief mourner'. One wonders what **Dan**'s wife thought of that!

Arthur was a gentleman and a gentle man, rather sedate, spreading abroad an air of serenity. A perhaps typical youngest son, he seems to have been liked and esteemed all his life by those around him. He worked assiduously at providing for his family in difficult times, and was always on hand when needed. But his idea of parental roles had probably been formed before the close of the 19th century. Hands-on fathering, 'quality time' spent daily with children would have been rather strange notions to him. His old-fashioned way made for a subtler intimacy: utterly committed, not distant, not even wary but reserved, a little formal.

Still, when possible, he would enjoy taking his children camping or fishing, to a picnic, or to a family farm at Oberon (his wife's family, that is) for Easter. The mountain roads at the time made that quite an outing in his canvas-topped 1928 Buick, the running-boards piled with luggage. While potatoes were the staple of that farm, the cuisine there is remembered for bread baked in a backyard oven after the dying fire was raked out, and what one child accurately described as 'kangaroo tail soup pie' – big on Worcestershire sauce but very tasty. On a good day there was even fishing on the estate. The fireworks for the annual backyard 'cracker night' seemed important to him (perhaps a big excitement in his own childhood?) and were never forgotten.

After a difficult birth not helped by that malignant midwife the Australian Agricultural Company, the town of Tamworth on the Liverpool Plains of northern NSW grew lustily. Graziers were there already, farmers were arriving, and with them came shopkeepers and providers of most services. From 1850 numbers of gold-seekers were also swelling the regional population.

The district was rich but the site was flood-prone. In 1878, when **Arthur** was about six years old, the railway from Newcastle reached Tamworth, so that he and the town grew up together. In his early years he saw the arrival of electric street lighting, reticulated water, constructed gutters and eventually paved streets. And later, to the quite vocal dismay of his brother **Oliver**, income tax of 'a shilling in the pound'.

From the beginning Tamworth was a feisty town, wanting to lead and to have all facilities as soon as, or sooner than, any comparable community. In the early 1920s especially, it was prominent in the New State movement, which offered one answer to the perennial question of whether Australia had too many governments or too few. If there was to be a New England state, Tamworth would like to be its capital. But the temper of this town was always businesslike and down-to-earth; a country music festival suits it to this day. Cities of the plain, indeed! Dreaming spires, if any, would fit more naturally in the ambience and climate of neighbouring Armidale.

Arthur Mason (in dark cap) and his bike in Peel Street Tamworth in the early 1920s.

In 1879, when **Arthur** was probably seven, his father **John Mason III**, whose exact birth date about 1816 is likewise uncertain, died from 'heart disease'. Soon after, in 1881, he also lost his 15-year old brother **Patrick**. That left him with three brothers, and his mother **Maria Maher** lived on in the town till 1905.

One early exploit remembered was his 'swimming a drayload of firewood and its horses across the flooded Peel River' so that the baker could bake and the town would not starve. On reflection, was either side of the river quite devoid of timber? Perhaps of suitable timber? Or dry timber? Well, feat of civic valour or just an unnecessary lark, it did happen, according to the closest of sources. Is it just an unrelated fact that among the **Masons** enrolled for Tamworth in 1899-1900 there was one **Joseph Mason,** baker, or was he perhaps the baker in need of firewood?

Arthur described his first formal job, in a hardware store, so: first a couple of months unpaid 'to see if you will do', 'then five shillings a week; give it to your mother, and if she gives you back threepence (pronounced thrippence, of course, some called it thruppence) for an ice cream, you'll think you're doing all right.' There is a distinct air of apprenticeship here. It may even be questioned whether ice cream had reached Tamworth by 1890, or 1900, but that is how he told it in the language of the 1930s.

In due course he established himself as a man of some substance with a house in Marius Street, elevated, close to the centre of Tamworth. It seems a reasonable guess that he was the **Arthur Edward Mason** enrolled in 1899-1900 as an ironmonger. By 1901-03 **Arthur Edmund** is recorded as a tobacconist, with fancy goods and a barber's shop (a common combination), employing a barber. Later he had a billiard saloon. An account-book remaining from 1915 shows both 'shop takings' and 'saloon takings', probably both at the same premises in Peel Street. His selection (even if self-selection) to play exhibition games against the travelling billiard virtuoso Walter Lindrum suggests he was of the town's best at that art. This was the simple game of billiards rather than the pool or snooker now more familiar, but Lindrum *was* the world champion, unbeaten for years and eventually beyond challenge.

In 1917 **Arthur** married **Maude Bailey**, then 24, who lived in Muswellbrook. Her childhood had been spent in a number of country towns including Carcoar and Cowra. Her father, sometimes a shearer, sometimes a barber, finally a hotelkeeper, accepted opportunity where it presented, and when settled sent for his family to follow. **Maude**, beautiful, strong, not assertive but very practical, provided a complement to **Arthur**'s somewhat unworldly qualities.

She was well worth waiting for, a valiant woman as the scripture evocatively puts it. The family next door at that time was still celebrating her pies fifty years later and far away — not for their undoubted excellence but because they saved that family from starvation. She pushed the pies under the fence, the family being quarantined in their home without provision for food, because of the influenza epidemic of 1919-20. Back in Muswellbrook the same epidemic claimed her younger brother's life.

Arthur Mason and Maude Bailey at the time of their engagement.

At his marriage in 1917, **Arthur** admitted to 39 years of age. The present writer, their son, does not know how accurate that was, and quite possibly he himself could not be too precise. All attempts to find an official record of his birth have been unsuccessful. His marriage and death certificates, and the incidental information in other family certificates (perhaps careless or even fudged), support various birth dates from 1872 to 1878.

Accordingly he would have been an adolescent or a young man during the notoriously hard times of the 1890s. After the series of gold rushes with their waves of immigration, their booms and busts, there was a lot of industrial unrest. Also the several colonies, labour groups and sectional interests were struggling confusedly to determine what shape of society might emerge. In the event it was the new, federated nation of Australia; the existing colonies became States, and remained autonomous in many important matters.

People in a country town probably fared better through that period than either the urban proletariat or casual rural workers. Given the limited communications then available, a go-ahead town would have made itself as self-sufficient as it could, creating a comprehensive mutual support; and there was the cohesion of his Irish-Australian community. Irish, yes, Australian, yes; he would be unlikely to reject either description, but also unlikely to define himself by either. His horizon was rather that of his town, its district and the people he knew directly. If he had aspirations, one might guess they looked to the life of a country gentleman.

While **Arthur** never became wealthy or really prominent, the early 1920s in Tamworth — the postwar years — were perhaps his palmy days. Before motorcycle clubs acquired the unsavoury air which, deserved or not, has hung about them for over half a century, he lined up his motorbike with those of the young bloods in Peel Street for mutual admiration: a small impromptu *concours d'elegance*. The proud owners must have felt that their move from horses, sulkies and buggies was decidedly upward, and entirely respectable. By that time he was hardly a young blood himself, either in age or by temperament. But on his motorbike and sidecar, the tradition says, he ferried his whole family of five about. Not too far afield, one supposes.

It would seem a social advance that at this time he was also an owner of trotting horses and secretary of the Tamworth Trotting Club. One horse in particular, Redland Bells, was very successful in races as well as shows, and was sought-after as a sire. There are records from the season of 1923 with a recurring stud fee of four guineas (£4.4.0), remarked on in the press at the time as surprisingly cheap. Some of the colts sold for up to £90 each. One could get a headache trying to relate those figures to present-day values.

His business premises, like others in Peel Street, were repeatedly flooded when the river rose, and this was given as one reason for his moving, about 1925, to Sydney. Floating down the street on a piano, round the shop on a counter, losing his account books, the stories vary. His children before leaving Tamworth were **Peg, Jack** and **Bob (Margaret, John Arthur** and **Robert Oliver)**, and the last child **Dorothy** was born at Ashfield in 1929.

A general tide of migration that flowed out to the country during the 19th century was returning to perceived opportunities in the big city through much of the 20th. **Arthur**'s brother **Will**, a railwayman, had left Tamworth many years before and was living in Bankstown with five of his six sons. A thought occurs that **Arthur** may also have had an eye on the wider competition of Sydney trotting, where some of Redland Bells' descendants had already been winning races. When departing Tamworth he left a number of horses on agistment at Duri in the nearby countryside. Some of them, or their progeny, remained his at his death twelve years or more later, but after payment of accumulated expenses barely any cash value was left.

This 1991 photo of Bob Mason is in front of the house called The Mount at Oberon, the home of the Arrows, the family of Maude Bailey, wife of Arthur Mason. It is understood that Maude Bailey was born there, as well as Maude's mother Euphemia (Curry) Arrow. It was thought to be an 1830s construction, but the roof and wall cladding in those years could not have been corrugated iron on such an isolated building, so must have been slab timber. It was recalled with affection by Maude.

By 1927 **Arthur** was settled in a new, unpretentious cottage in Frederick Street, Ashfield, with his wife **Maude** and three children. For a livelihood, he established a 'furniture shop' in the main street of Summer Hill, Lackey Street. It could have been called an antique shop had there been enough room to spread the stock around more elegantly. As it was, quite an amount of it was hauled out each day to the entrance and footpath so that customers could make their way in.

Parts of Summer Hill began the 20th century as 'the Woollahra of the western suburbs'. Lackey Street had been known as a fashionable promenade though it was a quite small space rendered rather tight by the presence of trams. In the 1930s few people had much money for collecting antiques; many of the big houses were being emptied of their treasures (whence the best of the shop's stock) or divided into flats, or both.

He ran that enterprise with unremitting application, no great flair and little enough reward — long hours, never a holiday except the standard public holidays — till his sudden death of a heart attack in the first week of the 1939 war.

In the meantime, however, about 1935, the family had rented out the Ashfield house and gone to live above a second shop, also in Lackey Street. **Maude** took on this shop for a year or so to bolster the flagging family income by selling cakes, teas and sweets — a move occasioned by the Great Depression. An arduous job for her, with 18-hour days being quite usual, and really not much of a bolster. Children agonised over the sweets — can we get 2 of those, 2 of those and one of those for tuppence ha'penny?

Maude Bailey Mason in the 1960s

The trams are now long gone, but in that street they outlasted the **Masons**. In **Arthur**'s few remaining years there were three more changes of home address, including one of the flats in the big houses. Many people at the time were trying new ventures and were on the move. Hanging on in hope....of....?

If in these moves there was any sense of panic it was not allowed to reach the younger children. They were aware that things were in short supply, that most of the people they knew were doing without something, and that many were much worse off than they. Yet it was a time by no means without enjoyment; real needs were well covered, there was no shortage of food, care or love. There was a wireless in the home, though not a telephone, and often, as an overflow of stock from the shop, a player-piano and a billiard table. There was also a feeling of security and stability — centred in **Maude**, but drawing strength from **Arthur**, from his perseverance and serenity.

Through the decade, as conflicts broke out in China, Abyssinia and Spain, as German rearmament escalated, as the Rhineland and then Austria were occupied, the sense of unease shifted from material shortage to the looming war. There was a helpless feeling, but also a hope against hope, as it drew ever closer. In memory those years appear as not a bad experience but subdued, a rather grey time.

After the carefree 1920s, the 1930s were a difficult time for Australia and for the world, but one is not disposed to make much of it in view of the carnage, destruction, disruption and displacement brought by the following decade. With the outbreak of the World War in 1939, austerity at home only became more austere as rationing of essentials was formalised. It was left to **Maude** to deal with that. Like the House of Lords throughout the war, she did it very well.

The last of the short-term addresses was the rather grand, slightly decayed mansion at 118 Victoria Street, Ashfield, where **Arthur** died. His children's ages at the time ranged from 9 years to 21. This house had been acquired shortly before and quickly put to use as a small-scale residential. Could this have been undertaken, could even the teashop a few years before have been undertaken because he had had warning of a threatening heart attack? No-one will ever know. Events in any case overtook the project. The house is still there (in 2009), no longer obviously decayed.

Arthur Mason was buried in the Roman Catholic section of Rookwood, mourned particularly by the Catholic people of Ashfield including the Sisters of Charity at Bethlehem College. In the tradition of his brother **Dan**, though on his own more modest scale, he had worked at raising funds for them. In all, an unadventurous, unremarkable small-town life, yet in its way exemplary. A life of love and practical service, lived with grace. And also with **Maude**!

Arthur was no mute inglorious Milton, no Cromwell either, and nobody minds that. Positive, ambitious and very effective people, who really leave their mark, are often not an unmixed blessing. On balance he probably contributed more to the general good of the world than Adolf Hitler. And, like as not, than Winston Churchill.

In the middle of and probably because of the War, on 6 Jun 1942, with the Japanese at the gates of Darwin and Sydney, **Arthur's** widow **Maude** married **Tom Nicholls**, a railwayman, son of a Cornish miner, who found fulfilment in growing very good vegetables. The family found pleasure

Chapter 3: John Mason II and III and their descendants

in eating them, long after the war ended. By his own lights a reasonable man, he was very different from **Arthur** and no soulmate for **Maude**. 'If I don't talk to him about horses and racing there's not much I can talk about'. He may well have felt intimidated.

But according to her quiet wisdom 'happiness is not getting what you want, it's wanting what you get.' Early in the marriage, **Tom's** work took them to live at Kiama, then at Wollongong. This certainly added interest to the lives of **Arthur's** children, mainly for holidays; with them, **Maude** continued to find mutual help and comfort. Soon **Tom** retired a second (and final) time, the couple's last 20 years being spent at and about Lidcombe.

After a somewhat turbulent time establishing a *modus vivendi* they settled down to a quiet, caring relationship of 32 years till her own death following a stroke on Christmas Day, 1974. That was the day after Cyclone Tracy destroyed Darwin. **Tom,** some years older, survived her by less than a year.

................et quorum pars magna fui

....wherein I myself had no small part.

Descendants of Arthur Edmund Mason

1 **Arthur Edmund Mason** b. 29 Apr 1872 according to DC Oliver. d. 9 Sep 1939 118 Victoria St Ashfield. m. **Maude Bailey** 14 Nov 1917 Muswellbrook municipality MC 12698 243. b. 9 Aug 1893 Oberon, NSW d. 25 Dec 1974 Lidcombe, NSW [daughter of George Bailey and Ann Euphemia Arrow]
    2 **Margaret (Peg) Mason** b. 14 Aug 1918 m. **Albert Butt** 31 Mar 1945 b. 5 Jul 1923 d. 5 Jan 198
        3 **Diana Butt** b. 19 Jul 1947 m. **Kevin Duff**
            4 **James Duff** 21 Jan 1971
            4 **Amanda Duff** b. 2 Feb 1972
            4 **Graham Duff** b. 2 Jan 1977
        3 **Kriss Butt** b. 20 Apr 1950 m. **Reg Feutrill** 12 Jan 73
            4 **Sarah Feutrill** b. 24 Nov 1976
            4 **Reon Feutrill** b. 12 Mar 1979
            4 **Wade Feutrill** b. 1981
        3 **John Butt** b. 9 Jun 1951 m1. **Judith Gates** 19 Jan 1974 b. 29 Aug 1954 m2. **Debbie Janssen** Aug 1984 b. 9 Nov 1960
    [Children of John Butt and Judith Gates]
            4 **Joel Butt** b. 7 Jun 1974
            4 **Megan Butt** b. 9 Aug 1975
            4 **Amy Butt** b. 23 Feb 1977
            4 **Luke Butt** b. 6 Apr 1979
    [Children of John Butt and Debbie Janssen]
            4 **Jerri Butt** b. 21 Sep 1987
        3 **Robert Butt** b. 28 Jun 1956 m. **Mona Lisa Reimitz** b. 22 Sep 1955
            4 **Vienna Butt** b. 25 Oct 1981
            4 **Jordan Butt** b. 19 Feb 1983
    2 **John Arthur (Jack) Mason** b. 16 Nov 1920 d. 10 Mar 2010 Lidcombe, NSW m. **Kathleen O'Connor** 1949 d. 15 Nov 2004 [daughter of Elizabeth Kathleen Magdalen(e) Menton]
        3 **John James Mason** b. 19 Jul 1951
    2 **Robert Oliver (Bob) Mason** b. 13 Feb 1924
    2 **Dorothea (Dorothy) Mason** b.12 Dec 1929 d. 23 May 1991 Calvary Hospital, Kogarah. m. **Leslie Jack (Jack) Loveridge** 11 Oct 1956 b. 19 Mar 1929 m2. **Jack** m. **Monica Burke** 1993 d. 23 Mar 2009
        3 **Peter Loveridge** b. 18 Sep 1957 m. **Mary Anne Clemson**. b. 24 Apr 1964
            4 **William Loveridge** b. 11 Sep 1999
            4 **Maitland Loveridge** b. 4 Mar 2001
        3 **Stephen Bruce Loveridge** b. 1 Nov 1958 m. **Julie Paget** b. 26 Jul 1958
            4 **Vikki Loveridge** b. 31 Oct 1990
            4 **David Loveridge** b. 29 Mar 1993
            4 **Nicole Loveridge** b. 29 Aug 1995
        3 **Paul Leslie Loveridge** b. 13 Dec 1962 m. **Helen Carroll** b. 3 May 1965
            4 **Amelia Loveridge** b. 13 Apr 2005
            4 **Eloise Loveridge** b. 13 Sep 2006
        3 **Andrew Loveridge** b. 16 Feb 1971 m. **Lynda Claxton** b.7 Aug 1973
            4 **Matthew Loveridge** b. 13 Jan 2005
            4 **Megan Loveridge** b. 30 Sep 2006
            4 **Jack Richard Loveridge** b. 21 Jul 2008

Chapter 3: John Mason II and III and their descendants

Peg's wedding to Albert Butt in 1945, attended by a pretty Dorothy as bridesmaid, siblings Jack Mason on the left, and Bob Mason on the far right. Their aunt Priscilla Mason can be seen centre rear.

The Masons and Loveridges
Bob Mason, Kathleen O'Connor Mason, Dorothy (Mason) Loveridge, John Arthur (Jack) Mason, Leslie (Jack) Loveridge, Jack Mason's son John. At Lidcombe about 1985.

Jack Mason in his youth

Peg (Mason) Butt in 1945 and in the 1960s

Celebrating Bob Mason's 90th in style: Peter and Bruce Loveridge, Bob Mason, Andrew Loveridge, John James Mason

Bob Mason at 90

David Loveridge at 21

2014

The later lives of us, **Arthur Mason**'s four children, while certainly worth living, have been hardly more remarkable to the outside observer than his. They have encompassed the Second World War (which directly involved only **Jack**), the nuclear standoff following, the attitudinal, mental and social upheaval of the 1960s, a long period of general prosperity and the rise of a cosmopolitan Australia. We allow ourselves to be old-fashioned if we want to. After all our grandfather was older than Queen Victoria (whose 200th birthday is almost upon us).

Peg was an accountant in Sydney till she met and married **Albert Butt**, and thereafter a farmer's wife near Cootamundra. She had come to know **Albert** as she pursued her interest in horse-riding in the Gundagai district. Conditions at first were primitive and difficult for them, without electricity or adequate piped water. **Albert** set about running the farm, improving it and its badly run-down house. Their first year of independence and hard work failed to produce any profit, though they had lived quite well off their own produce, as would be normal enough for a new farm. A big improvement came with the connection of electricity. Normal lighting and appliances could then be installed.

Unfortunately **Albert** developed a depressive illness, which added to **Peg**'s worries but brought her much closer to his mother **Madge**, remarried and now Mrs Coggan, as they worked together during many years to help him. The two women became best friends.

Later, when the family moved from the farm into Cootamundra, **Peg** worked for about forty years in a local law office — as conveyancer, tax-agent and office manager. Privately she was a financial nanny to family and a number of other people. **Albert** continued to work both on the farm and on building ventures in the town. But in 1981 she received a great shock with his unexpected death at the farm, apparently by his own hand. He was not yet 60.

Jack, sickly as a child and never strikingly robust but eager for life, could spare only limited time for schooling. Education and formation of character, however, can come in other ways. As an eldest son, he faced many responsibilities soon after his father's death, and dealt with them creditably. He filled successively a variety of roles: soldier (rising to sergeant), clerk (latterly on the Sydney waterfront), taxi-driver and taxi-owner. His first job on leaving school was in his father's furniture shop, an echo of that father's early stint in ironmongery. He was also the owner-builder of three homes; two of them, in Rose Bay and St George's Basin, on a very do-it-yourself basis. In the process he gained many skills and lost the end of a finger to a hungry machine planer.

His dearly-loved wife of 55 years was **Kathleen O'Connor**. She too carried on multiple jobs in and out of their home. During the long illness of her last years **Jack**, strong-minded, straightforward, practical yet judicious and rich in hard-earned empathy, shone in his crowning role as carer for her, and also for her sister. By this time all three were living at Parramatta, though not all in the same household.

Jack asked little of life, but he gave quite generously. Not that he ever had much available to give. Saving was not his thing, but neither was it his way to spend more money than he had. Among those who benefited were the surviving mates from his army unit. In poor health himself, he spent much time keeping them together, helping them deal with bureaucracy and in other ways. This he was still doing until 2010 when, at the age of 89, he died. He always retained his father's interest in woodwork and in good furniture, as also in the workings of nature.

Bob the younger son and, I confess, the writer of these notes, took refuge in impractical (and unremunerative) interests: language, literature, history, 'classical' music, all studied quite extensively, but with more enthusiasm than system. Except for the last 25 years in retirement he maintained himself as a hospital pharmacist. With this background and because of his age he can often clarify old-time pharmacy (and medical) practice — e.g. for family historians. To be blunt about it, saving *has* been *his* thing. He has enjoyed some limited time working in England and travelling in Europe. And in 2014 qualified as a nonagenarian. More agreeable than useful, he lives privately with a degree of assistance from family members. He has remained unmarried, to that extent untried. He usually sees both sides of any question and, feeling no need, seeing no hope, of an answer to *everything,* is uncommitted in many matters.

He talks a lot. A long if selective memory, developed when schooling consisted mainly of rote-learning, positively encourages him to trot out arcane facts, fascinating or distracting as you choose to view them, and quotations (apt or not) in five or six languages, many in verse. What a miserable education it would be that taught only practicality, efficiency, strategies, self-assertion and self-advancement (material advancement, of course)!

Sometimes, alarmingly, people will remember his observations and bring them back years later, to argue over or just chew over. The sage, or oracle, of Parramatta? Hardly. A vagrant mind, not very disciplined, not quick; it has been called labyrinthine. But while he holds forth and explores the labyrinth of *his* thoughts, his listeners may be peering into labyrinths of their own, hoping meanwhile that he will come up with something unambiguous and really illuminating. Small hope. His baroque, sometimes downright opaque way of expressing himself will not help. As is indeed the way of oracles.

He understands however that neither erudition nor succinct expression is wisdom. A short, crystalline sentence such as 'truth is what works' may give a neat answer to a complex or profound question, but seldom a satisfying one. That is what complex means.

People like, I think, to hear him talk, but often they wish he would stop. A family can perhaps afford one member like this.

Dorothy, the darling little sister but also a bearer of burdens, her mother's great support and (in Luther's phrase) a 'strong fortress' for all her family, was widely interested in people of all kinds — I would say the most gregarious of us. But sadly she was the first to die — unexpectedly, at 61, as she prepared for retirement after a full and demanding working life.

Her father's death when she was nine led to a somewhat disrupted adolescence involving several home addresses and schools — Pendle Hill, Five Dock, Kiama, Wollongong. But from her own childhood forward she knew what she wanted to do — to look after children. While not neglecting other interests, she was able to make that her personal and professional life's work. It began to fall into place when she started Nursing Training. Further study, for adult nursing, took her later to Hobart and Wollongong.

Dorothy married **Jack Loveridge** in 1956 and bore him four fine sons. Their first home being in Yagoona, she was then more in touch than her siblings with the Bankstown **Masons**, including their formidable — their cheerfully formidable — matriarch, her **Aunt Priscilla**. This geography also placed on her the largest responsibility for the day-to-day support of her own ageing mother. **Dorothy** and **Maude** both moved their households into a large house divided in two, at Lidcombe, an arrangement that lasted for the next 28 years. Ten years into that period, her mother **Maude**, and **Maude**'s second husband **Tom,** had died; and **Dorothy's** family was completed with the arrival of her fourth son, Andrew.

An excited 18 year old Dorothy, surrounded by streamers from the ship, as a friend leaves.

Over many years, before, during and after the raising of her sons, she was a highly valued Senior Nurse (mostly as a triage sister in Accident and Emergency) at the Children's Hospital, now at Westmead but then at Camperdown. When she died in 1991 doctors and nurses at the hospital held a memorial service in her honour. Beloved, I confidently believe, by all who knew her, her real memorial is seen in her sons. Of her ten grandchildren she lived to see only the first. Among them, she also has had Australian representatives in European handball.

Daniel Mason: b. 1832 or 1834 —?

SON OF JOHN MASON II AND JOHANNA QUIGLEY
BROTHER OF MARY, JOHN III, OLIVER, JOANNA AND MARGARET
MIGRATED WITH THE FAMILY ON THE CHINA, 1839

Information from Robyn Mason and Patricia Keevers

Daniel Mason came to Australia with his parents, **John Mason** and **Johanna Quigley** on the *China* in 1839, his age being reported as 7 years, the youngest of the six children. When his family were 'assigned' to **William Bucknell**, and to Sydney homes in the case of the girls, there is no mention of him, so it is assumed he went with his parents to Morpeth.

Our only sighting of him is this harsh note in the *Maitland Mercury* in April 1850, inserted by his father. He had evidently left home, for what reason we don't know — perhaps it was only the action of a rebellious teenager or a stern father. If **Daniel**'s age as reported in the *Maitland Mercury* is correct at 16½ when he 'absconded', his age on arrival in this country must have been only 5. One wonders why such a mistake, or misreporting, occurred. The ages for all the family seemed to change on each reporting.

> **Notice.**
> A YOUNG MAN, named DANIEL MASON, 16½ years old, fair hair, about 5 feet 8 inches in height, having ABSCONDED from his Parents without provocation, One Pound reward is offered to any person who will give any intelligence of him to his Parents, or who will inform the said Daniel Mason that his Sister, Mrs. Sheridan, has come from Port Phillip with the intention of taking him with her. Address to
> 532
> JOHN MASON,
> Swan Reach.

The sister referred to in this advertisement is **Mary, Mrs Thomas Sheridan,** living in Victoria for some 10 years, with one child and two miscarriages behind her, and some 20 years older than **Daniel**. For her to take responsibility for him was kind of her, for his father *not* to take responsibility for him was not. **Daniel**'s existence is not acknowledged in later official documents — for example the death certificate for his father **John Mason II** in 1858, on the information of his older brother **Oliver Mason,** or the death certificate for his mother, **Joanna Quigley,** reported by the same brother in 1857. Perhaps he changed his name and made a life for himself. One can only hope so.

Chapter 4

The migrating Oliver Mason

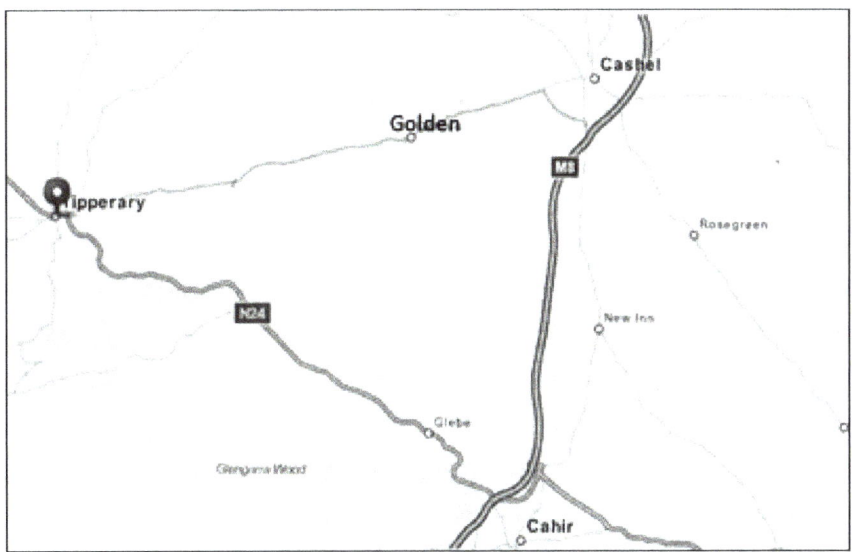

The triangle of Cahir, Golden and Cashel, in County Tipperary, Ireland where the young Mason males lived before they migrated to Australia

The areas in the Hunter Valley where the Masons settled in 1839.

Oliver Mason: b. Feb 1818 d. 7 Apr 1885

2ND SON OF JOHN MASON II AND JOHANNA QUIGLEY
BROTHER OF MARY, JOHN III, JOANNA, MARGARET AND DANIEL MASON
OLIVER, HIS PARENTS AND SIBLINGS MIGRATED TO AUSTRALIA ON THE *CHINA* ON 19 DEC 1839
M. ANN FITZGERALD 21 JAN 1853 ST MARY'S CATHEDRAL, SYDNEY B. 1825 D. 1 AUG 1891
FATHERED 7 CHILDREN, 41 GRANDCHILDREN AND MANY GREAT-GRANDCHILDREN
WAS ABLE TO BUY AND SELL LAND SOON AFTER HIS ARRIVAL IN AUSTRALIA

Written by Monica Mason
Material from Mason family members

Oliver Mason, with his father and mother **John II** and **Johanna (Quigley) Mason,** his brothers and sisters, migrated to Australia from Tipperary, Ireland on the *China*, arriving in Sydney on 19 Dec 1839. At 21, he and his brother **John**, then aged 23, were young and strong, and in a position to take on the challenges of this enormous disruption of their lives to migrate to the other end of the world. The family had shown a great deal of initiative in leaving what we were told was their poverty-stricken lives in Tipperary before the cataclysmic famine officially took hold of Ireland in 1845, but which had been escalating for some years.

Both **Oliver** and **John III Mason** had been employed (rare enough in Ireland at the time) as mill hands in the village of Golden, less than seven kilometres out of the bishopric city of Cashel, in Tipperary, an area owned by one of the great landowners, Lawrence Creagh, which they claimed as their home. The area is green and lush, but starvation was still the norm, though the young men of the **Mason** family were fortunate to have jobs which presumably assisted the rest of the family in Cashel to be strong enough to make the extraordinary effort – and expense – of getting themselves fitted out and onto a ship to Australia. The announcement in the official shipping documents at their arrival that **Oliver** and **John** were a 'ploughman' and a 'labourer' was probably a recognition of the perceived needs of the infant colony at the time.

They were both 'disposed' as they disembarked in Sydney from the *China*, at a standard rate of £21 per year plus rations, to **William Wentworth Bucknell** of Brecon, on the Paterson River, near Morpeth and Maitland. They therefore went straight out to Maitland with the male part of the family, the sisters being offered employment in Sydney and staying behind. **William Bucknell** (whose wife was related to the exploring politician **William Wentworth** who crossed the Blue Mountains in 1813) had been in the Colony since 1826, had been granted extensive land at Paterson, near Maitland, and continued to expand his holdings in that area. It is assumed that the **Masons** were employed on that property as agricultural labourers.

We have found no record of where or how they lived, however, nor of how or whether they served **Bucknell**, who had engaged them. We also have no knowledge of how or where **Oliver** met **Ann Fitzgerald**, his future wife, but **Oliver** had been consistently in the Maitland area in the intervening years. **Oliver** and **Ann Mason** had seven children between 1853 and 1865, and owned property at Woolamol (now Oxley Vale, a suburb of Tamworth), Morpeth and Cockburn River.

Oliver married **Ann Fitzgerald** on 21 Jan 1853 in St Mary's Cathedral in Sydney (MC V1853309 99). He appears, as his brother **John** does not, as witness/sponsor for weddings/baptisms etc. This seems to show an element of responsibility not otherwise obvious in the family. For example he witnessed the marriage of his sister **Johanna Mason** to ex-convict **Charles Tighe** in Sydney in 1841 (thus probably giving the marriage the family's mark of approval); the marriage of his brother **John** to his first wife, **Mary Hickey** in 1850; and the baptism of **John** and **Mary's** son **John** at Swan Reach in 1852.

That the **Masons** could define their occupations on individual documents themselves, means that the records occasionally deviate from the truth. However, **Oliver Mason** is named, reasonably enough, as a settler in Morpeth, and successively in Swan Reach and Raymond Terrace in the Maitland/Morpeth area;, then at his death in Tamworth in 1885 as a farmer and landowner in Tamworth.

The relationship with the huge land-owning company Australian Agricultural Company (AAC) may well have had an influence on the family. The AAC Company had been set up by the UK government, to whom Australia was still subject, and owned really vast tracts of land granted to them by the English government in the Port Stephens area nearer the NSW coast, under the influence in London of controversial Australian landowner **John Macarthur**. It had been hoped to run huge stocks of sheep there, but it was quite soon discovered that so close to the sea was inappropriate for sheep, and the AAC grant was transferred to the grant of two major tracts in the Tamworth area, *Warrah* and *Peel*, inland about 300 kilometres. This new land proved profitable.

The dates of the transfer from the Port Stephens area to the Tamworth district for the AAC are not too incompatible with the whole-family **Mason** migration occurring in the 1870s. That prompts the (unanswered) question — were some of the family employed by the AAC, or just opportunistically following this major development step? Tamworth had also had its gold rush in Tamworth in the 1850s and the development promised by the AAC's move to the Tamworth area forecast a bright future for new settlers, as the **Masons** became. The 4000-acre Woolamol grant was made to the Australian Agricultural Company, and was gradually sold off to small landholders. That Oliver bought 182 acres of this, however, was no mean feat from someone we had thought of as a landless peasant. So the **Masons** took the big step of transporting themselves over the mountains from the Morpeth area to Tamworth from 1870, when Oliver was 52, making lives for themselves there, as his sister **Margaret** and her husband **Patrick Creevey** had done in nearby Dungowan. Trains did not even arrive in Tamworth until 1878, though they served nearby Murrurundi in 1872.

Oliver's sister **Margaret Mason** and her husband **Patrick Creevey** had moved to Dungowan, 18 kilometres south of Tamworth, in 1863, and the **Mason** family moved to part of a new property, Woolamol, just north west of Tamworth, in 1870. The last child, **Joseph**, was actually born in Tamworth in 1865. Was **Oliver** there to discover opportunities? **Oliver** produced wheat – for which he must have had some experience on land at Port Stephens or in Ireland – and sent it to Gunnedah, as being a somewhat more navigable road than to Tamworth. There is a family story that a hammock was slung under the bullock dray for the driver to sleep in!

So at the time of his death in 1885, **Oliver** was a farmer and landowner at Woolamol, owned and operated by his family beyond his death. He bequeathed half of everything to each of his two younger sons, **Charles** and **Joseph**, and £30 to **Terence**. Other sons inherited nothing — were they old enough to be sufficiently settled? Two of them lived on a property at Cockburn River, near Tamworth, of which we know little to nothing. Since they were adults by the time of **Oliver**'s death, perhaps he felt they could cope on their own, since presumably **Ann (Fitzgerald) Mason** followed her husband's wishes and Will.

Oliver's Will was probated, and shows that he left property in the Tamworth area to his wife, **Ann Mason Fitzgerald**. She died six years after her husband, and her Will (probated 1891, *2467 Series 4*) written at her home at Rose Green Farm near Tamworth, left half of the 182 acres at Woolomol to each of their sons **Charles** and **Joseph**, and nearly £1000 worth of real estate — probably the properties at Marius Street and 98 Peel Street in Tamworth — also to **Joseph**. **Oliver**'s probate says he lived not at the Woolamol property, but perhaps more comfortably at Marius St/Manilla Highway, and at 98 Peel Street, Tamworth, both within the limits of the present town.

The move to the Tamworth district from the Morpeth area by **John**'s and **Oliver**'s families needs an explanation — which we don't have. Morpeth was more easily reachable by boat — a trip of about eight hours from Sydney — but Tamworth was a burgeoning, busy nearly-city, to which the AAC had transferred its properties from Port Stephens. It was becoming an important centre, though without direct transport to Sydney. The trip to Tamworth from Sydney went by coach from Morpeth, after the boat trip from Sydney. Schools, churches, businesses were growing apace in Tamworth, which by 1878 did have its own train service. This redistribution of AAC land to the Tamworth environment must have been another major pull factor for the **Masons** to settle there in 1870.

The migrating **Oliver**'s sons **John** (32 at his father's death), **Patrick** (29) and **James** (28) settled at nearby Cockburn River, outside Tamworth, about 10 kilometres away from Woolamol. Indeed the whole family at this stage seems to have changed its abode as a unit.

Oliver died at the age of 67, at Woolamol in 1885, of paralysis, which he had endured for over a year.

Burial record Oliver and Ann Mason at Tamworth Cemetery:

Name	First Name	Burial Date	Age	Relationships	Burial Place			
Mason	Oliver	7 Apr 1885	64	Husband to Ann	NSW	RC	V	86
Mason	Ann	1 Aug 1891	66	née Fitzgerald; Wife to Oliver	NSW	RC	V	86

Sacred to the memory of
Oliver Mason
Who departed this life April 7th 1885
aged 64 years
And Ann beloved wife of above who
departed this life August 1st 1891

This building, the old Royal Hotel, replaced the Freemasons Arms at
97 Swan St Morpeth

Chapter 4: The migrating Oliver Mason

2014

We have recently discovered a quite different background for this migrating **Oliver Mason**. We had believed the family to be 'landless Irish peasants', with no assets. We learn instead that earlier in Morpeth (and therefore probably in Ireland), **Oliver** owned a hotel, from soon after the family arrived. The *Maitland Mercury* advertisement and translation and the newspaper report of 3 Nov 1855 record the proposed sale of Morpeth property.

> **Cottage and Land,**
> *Opposite Mrs. Cornelius's Inn, Morpeth, and adjoining to Messrs Wisdom and Conlon's store, at present occupied by Mrs. Banfield as a Butcher's Shop.*
> Mr W A Dodds has received instructions from Mr Oliver Mason to sell by section, on the Premises, Morpeth, on Wednesday, 14 November, at Twelve o'clock.
> All that PIECE OF LAND adjoining to Messrs Wisdom and Conlon's Stores, Morpeth, and nearly opposite to the Hunter River New Steam Navigations Company's Wharf, having 62 feet frontage to Swan-street, by a great depth to a reserved road at the rear, on which is erected a Four Roomed
> VERANDAH COTTAGE,
> shingled; built of slabs, with brick chimney, three of the rooms being boarded. The cottage is at present let on a weekly tenancy, at 17s. per week; so that immediate possession can be given to a purchaser.
> The land is nearly all fenced in with an ironbark fence of three rails.
> Title good — Terms at sale.
> A.D. begs to direct the attention of builders, mechanics, and others to this sale of a well situated allotment of land at Morpeth, with a comfortable cottage thereon, yielding a rental of 17s. per week. The land has sufficient depth to divide it into two lots, one fronting on Swan-street, the other to a reserve road at the rear. The improvements cost the proprietor a great deal of money; and his only reason for parting with the freehold is because he has embarked in business in another district.

Lt. E.C. Close, the founder of Morpeth and veteran of the Napoleonic Wars, and his wife, built church and mansion in Morpeth, and sold land to **Oliver Mason** Yeoman of Morpeth in July 1853 for £155. Two years later on 19 Nov 1855, **Oliver**, now of Raymond Terrace, disposed of the land at the price of £350 – an excellent profit. It was a large block with frontage on Swan Street, the main street of Morpeth, facing the Hunter River.

In April 1855, **Oliver** became the licensee of the Freemason's Arms Hotel in Raymond Terrace. This licence was renewed on 22 Apr 1856. Raymond Terrace historians believe that the Freemason's Arms was in William Street and became the Royal Hotel, which no longer exists.

Oliver was thus a successful businessman, and had assets in this country very soon after their arrival. Those assets grew, particularly when he moved to Tamworth.

> **THE MAITLAND MERCURY**
> **3 Nov 1855**
> The undersigned most respectfully begs leave to inform his friends of Raymond Terrace, and the public of the surrounding district, that they can be furnished with clean, comfortable bedding, the choicest of Wines and Spirits and the very best of eatables, together with strict attention to civility, on the most modest terms. Travellers may depend upon finding first rate accommodation at:
> 'Oliver Mason's'
> Freemason's Arms – Raymond Terrace
> Note: Plenty of corn and hay – and Good Stabling

Descendants of Oliver Mason

Researched and written by Monica & Terry Mason
Much research also by Patricia Keevers

1 **Oliver Mason** b. Feb 1818 Golden, near Cashel, Tipperary, IRL. (21 on arrival 1839) d. 7 Apr 1885 Tamworth, NSW. DC 14440 (2525) m. **Ann Fitzgerald**. 21 Jan 1853 St Mary's Cathedral, Sydney. V1853309 99/1853 b. 1825 Stonehall, Limerick, IRL (calculated from DC) d. 1 Aug 1891 DC 14213/1891 Informant for DC son **Joseph Mason** [daughter of James Fitzgerald and Johanna Maun]

    2 **John F Mason** b. 14 Dec 1853 Morpeth, NSW. BC V1853 3971 d. 24 Aug 1926 Gayndah, Qld DC 5913421, Reg 1926/002707 003169 m. **Ada Evelyn Burnes** 1888 Narrabri, NSW. WC 6340/1888 b. 1872 Murrurundi BC 13704 1872 d. 9 May 1959 DC 1959/B31541 [daughter of Robert Burns and Emily Drysdale Burns]. At 20 in 1873, **John** and his younger brothers **Patrick** (17) and **James** (16) settled at Cockburn River, near Tamworth.

John's ten children (six boys and four girls) were born in Narrabri, Gunnedah or Quirindi, with one born in Boggabri. Their third child **Ann** lived only from 1892 to 1893. The remaining nine children moved with **John** and **Ada** to Queensland sometime after the youngest, **Ada Anne,** was born in 1909 — where, we don't know.

John is buried in the Gayndah Cemetery 200 kilometres west of Maryborough, Qld with a large headstone. He is the only family member buried there. He was 72 years old and died from chronic bronchitis, acute bronchitis and cardiac failure, listed as an Old Age Pensioner.

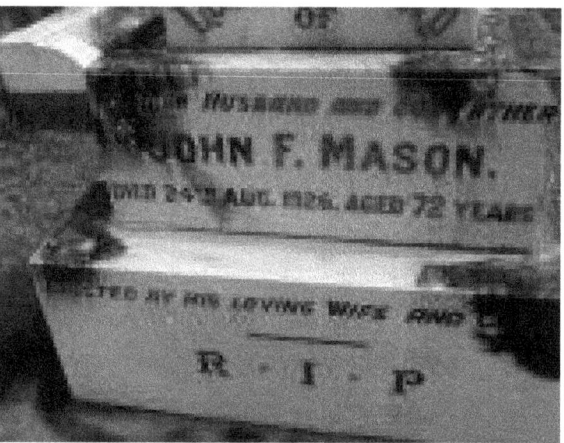

The rather unkempt Gayndah grave of John F Mason, who died at 72 in 24 Aug 1926. Erected by

        3 **Oliver Patrick Mason** b. 1889 Baan Baa, NSW (between Tamworth & Narrabri), reg at Narrabri BC 29106 1889 d. 15 Mar 1944 Qld DC 1944/B065569 m. **Amelia Emily Bourne** 21 Apr 1930 Qld, MC 1930/001782

Birth Record Oliver Patrick Mason

Reference	Name	First Name	Father	Mother	Birth Place
BC 29016/1889	Mason	Oliver P	John F	Ada E	Narrabri

Oliver Patrick enlisted with the Australian Imperial Forces (AIF) for World War I on 30 Apr 1915. He joined the 26th Battalion Infantry, Service No, 4905, and embarked for overseas service on 24 May 1915. His mother is listed as next of kin, giving her address as Ivanhoe, Baroona Road, Milton, Brisbane. **Oliver's** handwriting, in signing documents re his enlistment, is well developed and has style. His military record shows he was a signalman and a WWI hero, earning a Military Medal from the AIF in 1918 for:

conspicuous gallantry and devotion to duty in the operations at HERVILLY on night 17/18 September 1918. By his initiative and coolness Spr. Mason succeeded in maintaining communication in spite of heavy hostile shell fire. He set a splendid example and displayed untiring energy in the performance of his duty. (Sgd) Major General commanding 1st Australian Division.

Appearance: 5'11", 10 stone 11 pounds, chest 37 inches, fair complexion, blue eyes, hair almost black, copper coloured moustache, scar on small finger left hand (from WWI records).

Chapter 4: The migrating Oliver Mason

Oliver was discharged 14 July 1919, and was over age to serve in the WWII conflict. Three of his brothers – **James Edward**, at 42, **Joseph Charles**, 37, and **Edward John**, 36 — all served in WWII, and all returned home at the end of the war.

3 **Robert Joseph Mason** b. 1891 Boggabri BC 7224 1891

3 **Ann Mason** b. 1892 Narrabri BC 24416 1892 d. 1893 Narrabri DC 9839 1893

3 **John Leo Mason** b. 1894 m. **Freda Kathleen Hunting** 17 Jul 1933 Qld. MC 1933/B016079 b. c1912 d. 21 Apr 2004 Mudgeeraba, Qld

3 **Zillah May Mason** b. 1895 Gunnedah, NSW BC 32810 1895 d. 5 Feb 1949 Caboolture, Qld DC 1949/G020629 m. **Bernard Patrick McErlane** 20 May 1937 Qld, MC 1937/B028177 d. 22 Nov 1985 Caboolture, Qld

3 **Mary Philomena Veronica Mason** b. 1898 Gunnedah, NSW. BC 21734 1898 m. **Bertrand Frederick Evans** 11 Jun 1924 Qld MC 1924/001023 d. 23 Sep 1957 Qld DC 19957 B022171

3 **James Edward Mason** b. 9 Jul 1900 Quirindi, NSW BC 25589 1900. d. 1962 Qld DC 1962/5656 m. **Helen Isabel Leslie** 23 Mar 1929. Served in the Australian Army, WWII, Service No. 0208652, Enlisted in Maryborough, Qld, 9 Apr 1942, at age 42, 3rd of his brothers to enlist. Rank of Corporal, discharged 13 Jul 1944.

3 **Joseph Charles Mason** b. 12 Apr 1903 Baan Baa, near Narrabri, NSW BC 14197/1903 d. Record not found in Qld. WWII Enlisted in Maryborough in the Australian Army, 6 Jul 1940, age 37, 1st of his brothers in Maryborough, Service No. QX10718. Driver, discharged 15 Mar 1946.

3 **Edward John Mason** b. 12 Jul 1905 Quirindi, NSW BC 27092/1905 m. **Hilda Rosa Taylor** 22 Apr 1937 Qld. MC 1937/B027944 b. c1915 d. 30 Sep 2003 Pullenvale, Qld. Australian Army, Service No. QX23419, 2/5 Armoured Regiment Trooper. Enlisted Toowoomba, Qld, 27 Aug 1941, age 36, 2nd of his brothers to enlist. Discharged 29 Oct 1945.

3 **Ada Anne Mason** b. 1909 Quirindi, BC 18315/1909. Strangely, birth for another 'Ada' is registered at 18314/1909. Ada is listed on her father's DC 1944/B065569 as 17 years old. No further record found.

2 **Patrick Arthur Mason** b. 29 May 1855 Raymond Terrace NSW d. 1913 Temora m. **Margaret Toohey** 6 Sep 1883 St Nicholas Church, Tamworth NSW, MC 7055/1883. The marriage was dissolved by decree of the NSW Supreme Court on 27 Oct 1896, RG Dept. No. 96/4767, granted due to the violence **Margaret** was subjected to and for **Patrick**'s desertion of her and the children, then aged 7 to 11. **Margaret** brought up the three children on her own.

3 **Hannah May Mason** b. 9 May 1885 Tamworth NSW (Family bible) d. 23 May 1937, 20 Martin Place, Mortdale DC 9239/1937 from cerebral thrombosis m. **Edward J Smalley** 1914 Glebe, MC 5949/1914 b. 1884 Waterloo d. 1962 DC 29919/1962

War service

Arthur William Mason, son of **William** and **Priscilla Mason**, went to WWI

Vic Mason, son of **William Mason**, enlisted at 36 in the Navy before WWII started in 1939, and became a Lieutenant Commander (Electrical) in the RAN.

Bob Mason, Vic's 'little' brother who enlisted at 18, and served in WWII in the RAAF in Morse Code.

Jack Mason, son of **Arthur E Mason**, grandson of **William Mason**, served in WWII

Oliver Patrick Mason, eldest son of **John F Mason**, who served as a signalman in WWI, and won a Military Medal for his 'untiring energy in the performance of his duty'.

James Edward Mason, son of **John F Mason**, who served in WWII as a Corporal, enlisting at age 42

Joseph Charles Mason, son of **John F Mason**, who served in WWII as a Driver, enlisting at age 37.

Edward John Mason, son of **John F Mason**, who served in WWII an Armoured Regiment, enlisting at age 36.

Patrick Daniel Mason, son of **James Mason**, served in the Boer War and WWI

All these men who served came home at the end of their war.

3 **Bartholomew Theobald Mason** b. 16 Apr 1887 Tamworth (Family bible) BC 34838/1887 d. 6 Dec 1906 Drowned in billabong, Marsden, NSW, age 19 DC 12309/1906

3 **Veronica Pearl Mason** b. 1889 Tamworth, NSW d. 1956 Narrabeen, NSW DC 27694/1956 m. **Charles Oldham Johnson** 1916 Balmain South, NSW, MC 100039/1916 b. 1892 Bathurst d. 1955 Ashfield, NSW. DC 763/1955

2 **James Mason** b. 21 May 1856 Stroud, Raymond Terrace, NSW. BC 7469 d. 9 Mar 1915 Killed on the railway between Nemingha & Tintinhull, near Tamworth. m. **Jane E Purtell** (sister of **Catherine Purtell,** who married **James**' young brother **Joseph Mason** 1892) 15 Sep 1878 St Nicholas' Church, Tamworth MC 4843/1878 (Family Bible) b. 1860 West Maitland, NSW [daughter of Francis and Mary Purtell] d. 7 Mar 1936 Quirindi. In 1896 **James** was a labourer living at Duri, just south of Tamworth. His great grand-daughter **Patricia Keevers** found his wages in 1902 as ganger on Currabubula to Armidale to be 9/- (nine shillings, just less than $1) a day. **James** died as a result of injuries riding a tricycle on the line, knocked down by a light engine between Nemingha and Tintinhull. The Inquest of 10-20 Mar 1915 into the responsibility of the driver in Tamworth Courthouse found that too little care was taken by all – the driver, the fireman, and **James Mason**. The train men were committed to trial. The couple had an astonishing 13 children, though many died in infancy.

3 **Mary Therese Mason** b. 12 Jun 1879 Cockburn River Tamworth. BC 'Mary Thelma', Family Bible 'Mary Teresa' BC 23746/1879 d. 9 Jul 1965 Sacred Heart Hospice, Darlinghurst DC 24291/1965 m. **John Francis Joseph (Jack) Purcell** 15 Oct 1912 MC 15871 RC Church, Tamworth b. 1884 Morpeth BC 25211/1884 d. 1952 Petersham, Sydney DC 19904/1952 [son of John Francis Purcell and Sarah Vaughan]. BDM Register and Family Bible dates say she was 33, five years older than **Jack.** She was 86 when she died DC 24291/1965. Her father **James'** occupation is listed as linesman. Her son **James F** is the informant with her address: 80 Charlotte St Ashfield. Her husband **John** worked in Real Estate, and was born at Morpeth BC 25211/1884 MC says he was a farmer at Werris Creek.

3 **Patrick Daniel Mason** b. 27 Dec 1880 Glengarvon Station, Tamworth BC 26724/1881 (Family Bible says 29 Oct 1880) d. 1 Dec 1937 Western Suburbs Hospital, Croydon DC 23524/1937 m. **Elizabeth Gilmore** 22 May 1916 Mission Hall, Rozelle, Sydney MC 6100/1916 b. ? Durham, England d. 7 Mar 1917 Coast Hospital, Little Bay [daughter of Anthony Mears and Elizabeth Brown]. According to family member **Noel Mason**, when **Patrick** went to 'fight for the Queen' in the Boer War his father **James**, son of the migrating **Oliver**, would have nothing to do with him, so when he came back from that War, **Patrick** went to Western Australia as a teacher. His service in WWI also gained him a Belgian award.

MC 6100/1916 states that **Patrick** was 36 when he married **Elizabeth Gilmore**, a 47 year old widow, though his death certificate says he was 30 at the time. **Patrick**'s residence at the time of this marriage is given as Coffs Harbour, NSW. What was he doing there?

Patrick's DC 23524/1937 says that there were no children from this marriage. **Elizabeth** died only a year after their marriage, shown on DC 1917/573 as being from accidental injuries, falling down stairs, from an Inquest on 14 March 1917, with Informant **Patrick**, 2 Jarocin Ave. Glebe. **Elizabeth** is buried in the Church of England Cemetery, Rookwood, had been in NSW 11 years and had no children from the marriage. But her first marriage to **Harry Gilmore** in England had produced a son, **Arthur D**, 18 at the time of **Harry's** death. Buried at Rookwood: Mortuary 2; Area 14; Grave 2854. It is unknown whether the son was born in England or in Australia. (Informants: **Noel Mason, Patricia Keevers**)

After **Elizabeth**'s death in 1917, **Patrick**, at 38, married **Martha Austin** in Wembley, England c1918. b. c1877 Liverpool, UK, d. 15 Jun 1951 26 Roscoe Street, Bondi Beach DC 23524/1937.

Patrick Daniel Mason is buried at Rookwood Cemetery, Mortuary 2, Area 14, Grave 2854. (Informants: **Noel Mason, Patricia Keevers**)

3 **Anne Mason** b. 13 Oct 1881 BC 22782 Narrabri, NSW (Family bible) d. 7 Apr 1942. Perth. She was known as Sister Dolores and it is said she was killed by a tree falling on her in a cyclone in Broome. The St John of God nuns have no knowledge of anyone with these details.

3 **Margaret Mason** b. 1 May 1885 Tamworth BC 32871/1885 (Family Bible) d. 29 Dec 1921 St Joseph's Province, Albert St, East Melbourne DC 7383/1921

3 **John Charles (Jack) Mason** b. 8 Dec 1886 Tamworth BC 34845/1886 d. 1943 Warwick, Qld, DC 63023 m. **Alice Mary (Mary) Heyman** 1914 Tamworth MC 3698/1914 d. 27 Sep 1954 Balmain DC 17141/1954. **Jack**'s grandson, **Tim,** thinks Jack also spent time in NZ, living with **Jack**'s daughter and her husband, **Patricia** and **Cliff Keating,** after separation from his wife in the years before he died in 1943.

Jack and **Alice's** daughter **Patricia Amelia Thomasine Mason** was born in October 1915, the same year his father **James Mason** died on the railways. **Jack** left his wife **Mary** and their daughter at some later time, and the family recall that he was 'sent to St Martha's, to **Sister Thomasene (Jack's** younger sister, **Jane)**. It was probably later that he went to live in Warwick, Queensland — his niece **Joan** says he was a 'wanderer'. Later, probably about 1934, he lived with his younger brother **Vin (Charles Vincent Mason)** and his family in Tenterfield (north west of Grafton NSW) from c1934 to c1943, when he died. Apparently drink was a part of **Jack's** problem — he was walking home one night along the railway tracks and when crossing the rail bridge, fell off and was killed. He is buried at Toowong, Brisbane, Portion 1, Section 107, Grave No. 1. His grandson **Tim Keating** (son of **Patricia Amelia Mason**) who died some 63 years later, is buried in the same grave with him. Reasons for that are unknown.

3 **Ruby Myrtle Mason** b. 1 Jun 1888 Tamworth, NSW d. 18 Aug 1890 West Tamworth, NSW (Bible record) BC 35903/1888. DC 12396/1890 says she died from pulmonary tuberculosis which she had had 'for some months'.

3 **Jane (Sister Thomasene) Mason** b. 2 Feb 1890 Tamworth, NSW d. 24 Jul 1963 Hunters Hill, Sydney BC 33243/1890. Family Bible says 1st Feb 1890. **Sister Thomasene** was a Sister of St Joseph and worked in St Martha's boarding school in Lewisham, to which the three younger daughters of **Oliver Alphonsus Mason, Anne, Claire** and **Cath** were also sent for a time.

3 (Unnnamed male) Mason b. 14 Mar 1892 Tamworth BC 34102/1892, d. 17 Mar 1892 West Tamworth – a premature birth, living for only three days.

3 **Charles Vincent (Vin) Mason** b. 12 Apr 1893 Tamworth BC 34394/1893 d. 10 Nov 1963 DC 1963/029985 St. John of God Hospital, Richmond, Sydney m. **Winifred Margaret Mary (Win) Fletcher** 28 Jan 1920 St Mary's, Scone, NSW MC

Vin Mason, working on the railways, at Werris Creek with dog (Werris Creek Economic Development Committee)

3154/1921 b. 8 Jan 1903 Scone BC 7026 d. 17 Feb 1994 Scone District Nursing Home. After marriage they moved to Quippi, between Quirindi and Werris Creek, to Tenterfield 1934-1943, then Walcha Road, then Kootingal (north west of Tamworth) and retired from there. **Vin** died from Inanition, Dementia, Cerebral Arteriosclerosis stroke. Buried 11 Nov 1963 by Fr. James Hughes at Scone. **Win**'s parents, William R and Margaret M Fletcher, ran a boarding establishment in Scone, and **Charlie**, son of **Oliver Alphonsus,** boarded with them when he first went to Scone to work in the Railways Office.

3 **James Augustine (Gus) Mason** b. 23 Dec 1894 Tamworth, d. 19 Feb 1911. Family Bible says birth is 23 December 1895. He died from pneumonia in the Tamworth Hospital.

3 **Blandine Mason** b. 5 Mar 1896 Duri, NSW Reg. Quirindi, NSW. d. 20 Nov 1896 Tamworth DC 15368/1896. She died at 8 months from malnutrition and pertusis (whooping cough).

3 **Irene Mason** b. 18 Jul 1897 Duri, Reg. Quirindi NSW d. 20 Dec 1897 Duri, NSW. BC 25248/1897. Her brother **Jack** (as informant) was listed as a labourer living at Duri, nearby. DC 13745/1897 says she died at six months from gastroenteritis which she had had for 6 days. She was the only child registered to **James** and **Jane** who died at Duri — all the rest died at Tamworth or East Tamworth.

Chapter 4: The migrating Oliver Mason

3 **Dorothy Mason** b. 1900 Tamworth BC 7643/1900 d. 11 May 1900 West Tamworth. Informant **Joan Keevers** has said that her dad, **James**, had a great devotion to St Dorothy. DC 7117/1900 says she died from malnutrition at three months.

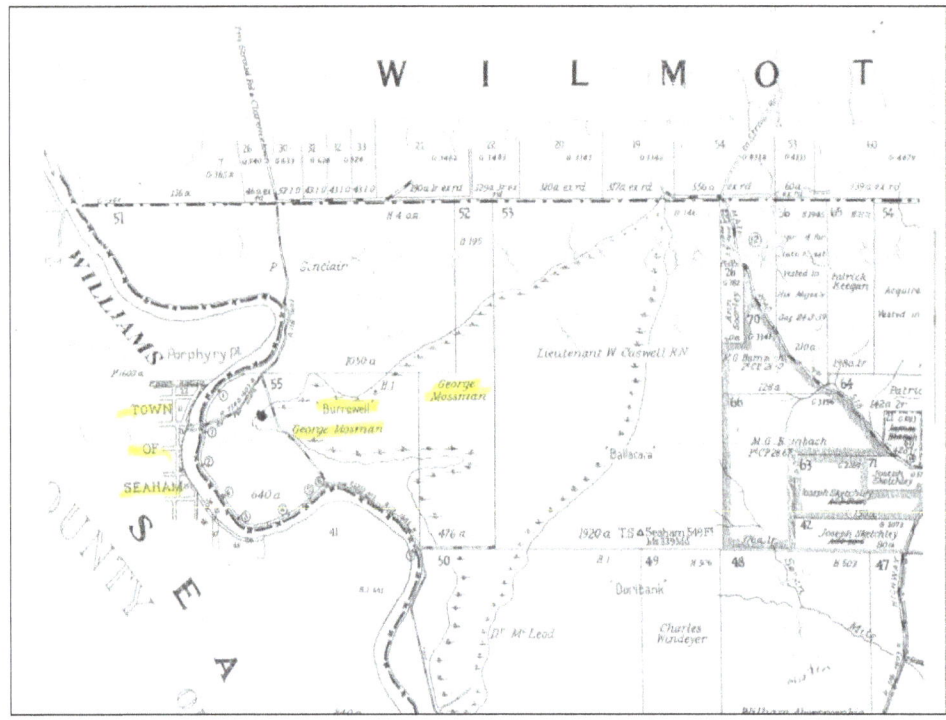

George Mossman's property Burrowell (highlighted), across the Williams River from Seaham, NSW, just north of Raymond Terrace, and east of Phoenix Park. We believe Oliver's father (the migrating Oliver Mason) was working on this property when his son was born in 1858.

2 **Oliver Mason** b. 24 Apr 1858 Burrowell, nr Seaham, Raymond Terrace NSW d. 28 Aug 1932 Cornwall Rd, Sandringham, NZ m. **Elizabeth English** 27 Feb 1878 Tamworth. [Daughter of Thomas and Mary English] d. c1879. m2. **Honoria (Nora) Dunn** 1907 Pukekohe, NZ b. 11 Dec 1872 Auckland, NZ d. 24 Oct 1943 Eden Terrace, Auckland. Burrowell was a property selected and owned by George Mossman's family at Seaham, so it is presumed that **Oliver** was in his employ. **Elizabeth**'s father gave consent for their marriage so she could not yet have been 21 years old, though on the birth certificate for their daughter **Margaret**, **Elizabeth** was said to be 22. Witnesses to the marriage are his father (the migrating) **Oliver Mason** and Agnes Bailey. **Elizabeth** is listed as a tailoress and **Oliver** says (a change for this farming family) that he is a saddler. Their daughter, **Margaret**, born 6 Dec 1879 at West Maitland BC 1879/16364, was ill for two months and died the next year from consumption and general debility. She was buried at Tamworth.

Terry Mason shows the (sadly untended) grave of his great-uncle Oliver and his wife Nora, in Auckland.

In loving memory of Oliver loved husband of Nora Mason and fond father of Charlie died 28 Aug 1932, and his beloved wife Nora died 24 October 1943

Oliver's second marriage on 10 Apr 1907, to **Nora Dunn**, was presided over by Father D. McMillan (priest from their local church, St Patricks, Pukekohe) in the grounds of her mother's residence at Ararimu South, Pukekohe (Auckland RC Diocese Offices). **Oliver**'s job, at 46, was a Quarryman and his father **Oliver**'s occupation had been Hotel Keeper (our first inkling that **Oliver** had assets). **Nora**'s occupation, at 34, was Domestic Duties and her father was a farmer.

Oliver and **Nora** had one child, **Charles Gerald**, baptised at their local church, on 16 Feb 1908. **Oliver** is buried at Waikumete cemetery, as a City Council Employee. **Nora** was 70 when she died at 5 Egerton St, Eden Terrace, Auckland. **Charles**

Chapter 4: The migrating Oliver Mason

became a painter, and was cremated on 9 Dec 1970 at 62. His last address was 96 Elliot St, Howick, Auckland. From his Will, we gather that he never married.

2 **Edward Terence Mason** was the sixth son of the migrating **Oliver** and **Ann Fitzgerald Mason**, b. 13 Dec 1863, at Port Stephens BC 138864/1864, registered at Narrabri. From his father **Oliver's** will, executed after his mother's death in 1891, he inherited $15 to be paid by each of his brothers **Charles** and **Joseph** to be delivered immediately. He worked as a painter, according to the census, in 1899/1900 at Woolamol. The *Morning Bulletin* of Rockhampton tells of the death in 1928 of **Edward** (we know him as **Terence**) **Mason**, who died at the age of 64 from being lost in the bush near Yeppoon, Queensland. He was unmarried.

> **DEATH OF EDWARD MASON.**
>
> Our Yeppoon correspondent telephoned yesterday. Three weeks ago an old man named Edward Mason, 64, was found wandering in the bush here. He had been lost for three weeks and for a fortnight had subsisted on prickly pear. He was taken to the Yeppoon Hospital, where Dr. Beaman and the nursing staff did all that was humanly possible for him. The hardships and privations he had endured proved too much for the old man, who rallied once or twice in a desire to live. Gradually he sank and finally passed away to-day. So far as is known, Mason had no relatives in the State."

2 **Charles Mason** b. 25 Oct 1862 BC 12711/1862 Wards River, registered at Port Stephens NSW d. 4 Apr 1954 North Sydney m. **Catherine Theresa Morris** 18 Jan 1888 b. 27 Jul 1858 Louth Park, Maitland BC 8825/1858 Ward's River near Port Stephens [daughter of Richard Morris and Bridget Cullinane] d. 29 Aug 1927 Cooroy, near Noosa, Qld. See

2 **Joseph Paul Mason** b.19 Mar 1865 in Tamworth d. 4 May 1918 Auckland NZ, m. **Catherine Purtell** 29 Jun 1892 Tamworth MC 7121/1892 with **Terence Mason** and **Teresa Purtell** as witnesses. **Catherine** died from leukaemia on 4 May 1918. The **Purtell** family (**Catherine's** background) consisted of seven daughters. **Mary** b.1857 BC 8544; **Jane** b. 1860 BC 8609 (married to **Joseph's** brother **James**); **Teresa** b. 1863 BC 9344, **Agnes** b. 1863, twin of **Teresa**; **Katherine** b. 1865 BC 10860; **Clara** b. 1870 BC 12109; and **Blandina** b. 1871 BC 12846. **Clara** became **Sister Mary Dolores**, Sister of Mercy, Auckland. **Joseph** and **Catherine** named their only daughter **Mary Dolores**. She joined the same Order of Sisters in Auckland and was known as **Sister Consiglio**.

Joseph and Catherine Mason's grave, Waikaraka Cemetery, Onehunga, Auckland NZ

Joseph Paul was born at Tamworth, as were his older brothers. He inherited land at Woolamol and chattels from his father **Oliver** in 1885, through his mother, when she died in 1891. He was perhaps seen as the one most in need of financial support. His wife **Catherine Purtell** was the younger sister of his older brother **James'** wife **Jane**, and they married in 1892 at Tamworth. The couple moved to New Zealand about 1897.

3 **John Cecil (Jack) Mason** b. 30 May 1893 Tamworth d. 11 Oct 1956 Pukekohe, Auckland, NZ m. **Ellen Genevieve (Cissy) Smith** 22 Jun 1919 St Benedict's, Auckland b. c1887 Auckland d. 13 Jul 1963 Auckland

3 **Oliver Louis Joseph (Brother Herman) Mason** b. 23 Jul 1895 Tamworth d. 21 Jun 1937 Naililili, Fiji from Parkinson's Disease. **Oliver** was educated at the Sacred Heart College in Auckland, run by the Marist Bros, and thus was inspired to join them. He was received into the Institute at Mittagong as **Brother Herman Mary** in 1913, where he began his training. His cousins **Terry** and **Oli (Brother Claudius) Mason** also trained there. The story from the Marist Order sees him as charitable,

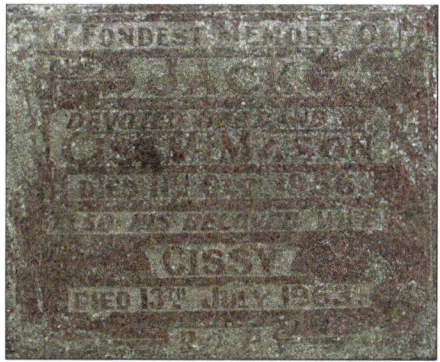

In fondest memory of Jack devoted husband of Cissy Mason died 11th Oct 1956 Also his beloved wife Cissy died 13 July 1963 RIP

amiable, kindly and humorous, and entirely uncomplaining, though 'suffering a martyrdom of pain'. He spent hours in his last years learning Hindi to keep alert and take his mind off his Parkinson's.

3 **Ronald Joseph Mason** b. Jul 1897 Auckland NZ d. 31 Jan 1898 Auckland. Buried at Waikumete Cemetery RC division C. Row 8, Plot 24, though no headstone has been found. This is the same cemetery where his uncle and aunt **Oliver** and **Nora** are buried.

3 **James Aubrey Mason** b. 1900 Auckland m. **Winifred Evelyn Nixon** 19 May 1962 St Benedicts, Auckland, NZ b. c1900 Wanganui NZ (both aged 62) d. 6 Nov 1986 Auckland NZ

3 **Joseph Mary Hillary Mason** b. 3 May 1903 Auckland d. 23 May 1969 Wellington NZ m. **Olga Alice Raynes** 26 Aug 1924 Ponsonby, Auckland. b.1902 Balclutha, south of Dunedin, NZ. He was a draper's assistant, she a milliner. They had two children, **Shirley** b. 1926 and **James** b. 1927 d. 9 Nov 1971 buried Mangere cemetery, South Auckland. After the breakdown of his marriage to **Olga Raynes**, **Joseph** married **Fiona Marion McClure Walker King** 17 Mar 1943 Wellington NZ, who was previously married to **Albert Victor King** 1926, divorced 1932. Their daughter **Lorna** married **Frank Bryant Taylor** in 1955.

Brother Herman —
Oliver Louis Mason

Joseph Mary Hillary Mason with daughter Lorna at her 1955 marriage to Frank Taylor

3 **Mary Dolores (Sister Mary Consiglio) Mason** b. 14 Mar 1905 d. 19 Mar 1990. Named after one of **Catherine (Purtell)**'s sisters, who became a Mercy Sister in Auckland known as **Sister Mary Dolores**. **Mary** joined the same Order of Sisters and was known as **Sister Mary Consiglio**, which translates as 'Our Lady of Good Counsel'. She was educated at St Mary's College, Ponsonby, Auckland, where her aunt was a member of the Community, entered St Mary's convent on 18 Dec 1921, and made her Final Vows on 2 Oct 1927. **Sister Consiglio** was a primary school teacher, but also cared for children in convents around Auckland, especially Otahuhu, Avondale, Henderson, Epsom, Takapuna, Papatoetoe and Manuwera. The nuns who remember her say that she was a great teacher, and that the kids loved her.

On her death, **Sister Mary Consiglio** was buried at Waikarake Cemetery, Hillsborough, Auckland, Area 5, Block F, No. 622, at the age of 85. She was a very gentle, peaceful and prayerful person, with a quiet sense of humour. Physically small and slim, she was always a quietly busy woman, even in retirement.

Sister Consiglio -
part of a blurred press photo.

> ## The Religious
>
> Many of Oliver's extended family entered religious orders.
>
> **Jane Mason, Sister Thomasene**, daughter of James and Jane Mason, St Joseph at St Martha's in Leichhardt.
>
> **Annie Mason, Sister Dolores**, daughter of James and Jane Mason, sister of Jane, the Order of St John of God, Broome
>
> **Terry Mason**, son of Oliver Alphonsus and Netta Mason, joined the Marist Order at age 13 in 1942 and served throughout Australia. Terry left the order in 1988 and married **Monica Murphy**, herself an ex-nun, later that year.
>
> **Oliver Benedict Mason, Brother Claudius**, son of Oliver Alphonsus and Netta Mason, brother of Terry, the Marist Order.
>
> **Annie Veronica Mason, Sister M Irenaeus**, daughter of Charles and Catherine Mason, Sisters of the Little Company of Mary
>
> **Catherine Gertrude (Gertie) Mason, Sister M Regis**, sister of Annie, daughter of Charles and Catherine Mason, Dominican Sisters Tamworth, then Rosary Convent, Waratah, Newcastle
>
> **Florence Maher, Sister Zita**, daughter of Maria Maher's brother Dennis, joined a religious group in Waratah, NSW
>
> **Mary Dolores Mason, Sister Mary Consiglio.** daughter of Joseph and Catherine Mason, Sister of Mercy, Auckland
>
> **Oliver Louis Mason, Brother Herman Mary,** son of Joseph and Catherine Mason, brother of Mary, a brother in the Marist Order. Using the name Mary in the religious name was then the practice
>
> **Odillo Clement (Clem) Mason,** son of Charles and Catherine Mason, was briefly in St Stanislaus monastery

Charles Mason: b. 5 Oct 1862 d. 4 Apr 1954

5TH SON OF THE MIGRATING OLIVER MASON AND ANN FITZGERALD
BROTHER OF JOHN, PATRICK, JAMES, OLIVER, TERENCE AND JOSEPH
MARRIED CATHERINE MORRIS 18 JAN 1888 B. 1858 D. 1927

Birth Records of Catherine and Charles Mason

Reference	Name	First Name	Father	Mother	Place
8825/1858	Morris	Catherine	Richard	Bridget	Mailtland
12711/1862	Mason	Charles	Oliver	Anne	Port Stephens

Charles Mason was born in 1862, at Wards River NSW BC 12711/1862, 75 kilometres north of Seaham, where his older brother **Oliver** was born. The birth was registered at Stroud, as were those of his younger brothers **Terence** and **Joseph Paul.**

In 1870 the family moved en masse to Tamworth. For **Charles'** father, **Oliver Mason**, this was a successful step. He had bought 182 acres of a 4000-acre AAC property, **Woolomol** just northwest of Tamworth (now Oxley Vale, a suburb of Tamworth), encouraged by the growth of that town and the possibility of owning farming land. Since **Oliver** died in April 1885 at his home in Peel

Street, where **Ann** lived until she died in 1891, **Charles** and **Terence** had run the farm. **Oliver**'s son **Joseph** migrated to Auckland, New Zealand, sometime after **Ann**'s death and the birth of his sons **Oliver Louis** in 1895 and **Ronald** in 1897.

Charles Mason and Catherine Morris, just before their marriage in 1888.

Charles Mason in his later years.

Charles was an inveterate reader and found that the local Presbytery had a large library. It was there that he met **Catherine Morris**, an assistant housekeeper. The two of them formed a close friendship which grew into courtship, and married in **Catherine**'s Parish Church at East Maitland on 18 Jan 1888. The family had a pew at that church, as did other large local families. **Charles** was 26 and **Catherine** four years older. Their marriage certificate has **Catherine** living at home with her parents at Buchanan, south west of East Maitland.

It was later that year that they welcomed their firstborn, **Oliver Alphonsus,** born on 24 Nov 1888, at Woolomol. **Charles** was then described in the census records as being a farmer in Port Stephens – the location of the AAC's original grant. Another eight siblings followed – four boys and four girls.

In 1891 **Charles**' mother **Ann Fitzgerald** died (her death certificate says from 'old-age-accelerated bronchitis', aged 66). She left **Charles** and his brother **Joseph Paul** half each of **Oliver**'s 182 acre property, part of Woolomol. **Joseph Paul** also inherited all her personal goods and chattels valued at £932, mostly unnamed real estate, reduced by a mortgage of £228. Her Will also stated that **Charles** and **Joseph** both had to pay their brother **Terence** £15 within three calendar months of her demise.

It seems that it was on the financial basis of that Woolomol property that **Charles** and his new wife **Catherine Morris** (called **Kate** by **Charles**), bought and settled at Carroll Gap, near the site of the later Keepit Dam. **Charles** is registered on the electoral roll as being a farmer at Woolamol in 1899, on the basis of his inheritance from his parents. In 1916 he was at Carroll Gap, on the Peel River, between Tamworth and Gunnedah, behind the Carroll Gap Public School. Between 1916 and 1918 he ran the local Post Office for the Carroll Gap community from this property, his daughter **Rene** following him as Post Mistress. **Rene**, only 16 years old, also taught at the local school there, and 'hated' it. **Rene** wanted to be in a draper's shop. In 1937 **Rene** married **Sydney Mostyn**, who was about 35, and they had no children.

Peter Lyons, Charles' eldest grandson, reported on the property at Carroll Gap:

> **Charles** and **Catherine Mason** bought land at Carroll Gap on the Peel River. A Public School was opened at Carroll Gap in 1882 until 1911 and later from 1913 to 1914. The building is still there today on the Keepit Dam road, just off the Oxley Highway before the river crossing.
>
> **Charles**' mother and father lived in Tamworth. The family had their own seat in the front row of St Nicholas Catholic Church, Tamworth. [**Terry Mason** sees nothing remarkable in this, it being a quite normal procedure in his experience for regular churchgoers (particularly those with large families, such as the **Masons**) to occupy the same pew at all services.] **Catherine Morris** was an assistant housekeeper at the presbytery, and **Charles**

visited her at the Presbytery as the church had an extensive library. They were married at that church.

The property behind the old school building was called The Keel, owned and being paid off by the **Masons**. It had previously been owned by Luchesford (Lands Dept No CP 76, 329 Portion 44 Parish of Moorowara), and was bought from the **Masons** by the Kenniffs. Mr Cupples of Somerton (postmaster 1939/59) knew the **Mason** name from older family members living at Carroll Gap. There was a Post Office on the **Masons**' property and the youngest daughter **Rene** ran it, as did **Charles** himself for a short while, from 1916 to 1918.

A building not far from the main house was sleeping quarters, and a barn built above flood level to store furniture from the rising river. Chinese families were living on the river when the **Masons** bought the property, and thought they would have to move when the **Masons** came, but **Charles** said he was quite happy if they stayed. There was a separate kitchen and bull-nosed verandahs on both the front and back of the main building, and possibly a covered walkway to the separate kitchen.

Whether there was a house already there or **Charles** built one has not been verified. This house (still extant) had an underground tank for water storage built above flood level, necessary before the later nearby Keepit Dam controlled the flooding and reduced the size of the property. **Charles** had a garden, turkeys, and a preserving shed, and decreed that the children should avoid the Chinese, since they used opium. There were sleeping quarters for visiting sons, a separate kitchen and verandahs. **Charles'** and **Catherine's** grandchildren say the property became part of family lore.

One of the stories told from the Carroll Gap time is of **Charles** helping his daughters out of the bedroom window to go to the local dance — was that **Charles'** sense of fun, leading the girls to believe that their mother didn't know? After **Catherine** died in 1927, **Charles'** was in Cooroy because their sons **Dick** and **Morrie** were cutting cane and **Charles** was working with them. 'Grandad loved the heat' says **Mick Lyons** quoting her dad. 'He wore a black singlet and would work all day — a billy can of tea and bread, plenty of sugar — worked sunup to sundown' when he was 63 or 64 years old.

Charles returned to northern NSW to his son **Jim** and **Jim's** wife **May** for a while. Certainly he was back in Sydney by the time **Netta** died in 1935. Thereafter **Charles'** son **Oliver** and **Netta's** children really got to know **Charles**, because he lived in the area until he died.

If ever anyone mentioned Grandad to **Mick** (the family name for **Marie (Mason) Lyons**), her face would light up and with a chuckle she'd say how much she loved him and what a fun-loving man he was. Her description of him was always, 'He'd wear his hat at a jaunty angle, swing his umbrella, whistle a tune and dance a few steps of a jig!'

Charles also had a more serious side to him too, as is shown by his devotion to his God. Every morning he would walk from Hornsby to Waitara, where their parish church was, for daily Mass — about half an hour each way. **Charles** at that time lived in various places — in Balmoral Street, Waitara, with **May**; his son **Clem** lived there too; granddaughter **Mick** also mentioned Alexandria Parade, Waitara; and Waitara Parade. After **May**'s death in 1935 family lore tells us that he 'lived at Captain Stewart's place, to do his gardens.' **Terry** adds that **Charles** lived in a 'hut' in the grounds.

Before **Rene** and **Syd Mostyn** married in 1937, **Rene** ran a beef and ham and sandwich shop, with the help of **Charles** and **May**.

In the early 1940s, **Charles** went to live with his son **Oliver Alphonsus Mason** and children at **Oliver's** home in Nursery Street, with the idea of supporting and helping **Oliver** out. He was fully occupied with helping keep the large vegetable garden productive — fertilising it with chook manure from under their perches, digging, planting and watering with water that he pumped from the well, as well as looking after rest of the grounds. **Terry** recalls that **Charles** slept out on the back verandah **Oliver** had earlier enclosed, making the windows for it himself. From here, **Charles** moved to 206 Miller Street, North Sydney, to live with youngest daughter **Rene** and husband, **Syd Mostyn**. He continued his daily devotion to morning Mass and it was on returning from Mass on 4 Apr 1954 that he walked in the door of their home, collapsed and died from a cerebral haemorrhage. **Charles** is buried in Northern Suburbs Cemetery.

> ### Children of Charles Mason
>
> 1 **Charles Mason** b. 25 Oct 1862 at Woolamol d .4 Apr 1954 BC 12711/1862 Buried Northern Suburbs cemetery, North Ryde. Son of the migrating **Oliver Mason** and **Ann Fitzgerald**
> m. **Catherine Theresa Morris** 18 Jan 1888 East Maitland b. 27 Jul MC 1858 8825/1858 Louth Park, Maitland d.29 Aug 1927 Cooroy, near Noosa, Qld
>   2 **Oliver Alphonsus** b. 24 Nov 1889, d. 4 Jul 1987
>   2 **Mary Monica (May)** b. 23 Mar 1890, d. 30 Jun 1938
>   2 **Annie Veronica (Sister M Irenaeus)** b. 24 Apr 1891, d. 3 Mar 1976
>   2 **Catherine Gertrude (Sister M Regis)** b. 4 Aug 1892, d. 20 July 1977
>   2 **Richard Percy (Dick)** b. Oct 1894, d. 6 Jul 1965
>   2 **Charles Morris (Morrie)** b. 16 Dec 1896, d. 29 May 1965
>   2 **James Kevin (Jim)** b. 18 Feb 1898 d. 17 Dec 1984
>   2 **Irene Clementine (Rene)** b. 4 Feb 1900, d. 26 Jul 1988
>   2 **Odillo Clement (Clem)** b. 4 Jul 1902, d.12 Oct 1987

Oliver Alphonsus Mason: b. 24 Nov 1889 d. 4 Jul 1987

B. 24 NOV 1889 WOOLOMOL, TAMWORTH NSW D. 4 JUL 1987
M1. NETTA OLGA GARRETT 4 SEP1920 B. 27 MAR 1895 D. 28 APR 1935
M2. ROSEMARY LOLLBACH 4 APR 1947 B. 17 SEP 1914 D. 12 FEB 1996 COFFS HARBOUR NSW

Oliver and **Netta** were married at the Temporary Catholic Church, Lithgow WC 19939/1920. **Netta** was born at Hartley, the daughter of William Garrett and Caroline Thaler, and died at St Kilda Private Hospital Hornsby of blood poisoning, having had nine children in 12 years. **Oliver's** second marriage was to **Rosemary Lollbach** 4 Apr 1947 MC 9367/1947 Holy Family Church, Lindfield, buried at Northern Suburbs Lawn Cemetery. Their story appears later in this book.

Mary Monica (May) Mason: b. 23 Mar 1890 d. 30 Jun 1938

B. 23 MAR 1890 TAMWORTH NSW, D. 30 JUN 1938 HORNSBY NSW

May Mason

May was known never to be strong. She didn't marry and was a very talented dressmaker, by which she earned her keep. Her niece **Leila** often remarked on **May**'s ability and was ever grateful for **May** having taught her how to sew. Before 1935, **May** worked with her aunt **Rene** and grandfather **Charles** at their ham and beef shop at Waitara. She left there to care for **Oliver** and **Netta**'s children for a short time and died from pneumonia in 1938. **May** is buried in the Northern Suburbs Cemetery, at North Ryde, Lot 43, Sec. G3

Annie Veronica (Sister Mary Irenaeus) Mason b. 24 Apr 1891 d. 3 Mar 1976

B. 24 APR 1891, TAMWORTH, D.3 MAR 1976

Sister Irenaeus (Annie), Oliver Alphonsus Mason, and Sister Regis (Gertie)

Annie entered the Sisters of the Little Company of Mary (LCM) as **Sister Irenaeus** on 7 Jun 1922, taking her final vows on 20 Jan 1928. Her reference to be taken into the convent indicates that the family had lived in the Gunnedah parish for some years previously, and that she had been employed as a typist in Ballina by Mr. G.T. Howarth, The Strand Stores from Jul 1918 to 30 Mar 1920, because she needed a dowry to enter the convent. **Annie** completed her General Nursing training In the convent. She was in community at Lewisham for some 20 years to 1943, again from 1947 to 1956, and in between at Lake Macquarie. She was an organiser and supervised the laundry at Lewisham, also working in Medical Records. When at Wagga, she was in charge of the convent chapel. She is buried at Wagga Lawn Cemetery, and has a different headstone to all the other Sisters. **Terry**'s comment, with a chuckle: 'That's fitting. She was always a bit different!'

Catherine Gertrude (Gertie, Sister Mary Regis) Mason: b. 4 Aug 1892 d. 20 Jul 1977

B. 4 AUG 1892 BC 34277/1892 D. 20 JULY 1977

Catherine was known in the family as **Gertie**. Her father **Charles** would call for **Kate** and **Gertie** would reply, asking 'Which one?' **Charles** got so sick of it that he called her **Gertie** and **Gertie** she remained. She obviously was quite spirited and was a great friend of her younger brother, **Dick**, another very lively member of the family.

Gertie became **Sister Mary Regis** in the Dominican Sisters, having been educated by them at Tamworth. As with many of the members of this branch of the family, her stories and recollections of her childhood are affectionate, rural and lively. In the convent she often enlivened Recreations with her stories — for instance on sale days when their parents had driven by sulky to Tamworth and the 'big ones' were left to hold the fort, take care of the younger children and keep the cow out of the lucerne — this last not often achieved.

Gertie, at 18, before she became Sister Mary Regis

She took her love of the land into the convent, finding long-lasting pleasure in tending convent gardens. After entering the convent in Nov 1912 and being professed on 6th Apr 1915, **Sister Regis** worked with deaf pupils at the Rosary Convent, Waratah, acquiring considerable skill in sign language and a deep empathy with her students, which they reciprocated.

Sister Regis was Prioress at Waratah for a time, and towards the end of her life lived at Santa Sabina in Strathfield. She was blessed with a deep spirituality and a balancing sense of fun. She was very frail in her later years, and returned to Waratah, her first and most loved mission. **Gertie** died there 20 Jul 1977 and is buried in Sandgate cemetery, near Newcastle.

Richard Percy (Dick) Mason: b. 8 Oct 1894 d. 6 Jul 1965

B. 8 OCT 1894, D. 6 JUL 1965 NEWCASTLE
M. ALICE EILEEN SCANNELL 29 OCT 1926 B. 1898 MOREE D. 1956 MAYFIELD
PARENTS OF MARGARET B. 1930 AND PAUL B. 1931

Dick was known in Newcastle as Ginger Mason, having inherited his red hair from his father, **Charles**. **Charles** gave **Dick** a horse to go droving during a drought in Tamworth, and **Dick** eventually made enough money to go to Queensland. He got a job cutting cane at Cooroy and his brother **Morrie** followed him there.

In 1923 **Dick** joined the Police Force in Sydney, and transferred to Newcastle. There he met **Alice Scannell**, daughter of Patrick Scannell, Inspector of Police. **Dick** married **Alice** in 1926 at East Maitland. After he retired from the Police Force in 1954, **Dick** was employed as Night Watchman on the Newcastle wharves. His employers lost a good few of their workers there – they disappeared because they recognised **Dick**!

Dick Mason

Mick recalls **Uncle Dick** as a very large man with enormous arms and hands. The kids used to hold on to a finger each for **Uncle Dick** to swing them round. The local children in Newcastle used to call him Da Mason – the name given him by his grandson **Richard Bergholcs**, who was at the time unable to say 'Grandad'. One of those local children, **Anne (Nolan) Keating** (**Larry**

Keating, her husband, was **Terry Mason's** principal at St Clare's in Taree) refers to **Dick** as 'Ol Da Mason' and can see the resemblance in **Terry** to **Dick**.

Dick and **Alice**'s son **Paul** Mason, an accountant, worked for Qantas for most of his working life. He and his wife **Robin Vidler**, a nurse he married in 1960, discovered that **Robin's** grandmother **Mary Vidler** was the sister of **Annie Bezant Mason**, wife of his relative **Oliver Peter Mason**, who lived together as widows for some 33 years. Robin was educated at the same school as **Sister Mary Regis**, who became godmother to her daughter **Felicity**.

Dick eventually developed Parkinson's disease and admitted himself into St Joseph's Nursing Home at Sandgate. He was moved to St John of God at Lake Macquarie where he later broke his hip, developed pneumonia and died. Before he died he told his family not to bother with a headstone on his grave but to have Masses said for him. Both **Dick** and **Alice** are buried at Sandgate Cemetery, Newcastle.

Charles Morris (Morrie) Mason: b. 16 Dec 1896 d. 29 May 1965

B. 16 DEC 1896 TAMWORTH D. 29 MAY 1965 MT OLIVETT HOSPITAL, BRISBANE
M. VALERIE CAMPBELL 1924. B. 27 MAY 1896 BALLINA D. 16 NOV 1956

Morrie spent most of his life in northern NSW, his main base being Murwillumbah. Earlier he had been a share farmer at Dunbible, most likely a dairy farmer. It is well known that **Morrie** was lame and there are various versions of how that came to be. He married **Valerie (Val) Campbell** in 1924

The first two of **Morrie** and **Val's** four children were born in Cooroy: **Brian** in Feb 1926 and **Catherine Carmel (Carmel)** in Oct 1928. At around this time, **Morrie's** parents **Charles** and **Catherine** moved to Cooroy. In August 1927, **Morrie** was at work when he got the message to say that his mother, **Catherine**, was sick, but OK. He visited her and immediately got a priest for her. She died a half hour after being anointed. She was buried in the Catholic section of the Cooroy cemetery with no headstone. **Terry** and **Monica Mason** visited the site, did some research, found her grave site, and decided to mark the spot with a small plaque.

Morrie Mason

From Cooroy, **Morrie** and family moved to Roma, while **Charles** returned to Coolangatta to be with **Jim** and **May**. At Roma **Val** gave birth to a little girl, **Valerie May**, stillborn. Then in November 1931 they had another little girl, **Valerie Regis (Val)**. As an adult, **Val** cared for her father until he decided to admit himself to Mt. Olivett Hospital so that **Val** could follow her dream to join the order of Sisters begun by Mary McKillop (the Brown Josephites, as they are affectionately known) in 1958. **Val** says that **Morrie** suffered a partial stoke about this time. He spent many years on his back, dying in 1965. He is buried in the Catholic Cemetery at Murwillumbah.

James Kevin (Jim) Mason: b. 18 Feb 1898 d. 17 Dec 1984

B. 18 FEB 1898 TAMWORTH D. 17 DEC 1984 JOHN FLYNN PRIVATE HOSPITAL, TUGUN, QLD
M. MARGARET MARY (MAY) DAY ST AUGUSTINE'S COOLANGATTA 2 FEB 1928 B. 1904 CATTLE GULLY, DARLING DOWNS, QLD, D. 11AUG 1996 JOHN FLYNN HOSPITAL TUGUN.
BOTH BURIED AT TWEED HEADS LAWN CEMETERY, RC SECTION

When **Jim** was 29 years old he lived at 59 Bruce St., Newcastle, where he worked for a produce firm as a carrier. He had already met **May Day** from Coolangatta and had become engaged. When later he was made redundant from the produce firm, he felt that they couldn't get married. But **May** insisted they go ahead, so they moved north to live with her parents on dairy property *Cressvale* at Piggabeen, Northern NSW, in 1931. It was a very full household, with **May's** parents, **Jim** and **May**, three of her siblings and **May's** new baby!

Jim Mason later in life.

Jim and May at their wedding, 1928

Jim and May left Piggabeen in 1938 to live in Coolangatta. He purchased a banana plantation at Cobaki in NSW but it wasn't making much money so May went to work in the Haberdashery department of Stafford's General Store, in Coolangatta's main street. In 1952 they moved to Mitchelton, Brisbane, purchasing a small crop farm where he and son **Kevin Mason** grew strawberries, until they all moved to a dairy farm at Terranora, in 1962.

They raised three children in Terranora — **Monica**, **Kevin** and **Leo**. **Jim** and **May** lived there until **Jim** died on 17 Dec 1984 from cancer, in John Flynn Hospital, Tugun, Queensland. **Jim**'s widow **May** died 11 Aug 1996. Both are buried at South Tweed heads Garden of Remembrance.

Jim's daughter in law, **Denise**, says that he was a quiet man, serious, very kind, 'but don't argue with him!'

Irene Clementine (Rene) Mason: b. 4 Feb 1900 d. 26 Jul 1988

B. 4 FEB 1900 TAMWORTH BC 16953/1900 D. 26 JUL 1988 TURRAMURRA
M. SYDNEY MOSTYN 10 JUL 1937 ST MARY'S NORTH SYDNEY B. 7 FEB 1899 HELENSBURG NSW
D. 6 APR 1964, DC 22471/1964

When **Charles'** family lived at Carroll Gap, **Rene** (as the family called her) ran the Post Office for a time. Later she worked at the Gosford Railway Station Refreshment Rooms and Central and at Broadmeadow Stations. At one of these places she worked with **Molly** who became a life-long friend and was always referred to by **Rene**'s nieces and nephews as '**Aunty Mol**'.

Before **Rene** and **Syd** married in 1937, **Syd**, a scrap metal Merchant, had a Milk Bar café and lived with his mother at the back of the shop (about 1935-37). After their marriage, **Rene** and **Syd** lived at 206 Miller St, North Sydney. They had no children and **Syd** did not want to adopt, so after brother **Oliver**'s marriage to **Rosemary Lollbach**, **Oliver**'s two youngest daughters by **Netta**, **Anne** and **Cath**, went to live with **Rene** and **Syd**. After they moved on, her father **Charles** lived with **Rene** and it was there that he died in April 1954.

Rene ran a ham and beef shop with the help of her older sister **May** until after **Oliver Alphonsus'** wife **Netta** died. **Rene**'s brother **Clem** lived with them and wanted to buy the shop, but that didn't happen. **Clem**'s future sister-in-law, **Eileen Kelly**, went to work there to replace **May,** who went to look after **Netta**'s children after **Netta** died.

Sometime after **Syd Mostyn** died in 1964, the local council wanted to redesign the area which meant their home at 206 Miller St was to be demolished, along with many others, to make way for a motorway. **Marie** and **Bernie** built a flat on to the back of their home at 16 Nursery Street, Hornsby, and **Rene** lived there for about four years before she decided to move to Nazareth House in Turramurra, where her long-time friend, **Mol**, had already moved. **Rene** died there in 1988, about a year after **Mol**, and is buried in the Catholic Section of Northern Suburbs cemetery, with **Syd** Row 23-0013.

Rene Mostyn in her later years

Odillo Clement (Clem) Mason: b. 4 Jul 1902 d. 12 Oct 1987

B. 4 JUL 1902, TAMWORTH BC 26686/1902 D. 12 OCT 1987 KIAMA NSW
M. WINIFRED (WIN) KELLY 19 OCT 1935 B. 4 MAR 1903 LAUNCESTON D. 17 FEB 1994 KIAMA

Clem Mason

At 16, **Clem** wanted to be a priest and so made contact with a Christian brother he knew, who arranged for **Clem** to board with the Kelly family in Launceston. This didn't work out (there were two daughters in the family) and the Bishop of Hobart sent **Clem** to St Stanislaus in Bathurst, NSW for two years. He failed Latin so no priesthood for him.

Clem returned to his family in Queensland when his mother **Catherine (Morris) Mason** died in Cooroy in 1927. He decided to join the Police Force but wasn't tall enough, so he joined Sydney Fire Brigade for about 19 years. He then transferred from Hornsby to Crows Nest, and in this period revisited Launceston, looking up **Win Kelly** whom he found to be engaged. She eventually broke it off and married **Clem** on 19 Oct 1935 at St Patrick's Sydney. They delayed their marriage until then, following **Clem**'s sister-in-law **Netta**'s death. They lived at 36 Brook St, Naremburn, and had no children.

Clem left the Fire Brigade in 1945, and they moved to Robertson-Fitzroy Falls NSW to grow cabbages. It was an extremely tough life which they battled for eight years. They left there following **Win** being very ill and the farm a failure. 1953 saw them at Dunmore, Shell Harbour, where they leased land for 21 years which **Clem** ran as a dairy. They sold up in 1974 and moved to Kiama to a property **Clem** had bought in 1953. They lived at 63 Barney Street until they both died.

For 60 years, well into his retirement, **Clem** worked tirelessly for the St Vincent de Paul Society, and **Win** was hugely proud of the Papal Award he was given for this charitable work.

Clem developed Parkinson's disease and died in a Nursing Home in Kiama.

Win's lifetime was filled with a love of music. As a young woman she played piano with the Sydney Symphony Orchestra and, while at Dunmore, would join a few friends to play at Friday and Saturday night dances. **Win** spoke of walking a mile from the house to the roadside to be picked up by these friends and then the long walk back home afterwards. She taught music and singing at the local Catholic school and for many years played the organ at Mass. She was diagnosed with cancer while she was caring for **Clem**. It eventually caught up with her and she died in May 1993, having celebrated her 90th birthday with many of her nieces and nephews. She'd had a tough life but was an ever cheerful and chatty person. **Win** is buried with **Clem** in the Catholic Section of Kiama cemetery.

Oliver Alphonsus Mason: b. 24 Nov 1899 d. 4 Jul 1987

SON OF CHARLES MASON AND CATHERINE MORRIS
GRANDSON OF THE MIGRATING OLIVER MASON AND ANN FITZGERALD
B. 24 NOV 1889 WOOLOMOL, TAMWORTH NSW D. 4 JUL 1987
M1. NETTA OLGA GARRETT 4 SEP1920 B. 27 MAR 1895 D. 28 APR 1935
M2. ROSEMARY LOLLBACH 4 APR 1947 B. 17 SEP 1914 D. 12 FEB 1996 COFFS HARBOUR NSW
FATHER OF 14 CHILDREN

Birth Record for Oliver Alphonsus Mason

Reference	Name	First Name	Father	Mother	Date	Place
34344/1889	Mason	Oliver A	Charles	Catherine	24 Nov 1888	Tamworth

Oliver Alphonsus was born at Woolomol in November 1888, on his grandfather (the migrating) Oliver's 182 acres — just north-west of Tamworth, now the suburb of Oxley Vale.

In the late 1890s/early 1900s, his father **Charles** moved the family to nearby Carroll Gap, after his father died and he inherited half of the Woolamol acreage.

Oliver left the family's home at Carroll Gap when he was about 26 years old because he felt that there was insufficient income from the farm to keep them all. **Vin Mason**, a first cousin (son of his uncle **James** and aunt **Jane Purtell**) influenced him into working on the railways since he himself was already employed there, and was instrumental in getting **Oliver** a job.

Oliver worked all his life on the railways. His first job in Jul 1915 was in the **Murrurundi** District as a Porter for the pay of 8/- a day. By Feb 1916 he was 3rd C Shunter with an improved pay of 9/- a day. In Aug 1917 he was dismissed by Proclamation because he left work on strike.

> *The general strike occurred because the government, through the NSW Department of Railways and Tramways, introduced an American costing system, to determine where its workers could increase efficiency. The railway workers were the first to strike but this soon spread to other unions.*
> Curator's notes on the general strike 1917

Oliver Alphonsus' Railway placements	
1916	MURRURUNDI
1917	ESKBANK
1920	WIMBLEDON
1922	JUNEE
1924	ESKBANK
1925	LITHGOW
1926	SYDNEY DISTRICT
1927- 29 NOV 1953 (RETIREMENT)	ASST STATION MANAGER AT TURRAMURRA
SERVED 38 YEARS, 2 MONTHS, 13 DAYS	

Reinstated In August 1916, **Oliver** had a job as Shunter and then Signalman at Eskbank near Lithgow, where he boarded at an establishment run by Mrs Caroline Garrett and her daughter, **Netta**, whom he was eventually to marry.

The story is told that one Sunday, after having attended Mass, **Oliver** was sitting in the sun reading the paper. Apparently **Netta** wanted his attention and when it wasn't forthcoming, she threw the dishcloth at him. The attraction was there, but **Oliver** would have probably thought there would be difficulties in their relationship going any further for he was a committed Catholic and she a Methodist. In those days 'mixed' marriages were very much frowned upon by the Catholic Church.

In June 1918, **Oliver** qualified as a 7th C Signalman. In March 1919 he moved on to Wimbledon, a little place west of Blayney, as Night Officer. It is presumed it was during this time that **Netta** had been in communication with **Oliver**, because he received a letter from her informing him that she was taking instructions in the Catholic Faith.

In February 1920, **Oliver** returned to Eskbank as Signalman and it was just a few months later that he was sent to Junee as 4th C Relief Night Officer. His pay was £245 per annum. In Aug 1920

Chapter 4: The migrating Oliver Mason

A youthful Oliver Alphonsus Mason

Netta Garrett at the time of her engagement to Oliver

Oliver Alphonsus Mason and Netta at their wedding in 1920.

Netta and **Oliver** became engaged. They married in the Temporary Catholic Church on 4 Sep 1920.

Netta was born at Lithgow on 27 Mar 1895, one of eight siblings. Her mother was born in Germany and had, at the age of 13, migrated to Australia with her mother and step-father. **Netta's** father was born in England, according to his marriage certificate, and he was the informant on three of his children's birth certificates.

Oliver and **Netta's** first child, **Marie Olga (Mick) Mason**, was born at Junee Private Hospital in Jul 1921. In October, **Oliver** returned to the Eskbank District as Relief Officer. The next few children – **Charles, Leila** and **Pat** — were born at Blayney.

The end of Nov 1926 took **Oliver** as 4th Relief Officer to Sydney, where the family lived in rented accommodation in Hunter Street, Hornsby. Their son **Oliver Benedict** (now referred to as **Oli**) was born at St Kilda Private Hospital. By the time **Terry** was born in 1929, the whole family was living at 12 Nursery Street, where **Oliver** lived for the rest of his life.

Oliver held the position of Relief Officer for the next ten years and in that time **Claire, Anne** and **Cath** were born. In April 1935 tragedy struck with the death of **Netta** from septic pneumonia. She was only 40, and had given birth to nine children in only 12 years.

Oliver battled on with the help of close family members. **Aunty May, Oliver's** sister, stayed for a time, but **Marie**, as a 13 year old and the eldest, took on the mothering role. After she completed her schooling at Monte St Angelo in Sydney, **Marie** took a job at a telephone exchange.

In 1940 **Claire**, aged eight, **Anne**, aged seven and **Cath** aged four, became boarders at St Martha's in Leichardt, where a cousin of **Oliver's, Sister Thomasene**, was on the staff. The girls returned home for all school holidays. Their aunt **Marie (Mick)** would visit them every second Sunday and take them out for the day. **Claire** was known to do some not-too-serious damage to her glasses so that she would gain another day in town with **Marie** to get them repaired. There were also the less-regular visits from **Leila, Pat** and **Oli**. The girls loved it when their Dad would get a day off and come to visit them and take them out, taking them to Lithgow on one outing. Of course a day off school was an added bonus. Once their primary school education was completed in 1945, they lived at home with **Claire** attending studies at the Mount Street school in Home Economics.

16 Nursery Street, Hornsby

Anne and Cath went to secondary school at Mount St. Bernard's in Pymble. After Granddad Charles died in 1954 at Aunty Rene and Uncle Syd's place, Anne and Cath went to live there.

During this time, Netta's mother, usually referred to as Grandma Williams, would come and stay for a time. Her grandchildren recall her taking them for walks in the Ku-ring-gai Chase bush. She always carried a stout stick in case they should disturb a snake, and told them about the various plants. Sometimes she took them to Higgins' orchard to buy some apples. Terry recalls that on these occasions, he used to pull faces in the hope that old Mr Higgins wouldn't recognise him, after he and his mates daring each other to steal some apples from under the trees! Grandma always fitted in with whatever was going on at the time, even to making sure that when the grandchildren came in after playing outside in the summer evening after tea, they said their night prayers — the Rosary.

Oliver's Railway employment card, from 16 May 1929 to 29 Nov 1953

Oliver was appointed 4th C Relief Assistant Stationmaster at Turramurra for a year in 1936 and then as a permanent position until he retired in November 1953 — a total service of 38 years, 2 months and 13 days. It was some 24 years after he retired that a gold watch for long service was presented posthumously to Rosemary, his second wife. Rose wore that watch every day until she died in 1996.

Life at 16 Nursery Street, with two blocks of land on one side of the home, enabled them to be almost self-sufficient (all the more necessary, as the depression progressed) with a wonderful vegetable garden and fruit trees tended by Oliver during the day since he worked at night — 3pm to 11pm. Produce from the garden, eggs from the chooks and milk from the cow were all shared with neighbours if they had a need. Oliver was handy in making things. Terry recalls that his Dad added to the size of the family home by closing in the verandahs and making the windows for the enclosure.

All the children had their chores. Charlie looked after the chooks and milked the cow until one day he cut the top off one of his fingers. Oli took on the chooks and Terry the milking of the cow. The girls had the inside-the-house jobs. Terry recalls that the neighbours all let their chooks out into the creek that their homes backed on to so they could get good pickings. He noticed that a neighbour's duck always came into their chook pen and ate the food put out for their hens. He and a kid from next-door decided to solve the problem. Result, a barbecued duck down in the bush! The next day the owner of the duck asked **Terry**, 'Have you seen my duck?' Honest answer, 'No, not since yesterday.'

There are many delightful stories told of adventures had during those years. **Terry** the story-teller (siblings might indicate that some of the stories are a bit stretched) tells of fun and games with the other kids from the street, who gathered in the cow paddock for games of Countries where each of them took the name of a country and a nominated person, usually **Charlie**, would begin by throwing a tennis ball into the air and calling the name of one of the countries. That person would have to run and retrieve the ball calling 'Stop' when they had it in hand. This was followed by a negotiation with another participant as to how many steps could be taken to get closer to be able to tag them with the ball. Once tagged, that person was 'In'.

There were the games of marbles played on dirt road, sometimes with the men from the neighbourhood (who worked on the railways too) who would stop and have a few shots with the boys. Then there was **Uncle Dick**, **Oliver**'s younger brother, a policeman of large stature, visiting after having brought prisoners from Newcastle to Long Bay. He'd swing the kids around and join in kicking a football around only to kick it so hard one time that the ball collapsed, much to **Terry**'s disappointment. And of course there was always the Ku-ring-gai Chase bush, where the boys spent hours playing, catching tadpoles and yabbies. In the summer, there was swimming in the local water holes. On 24 May, Empire Day, there was always the street bonfire which the kids of the street spent weeks collecting tree branches for. There was an unspoken competition between the kids of the various streets.

Oliver Alphonsus Mason, very comfortable at 90.

The recollections of his children (admittedly of **Oliver** as an older man) show him as perceptive, intelligent and wise. His authority was not questioned especially by his sons – they *ran* when he whistled for them to come home from playing in the bush. **Oliver**'s son **Terry** sees him as a strong Labor man, with a thirst for knowledge and very open to other's opinions. **Terry** adds that he and his brothers learned many life skills from their Dad by working alongside him and being trusted to continue a job alone.

In 1941 there was a very dry period, even a drought, which stands high in the family's recollections. **Terry** recalls that at one stage they had to fill all the receptacles that they could to provide for their daily needs. You weren't allowed to turn a tap on after a certain time, e.g. 9 a.m. **Charlie**, **Oli** and **Terry** worked together digging a well at the bottom of the property, near the creek. **Charlie** was in the well, as **Oli** and **Terry** would lower and lift the buckets bringing the soil out. There's no doubt that **Oliver** would have worked on this project during the day, making sure it was properly shored up.

About this time **Grandad Charles** came to live with them. **Terry** tells of him, while pumping water out of the well by hand, filling a 44 gallon drum of water near to the vegetable gardens, saying the Rosary. Prior to having this pump, the boys were expected to use buckets their Dad gave them to cart the water from well to garden, but the boys decided that kerosene cans meant fewer trips. These vegetable gardens had all been edged with sandstone that **Charlie**, **Oli** and **Terry** had chipped from the bush and then wheel-barrowed all the way home.

In 1946, **Oliver** married **Rosemary Edna Lollbach** at Holy Family Church Lindfied, with **Mick**'s husband **Bernie Lyons** as best man. The reception was done by the indefatigable **Mick**, long the mother figure to her brothers and sisters. She kept the strong feeling alive between the two halves of the family, since **Rosemary** and **Oliver** had five children – **Colleen**, **Josephine**, **Judith**, **Tony** and **James**.

After his retirement inn 1953, **Oliver** followed his father's footsteps and walked half an hour every day to Waitara to open the church and attend daily Mass. When **Oliver** turned 90 in 1978, **Terry** recalls that he was still working in the garden, and still involving himself intensely in family affairs.

A patriarch. Revered. Much loved.

Children of Oliver Alphonsus Mason

1 **Oliver Alphonsus Mason** b. 24 Nov 1888 Woolamol, Tamworth d. 4 Jul 1987
m1. **Netta Olga Garrett** 4 Sep 1920 Temp Catholic Church, Lithgow. WC 19939/1920 b. 27 Mar 1895 Hartley, near Lithgow BC 13984/1895 d. 28 Apr 1935 St Kilda Private Hospital, Hornsby, blood poisoning [daughter of William Garrett and Caroline Thaler]
m2. **Rosemary Lollbach** 4 Apr 1947 WC 9367/1947 Holy Family Church Lindfield b. 17 Sep 1914 d. 12 Feb 1996 Coffs Harbour NSW. Buried Northern Suburbs Lawn Cemetery.
[Children of **Oliver Alphonsus Mason** and **Netta Olga Garrett**]
  2 **Marie Olga (Mick) Mason** b. 11 Jul 1921 Junee NSW d. 4 Nov 2002 Hornsby m. **Bernie Lyons** 12 May1947 Our Lady of the Rosary, Waitara NSW b. 3 Apr 1917 Coogee, NSW d. 29 Apr 1997 Hornsby
  2 **Charles Francis (Charlie, Chick) Mason** b. 4 Feb 1923 Blayney NSW d. 23 Feb 2007 Public Hospital Muswellbrook m. **Marj Norma Daniels** Muswellbrook b. 6 Aug 1927
  2 **Leila Monica Mason** b. 12 Dec 1924 Blayney NSW d. 8 Apr 2009 Holy Spirit Home, Carseldine, Brisbane, Qld, stroke m. **Neville Gilbert** 5 Oct 1946 Our Lady of the Rosary Church, Waitara b. 11 Jan 1921 Wynnum Central, Brisbane Qld d. 3 Jan 2012
  2 **Kathleen Patricia (Pat) Mason** b. 17 Sep 1926 Blayney NSW m. **John Edward O'Grady** b. 6 Nov 1919 Fremantle d. 19 Sep 1989 Hospital, Katoomba, NSW
  2 **Oliver Benedict (Brother Claudius) Mason** b. 28 Feb 1928 Hunter St.
  2 **Terence Joseph (Terry) Mason** b. 7 Sep 1929 Hornsby NSW m. **Monica Clare Murphy** 5 Jul 1988 Taree NSW b. 4 May 1945 Norsewood, NZ
  2 **Claire Frances Mason** b. 14 Jan 1931 m. **Michael (Kazimerz) Kurzawaski** 27 Apr 1968 Our Lady of the Rosary Waitara, NSW b. 22 Dec 1927 Poland d. 27 Mar 1990 Gwandalin, NSW
  2 **Annette Philomena (Anne) Mason** b. 10 Aug 1932 Hornsby NSW m. **Peter (Pius) Hartman** 16 Apr 1968 St Mary's Catholic Church, North Sydney NSW b. 11 Jul 1929 Switzerland d. 12 Aug 1990 Nabiac
  2 **Catherine Eileen (Cath) Mason** b. 29 Dec 1933 Hornsby NSW m. **Maurice Tully** 21 Jan 1963 Catholic Church, Kirribilli NSW b. 28 Aug 1937
[Children of **Oliver Alphonsus Mason** and **Rosemary Lollbach**]
  2 **Colleen Mary Mason** b. 6 Jan 1948 d. 13 Oct 2010 m. **Brian Lester** 13 Dec 1969 Our Lady of the Rosary Waitara b. 21 Nov 1946 Mater, North Sydney
  2 **Josephine Gertrude Mason** b. 19 May 1950 m. **Paul Parrish** Our Lady of the Rosary, Waitara b. 19 Aug 1956
  2 **Judith Rosemary Mason** b. 1 Jul 1951 m. **Merrick Rhone** 9 Dec 1980 Gosford b. 14 Nov 1952 Central Coast
  2 **Anthony John (Tony) Mason** b. 29 May 1954 Sydney m. **Deborah (Debbie) Robb** 12 Mar 1987 Georges Gold Mine, Lowanna b. 20 Feb 1963 Coffs Harbour NSW
  2 **James Oliver Mason** b. 25 Apr 1958 m. **Wendy Barnard** 16 May 1985 Durham House, Carlingford b. 13 Jul 1954 Auckland, NZ

The Railways

As an employer and a source of accidents, the Department of Railways was very strong in the Mason family — mostly Oliver Alphonsus and his descendants.

Oliver Alphonsus Mason worked for the Railways for 38 years. Eskbank, Cootamundra, Junee, Lithgow, Newbridge, near Blayney, Hornsby, Turramurra and Waitara. A notable record, for which he was posthumously awarded what the family knew as 'the railway watch'.

Charles Mason, Oliver's father, was Senior Clerk at Muswellbrook.

Bernie Lyons, husband of Oliver's daughter Marie Mason, was a career railwayman as a guard.

Kevin Lyons, son of Marie Mason and Bernie Lyons, also served.

William Mason, husband of Priscilla Smith, was a Railway Guard all his working life, from 1901 to his death in 1932.

Hilton Mason, William and Priscilla Masons's son, was briefly with the Railways early in his career.

Charlie (Chick) Mason retired at 61 'because of tax'. He was at Muswellbrook.

Clem Mason, very briefly.

John Patrick Creevey, died on the rail line 18 Sept 1901, by a train at Redfern Station, Sydney.

John Charles Mason fell off a railway bridge and died in 1941. Death date given as 1943.

James Mason died at the age of 21 in a shunting accident.

Maria (Maher) Mason's brother Dennis Maher was killed in 1889 in a shunting accident on the railway.

Children of Oliver Alphonsus Mason

Marie Olga (Mick) Mason: b. 11 Jul 1921 d. 4 Nov 2002

B. 11 JUL 1921 JUNEE NSW D. 4 NOV 2002 HORNSBY
DAUGHTER OF OLIVER ALPHONSUS MASON AND NETTA GARRETT
SISTER TO CHICK, LEILA, PAT, OLIVER (BROTHER CLAUDIUS), TERRY, CLAIRE, ANNETTE, CATH
STEP-SISTER TO COLLEEN, JOSEPHINE, JUDITH, TONY, JAMES
M. BERNIE LYONS 12 MAY 1947 B. 3 APR 1917 D. 29 APR 1997
MOTHER TO PETER, MICHAEL, JOHN, MARY, JOE, CARMEL, JENNY, KEVIN, ANGELA
MOTHER FIGURE TO VERY MANY MASONS.

Claire Mason and her 'big sister' Mick Mason, in town for a cherished day off school.

Marie Olga Mason, known as **Mick**, was the mother figure for the large family of her father **Oliver Alphonsus Mason** when her mother **Netta** died in 1935, when **Mick** was only 13. Her mother's death hit **Mick** very hard – her family describe her as 'going through heck'. She is reported as saying she could cope, however, 'as long as Dad is OK'. **Marie** flatly refused to have the family split up and moved away, so cared for them all, creating a bond that lasted through the lives of all of them. She became so indispensable that when she announced she was getting married to **Bernard Lyons,** her father exclaimed 'What do you want to get married for. You have all your family here!'

Bernie's background had been on the Macleay River, trading horses. **Marie** and **Bernie** had nine children. **Marie** mothered them as well as her own sisters and brothers, plus the five children produced after her father married **Rosemary Lollbach** in 1946, making a close family bond through a very large family. She even catered for her own wedding reception, and that of her father's second wedding.

Marie's caring nature was evident in her own children – six of the nine had careers helping those less fortunate – **Carmel**, **Jenny**, **Kevin**, **Joe** and **Angela** all worked with the disabled and **Peter** worked with disadvantaged families.

The three youngest of **Oliver's** first family, **Claire**, **Ann**, and **Cath**, boarded at St Martha's at Leichhardt, where **Sister Thomasene** (their cousin **Jane**) was also a member of the community, a Sister of St Joseph. When **Cath** went off to boarding school, **Marie** cried, because there was now no one for her to look after. **Claire** however had the family initiative: family lore says she broke her glasses so that she'd be able to have a day out of school with **Marie**. The photo of a very elegant **Marie** (about 20 at the time), escorting **Claire** in the city shows however that they both enjoyed the opportunity thus made.

Marie found the death of **Rene Mostyn**, her aunt, on 26 Jul 1988 also very hard to deal with, her father **Oliver Alphonsus Mason** having only died the previous year. She did however manage to attend the wedding of **Terry** and **Monica** in 1988, which was most important to all of them. She was told just before the wedding in Taree that she had breast cancer, and had to be hurried home before the very special family celebration arranged for next day. She lived at 12 Nursery Street Hornsby until her death in 2002.

Masons meet in Taree 1993
Helen (Mason) Malcher, Monica (Murphy) Mason,
Marie (Mick) (Mason) Lyons, Bernie Lyons, Terry Mason

Terence Joseph (Terry) Mason: b. 7 Sep 1929

B. 7 SEP 1929
6TH SON OF OLIVER ALPHONSUS MASON AND NETTA GARRETT
MARIST BROTHER 1942 – 1988
M. MONICA MURPHY 5 JUL 1988 B. 4 MAY 1945
BROTHER TO MICK, CHICK, LEILA, PAT, BROTHER CLAUDIUS, CLAIR, ANNETTE, CATH
STEP-BROTHER TO COLLEEN, JOSEPHINE, JUDITH, TONY, JAMES

Terry Mason was born at the family home in Hornsby, in 1929, when his father was 40, his mother 34. He recalls a most pleasant, blessed childhood. Hornsby was still semi-rural, and their property was very nearly self-sufficient for food: the family had a dairy cow which had to be taken down the road to be serviced, plus chickens, fruit, and chooks let out down near the creek where an old duck would pinch their food, so the boys saw it as a given duty to barbecue and eat said duck hidden in the bushes — a feast they still recall with relish. Camping out overnight. Fruit trees (plums, blackberries), and pinching the neighbour's fruit and vegetables then '**Grandma Williams**' (the family of their mother, **Netta**), taking them to visit the same neighbour's orchard when the kids had nearly got caught the previous week. Cowboys and Indians, and cars very rare. 6d allowance. Spuds, toast and tea in the bush. **Marie**, the oldest, caring for them all (and doing it for many more years). Swimming in the waterhole, now polluted beyond recognition. *Ginger Meggs* country — the character was based in the Hornsby area – this was it, to a tee.

But at just 13, in January 1943, **Terry** left home and entered the monastery as a cadet Marist Brother, and rather sadly recalls that home visits thereafter were formal affairs, in stiff formal clothes, visiting elderly relatives and Religious, rather than recapturing forbidden pleasures with the local kids. His childhood had, in effect, finished at 13. In later years, he and his brother **Oli (Brother Claudius)**, returning home from their monasteries in their monks' robes, were held in some considerable awe by young **Peter Lyons** (18 years younger), and **Kevin** (31 years younger), the sons of their older sister **Mick**, married to **Bernie Lyons**. The awe has disappeared, the mutual affection has not.

by Terry Mason

I was born on 7 Sep 1929 to **Netta** and **Oliver Mason** in St. Kilda's Private Hospital in Hornsby. I was lucky to survive diphtheria in my first year of life. My older sisters, **Marie (Mick)** and **Leila**, recall that I was a baby who cried a lot.

Mum/Netta died when I was five and I only have a couple of memories of her. One was when I had a blue-bottle tick imbedded in my shoulder. It was discovered when I was in a 'rough and tumble'. Mum dealt with it. The other occasion was on a Sunday afternoon and a storm was about to break. We were playing in the front yard and I went to get a drink from the garden tap. Suddenly there was a clap of thunder with a simultaneous flash of lightning. It scared the hell out of me and I ended up on the ground. **Mum**, again, looked after me. Apart from those two occasions, I have no recollections of **Mum**. Her death was a non-event but the effects, long-lasting. The impression given from the rest of the family is that I was a bit of a tearaway kid.

Early schooldays were at Our Lady of the Rosary Waitara, under the guidance of the Mercy Nuns. Sister Assision was my first teacher and the classroom used to be a house. A lemon tree grew in the yard and I recall Sister getting me to collect lemons. She was a good mate. We walked to school which was next door to the church, taking about half an hour. That took us past Barker College which meant twice a day we had to walk against large numbers of high school students coming from (or to) the railway station. We were often banged with their Globite cases. At one stage, when I was older, I had had enough of it and grabbed a boy's boater hat and tossed it away. It flew like a Frisbee out on to the road! Consequences? I don't remember. It gave me a sense of satisfaction, though!

The playground was divided into a boys' and girls' area. The boys' area was the car park for the church next door. The girls were given a basketball to play with and the boys were given no play equipment. One day, when the nuns on supervision were swapping duties, we boys made a raid on the girls, securing the ball and quickly returning to our territory with the resulting consequences.

Following this raid on the girls' basketball, Fr. Hoare, Parish Priest, turned up at the **Mason** household and suggested to Dad that it was time the boys (**Oli** and I) would be better off (or was it the Sisters?) at the Brothers. We had a choice of St. Pat's in town, Marist brothers in North Sydney or Eastwood and the Christian Brothers at Chatswood or Strathfield. Eastwood was nearest and at that time train travel for all students was free. And so the decision was made.

Terry's Marist postings	
1943 - Aug 1949	Mittagong
Aug 1949 - 1952	Lidcombe - started teaching
1953 - May 1954	Maitland
May 1954 - 1961	Darlinghurst
1962 - 1967	Rosalie, Brisbane
1968 - 1972	Cairns (Deputy)
1973 - 1974	St Joseph's College, Hunters Hill ('Joey's')
Xmas 1974	Study in Rome
1975	Melbourne (Study)
1976	Deputy, St Gregory's College Campbelltown
1977 - 1981	Pagewood
1982 - 985	Armidale, study
1986	Marcellin College, Randwick
1987	Left Brothers
1987 - Oct 1999	St Clare's Taree

1941 and 1942 saw **Oli** and me at Marist Brothers', Eastwood. Brother Leopold was Principal. Others on the staff were Brothers Leonard, Cuthbert, Michael, Wilfred, Maximus and Cosmas. I completed Sixth Class and 1st Year Secondary, there.

In May of 1942, Brothers Arcadius and Andrew came to the school to recruit boys for the Marist Brothers' Juniorate. We were all sent in to see them individually. I expressed interest but said nothing to anyone. They came again in August or September and asked me if I had talked about it at home — that would have been the greatest joke of all time because I was not noted for being 'the type' but rather as being a bit of a rebel. The Brothers sent me home with a letter. About 11am I caught the train from Eastwood to Hornsby and walked home from there. I had had time to think about what the reaction at home would be like. Dad was down in the garden as he usually was each day and **Marie**, my eldest sister, was in the kitchen. 'Have you been expelled?' **Marie** asked. My prediction about my arrival proved to be right! I shook my head and handed over the letter. I returned to school without any more conversation. Arriving back at school Brothers Arcadius and Andrew asked me what the response was — I said I didn't wait for an answer.

The next day it had all been set up for me to go to Mittagong to the Juniorate. I had a problem in convincing my mates that it was so - they probably thought I was more likely to be going to the Farm Homes for Boys at Mittagong. Decision-making for me was nil.

On 26 Jan 1943, I was taken to Central Station by someone, presumably family, and handed over to the Brothers, where I met about 24 other boys. We travelled by train to Mittagong which took about three hours. This was my first time away from home.

The years I spent at Mittagong were war years with things pretty austere and regulated, but with hindsight, that is what I needed. I learnt many survival skills — general household chores such as cooking, mending socks, sewing on buttons, ironing; as well as gardening, growing vegetables, and many others. There were about 150 boys from 1st Year Secondary to Leaving Certificate on the property and there were only two paid employees — one was a chef for the Juniorate and one ran the Dairy farm. The rest of the work was done by us boys. These jobs were done in out-of-school hours and I developed a great love of physical work.

In 1944, at Easter time, **Oli** joined me. I only found out that he was coming the afternoon he was to arrive. I found it difficult to convince my mates that we were brothers. **Oli** was in Fourth Year and I was in Intermediate.

Mittagong, being a cold climate especially in the winter, required heating and hot water which was generated from a large boiler. All cooking was done on fuel stoves which meant that firewood was an essential. Firewood was obtained from an extended part of the property, about two miles from our living quarters. Bush drives were part of the routine whereby trees were felled, sawn up and, using a hired truck, brought in from the bush. One of the rostered duties for us boys was the wood heap, which involved sawing up the logs into lengths suitable for the stoves and the boiler, using cross-cut saws. Each wood drive would see anything up to ten truck loads in a day. Another rostered duty was the boiler. This involved making sure there was plenty of steam was available for hot water for the kitchen, laundry and showers.

Sport played an important role – we played hockey, soccer, Rugby League, Aussie Rules, cricket, tennis, handball, and swimming (in a dam). Athletics, including field events, were a part of it too.

Captain Terry Mason —a 'hands-on' OC Cadets

A major part of life here was to develop our spirituality with very traditional daily Mass, Rosary, morning and night prayer, spiritual reading etc. I acquired a great love of good classical music, including the Gregorian Chant which we used to sing parts of in church Liturgies. I was one of the twenty boys who were in the Schola. This involved learning and then singing the 'Propers' of the Mass in Gregorian Chant until our voices 'broke'. Brothers Gregory and Paul were our teachers and inspiration in this.

My leaving certificate results were not great but miles better than if I had stayed at home. The Juniorate had many more positives than negatives, but the main negative was the loss of family ties. The training centres were very self-reliant. A dairy farm provided milk and meat, an orchard mainly for apples, vegetable gardens, potatoes, and wood for heating. All of these provided great learning opportunities for all of us and kept the cost down. When I reflect on these times, I believe that there's more to education than the three Rs.

I enjoyed my time at the Juniorate and it was a good preparation for life. I was kept back, as a Postulant, for six weeks longer than the other boys of my group. It didn't really bother me once I learned it was for levity.

I left the Novitiate on 20 Aug 1949 and travelled by train to Lidcombe to be met by Br. Leonidas. We walked to Mills Street to the Monastery, had lunch and set off for the SCG to watch Souths versus Cronulla. The Brothers' house was designed for the purpose and was excellent. For the first time in my life (19 years) I had a room to myself. For a first Community, it was a good place to be and broad minded enough to allow initiative.

With every reason to fail in the classroom because I had no teacher training, it was with a determination to succeed motivated by a fear of failure that I began my teaching career. I was assigned a 5th class of about 70 boys. I was happy with how the rest of that year finished. The monks were very supportive, especially Br. Verius. In 1950 I took that class on to Year 6, which was a great help already knowing the boys. I introduced them to State Bursary and Brian Whittaker won the first Bursary for that school. I took the 6-stone football team in the MBSA (Marist Brothers Sports Association) Competition. We did well. I took the Under 14 cricket team, also. Many years later at Darlinghurst, I was assigned the coaching of an Under 15 team which the year before had been beaten every week. In order to give them something to aim for, we made a resolution that no team would beat us by more than ten points. If a team was ahead by more than ten then we aimed for fifteen and so on. At the end of many subsequent games, although beaten, we had achieved our goal and they came off the field celebrating. Opposing teams found it hard to understand. There's more to sport than winning!

My confidence in teaching continued in 1951 when the Marist Scholasticate was moved to Drummoyne. My class was selected for demonstration and practice teaching lessons. In a practice session, trainee teachers taught three lessons and class teacher taught three. For me, this was a real learning curve and continued through the next year. I have fond memories of Lidcombe and still have contact with some of those ex-pupils.

Chapter 4: The migrating Oliver Mason

Brother Albanus, who was appointed to Lidcombe staff in 1951, often talked about Maitland so when the next year's appointments were read out at the end of 1952, I was pleased to be appointed there. The old cathedral had been converted into a hall and above it, four classrooms. Mine was 6th Class. The primary school was quite separate from the secondary. This was a wonderful place to teach in, and that class obtained five State Bursaries. I had the 6-stone footy team and Barry Graves, younger brother of 'Wakka' Graves of Souths, was the 5-8s coach. In 1954 I was invited into secondary, teaching Maths but that came to a sudden end in May, when I was transferred to Darlinghurst right next to Kings Cross. What a contrast! Brother Wilfred was to take my place and me, his. The day our swap took place, Brothers Michael, Gerald and Venard transferred Wilfred up but before they took me down, we played a game of golf at East Maitland — my first game. I am still in touch with a few of those I taught in that short time!

1954, Term 2 at Darlinghurst, I took over a combined 5th and 6th class of about 75 in the hall. The following year, 1955, there were 110 boys in the 5/6 class. The Provincial (Senior Brother in charge of NSW Marist Brothers) came to check the situation, so I put a step ladder in front of the class. He asked me what the ladder was doing there and I explained that it was so I could see the boys at the back of the class. The result was a large, thick curtain suspended the hall, splitting it in half. Paddy Larkin was given 5th Class in one half and I had 6th Class in the other.

Brother Fergus asked me to take on the running of Cadets in 1956, with no experience. The Brothers' house was primitive but was made bearable by the quality of the Brothers there. The community/staff changed many times but Pat Butler and I had eight years there together. We were both transferred on the same day and both came from Hornsby. I had 7⅔ years there, teaching Year 6 Primary. I have very fond memories of my time at Darlinghurst and again, there are ex-students who keep in touch with me.

I was transferred to Rosalie in Brisbane, Queensland in 1962. It was here that I made my first move into Secondary, teaching mainly maths, science and history in lower secondary classes. Brother Ernan gave me the chance to teach physics to senior classes and I took the opportunity. I have long and lasting memories of this school, its pupils and parents and friends. Seven of my students gained highest passes in Junior Secondary Maths. The author of a maths text book rang and asked me what I put their success down to. I told him it was because I used his text book!

In the early 1960s, the Marist Brothers bought a dairy farm about two miles from Currumbin Creek from Henry Waters. Brother Harold, on the staff at Rosalie, was responsible for the farm. He shifted a building from the property at Mt. Tambourine, which had been used to house the boys from the school during the war and had it reassembled as living quarters for the Brothers at the dairy farm. All this was done by us Brothers in holiday time. For the next 20 years this was my holiday home. Greg and Gwen Waters became the share farmers, as well as my good friends. I enjoyed the work on the farm and used do the milking for two weeks during the Christmas holidays so that Greg, Gwen and children could get away for a break. The place was also used for father/son weekends, which were really working bees. These involved harvesting, replacing the old dairy with raised herringbone bails with overhead feeding and concrete yards — a big job, replacing fences, painting the house etc.

Back at 'Rosa' I coached the first cricket and rugby teams, as well as athletics. These were a constant commitment of time and energy. I was appointed Officer in Charge (OC) of Cadets and this on top of a full teaching load, gave little time for other things. 'Rosa', like 'Darlo' kids, came from low socio-economic backgrounds and had a determination to do well. Looking back, I rate them as the two best schools I taught at. I remain in regular contact with the dads of these boys who became firm friends from these working weekends. So much so, that when **Monica** and I married, they put on and invited us to a special barbecue so that they could meet the woman I married!

My appointment to Rosalie enabled me to really catch up with my sister **Leila** and her husband **Nev**, as well as their family. This was a real highlight of my time there.

After six years at 'Rosa', I was appointed as deputy Principal at St. Augustine's, a boarding school in **Cairns**. There were about 300 boarders, housed in six dormitories. They were two-storied, weatherboard buildings, accessed by external wooden staircases. This was my first experience of being in charge of senior boarders. There were about 45 seventeen-year-old young men. I was amazed that there were no fire drills practised and no fire-fighting equipment available.

I was OC of Cadets, and had the first-grade footy coaching and athletics coaching. My teaching programme was religion, maths and physics. During school time, I was lucky to be in bed before 11pm and expected to be up at 5.30am. Supervision of dormitories, dining room and studies occupied any other time. The building programming had begun — four new laboratories, a new air-conditioned library and a new classroom block. It was a stressful time.

I created a new band, this time a full brass band. There was a large number of Italian boys who were wonderful musicians. Many requests were forthcoming which gave the lads a good break from the College.

The Principal, Laurie Garnaut, was keen on sailing and having the College take part. With so many boarders bored on Sundays, it seemed a good thing for them. Laurie gave us a Heron sailing boat. In a short period of time (12 months) we had acquired four Herons. I built one which took me six months. This meant that about 20 boarders could spend time on Trinity Bay sailing in competitions under supervision of the yachting club. The kids loved it. Lots of these boys were from huge inland properties and many a parent found it astounding/amazing to see their boys so competent at sailing. Boarding schools are tough assignments! Even so, the Cairns and North Queensland were great and exciting years. The tobacco and sugar cane farmers in the area were inspiring people in all aspects of life.

The Dominique, built by Terry Mason

After five years at Cairns I was appointed to St. Joseph's College in Hunters Hill and so back to Sydney. I took up residence in January 1973. No cadets, thank God, but I was made fifth form master in charge of about 160 seventeen year old boarders in three dormitories. The College had just gone through a major building programme.

My teaching load of maths, physics, biology and religion was very constant and as senior master I was expected to know where every boy was at any given time. Weekends were hectic. I coached the Under 16 A and B Rugby teams. On Saturdays the college would have up to 45 rugby teams in the field. Refereeing was always on. Supervising dining rooms and free time was draining. During 1974 I was informed that some students had drugs at the college. This caused a number of repercussions among some parents. I had been out of town during the 60s and life in the city had changed — in this case, not for the better.

After 25 years of teaching, I was offered a course in Rome over Christmas of 1974. The 10 weeks in Rome were good and raised some challenges for me. I had a few days in London on the way home as well as Tel Aviv and Old Jerusalem, all of which raised more questions for me. I talked to the ordinary people about ordinary life issues. In all, it was a real eye-opener as was Bombay (Mumbai) and Calcutta. Amazed!

Terry helped build an enormous shed on the cattle property belonging to the Balgo Aboriginal Mission.
A nice change from teaching?

1975 saw me at the National Pastoral Institute in Melbourne, doing my first formal study since Leaving Certificate in 1949. There were many challenges from fellow students as to what my vision was. All in all, it was a most valuable year in my personal and spiritual development. As part of the year's study, we had lectures on indigenous peoples' spirituality. I asked the lecturer if he had lived or worked amongst the Aboriginal people. He hadn't. Another student asked me if I was interested in going to an Aboriginal Mission. I was and that Christmas I flew into Balgo Hills Mission, which is halfway between Derby and Alice Springs. These six weeks raised more questions for me and so I returned to the mission each Christmas break for the next eight years.

We volunteers would help run the Mission while some of the regular staff was able to have a break away. Most of our time was spent in occupying the children while the Big Meetings were on. I found it a very interesting time, trying to understand their culture. The people were more than happy for us to share some experiences with them. One thing that was most obvious was that they were very much survivors in a very harsh environment.

I was appointed to my third experience of a boarding school, Campbelltown, in 1976. I had asked to just have a teaching position but was appointed as deputy principal. After one year, I was shifted to the staff at Pagewood, in 1977. I enjoyed my five years there. In my last year at Pagewood, I enrolled at Armidale Uni as a mature age student completing a unit on maths. The next four years I attended uni full time and boarded with the De La Salle Brothers. Finally I had my qualifications B.A.; Dip. Ed.; Dip. R.E.

With qualifications in hand, I was appointed to Randwick for 1986. No boarders but students from wealthier socio-economic backgrounds. It was during that year I made the decision to leave the Brothers — the life was no longer life-giving for me. This meant that I had to apply for my first job ever. Fortunately I heard that St Clare's in Taree were looking for a maths/physics teacher because they were moving into Years 11 and 12, having previously just been Years 7 to 10 school. I was in the right place at the right time. I got the job, beginning January 1987.

This meant that I had to find somewhere to live and to furnish it. I had never even made a decision as to what curtains to put in a room, let alone choose furniture and all that I needed to set up home. Luckily I had my sister, **Anne** living locally so she and **Cath** helped me to do this. I taught at St. Clare's for twelve years and thoroughly enjoyed teaching without all the other add-ons of past schools.

In 1988, **Monica** and I married. We had first met some years before, in Auckland at a summer course for those who had been in religious life for some years. **Monica** was fortunate to get a teaching job at St. Joseph's Primary School, at the end of that year.

In the last two years of teaching at St. Clare's, I reduced my teaching down to 0.6 of a load. This enabled me to do a much more thorough job at the chalk-face. It meant that I spent the full day at school but only teaching five periods out of seven, and I continued working till I was 70.

In October of 1999, when I put down the chalk in the last class for the last time, one of the girls came up to me and asked for the piece of chalk. I wondered what she wanted it for and was told that she wanted it 'because it was historic'! Later on there was a celebration organised by Larry Keating, Principal of St. Clare's, with the help of some staff members, for a wider group than that of St Clare's, unbeknownst to me! It involved a Mass of Thanksgiving, followed by a meal. I was stunned when I arrived, to find many of my siblings and their

Terry and Monica Mason at their wedding in 1988

spouses, a few cousins, ex classmates from Mittagong days as well as some past confreres from around the eastern coast of NSW and Queensland.

And so I retired having achieved 50 years of teaching. But not quite! **Monica** was still teaching at St Joseph's, now just down the road from our home. To help her out, I used go to the school once a week and take 10 to 12 of her Year 4 students to extend their maths. There was always plenty of competition between them to have this chance. **Monica** retired at the end of 2004.

My retirement and **Monica**'s 10-week long-service leave coincided. We decided it was the chance we had long looked forward to, to travel overseas. We chose a couple of guided tours which took us to England, Scotland, Wales and Ireland. We then did a similar thing in Europe — France, Barcelona, Italy, Greece, Austria, Switzerland, Holland and Belgium. We were fortunate in having a near neighbour who was a travel agent and one day in 2002, as we were talking to her she showed us a flyer about a ten-day tour she was taking to China. I was instantly keen to take up the challenge, as was **Monica**. There were lots of local people on the trip including some staff from St Clare's and St Joe's, which added to the joy of the trip.

Following our marriage in 1988, **Monica** and I made a point of regular tips to New Zealand to spend time with her parents and siblings. Christmas was usually celebrated at the family home and eventually on one of **Mon**'s sibling's properties, with the whole clan gathered for three days. These were always great fun especially when we stayed with her brothers who both had sheep properties. We enjoyed getting out on the quad bikes in the busy seasons and helping where possible. They were great bonding times, especially with the next generation. We also made a point of having some time to ourselves which meant we would explore some part of New Zealand that we hadn't visited before. Fantastic! We are now very grateful for these opportunities since I can no longer travel that distance, having had a stroke in March of 2009.

Monica Murphy Mason: b. 4 May 1945

B. 4 MAY 1945 NORSEWOOD, NZ
M. TERRY MASON 5 JUL 1988
DAUGHTER OF JIM AND MARY MURPHY
SISTER TO PETER, MARIE, ANNE, ROSALIE AND KEVIN MURPHY
NUN FROM 1963 TO 1987

By Monica (Murphy) Mason

I am the third child of six, born to **Jim** and **Mary Murphy.** The eldest is **Peter**, followed by **Marie, me, Anne, Rosalie** and **Kevin**. From the time I was about 11, we lived on the same property and house where Dad grew up. It was a small dairy farm with sheep, several horses and plenty of working dogs.

The local district was known as Norsewood, since a group of Norwegians, brought out by the Government in 1872 to clear the native rainforest, make roads and create settlements, made this their home. The Danes, who were also part of this, settled in the area that is now known as Dannevirke. I grew up with classmates whose names were Olsen, Johansen, Andersen, Fredericksen, Swensen, Eriksen, Pedersen and many others.

Terry and Monica Mason

Dad's older brother, John Murphy and family, lived on a neighbouring property, and we enjoyed the many times our families got together, collecting each other's hay or whatever. Of course all the children attended the same local State school and so **Dad** and **Uncle John** shared the job of either taking us up to school or bringing us home.

When I first started school, there were only four teachers on staff, which meant that we had composite classes in each room. In the middle 1950s the school roll increased, so another classroom had to be built to accommodate children and a new teacher. I was in the class that started the year in a shelter shed for a very short time. To me it seemed to be weeks! We were then moved to one end of the corridor outside the other classrooms. Eventually we were moved to the other end of the village, into a building that was called the 'Reading Room'. The 'long drop' toilets were specially dug for us — one for boys and one for girls. Each recess, we were marched in twos up to the main school. I was a timid kid and one memory stuck, because it was the only time I recall being chosen to be the leader of the girls. Johnston Wehi was the leader of the boys. The fun part of it was Johnston challenging me to take long strides like his, with the rest of the class trying to keep up. No teacher was really supervising – he was driving the very short distance in his car.

On leaving primary school, I was sent to boarding school in Masterton (80 miles away) where my sister **Marie** was already. **Mum**, a retired teacher, felt that we would be better able to study in the time provided for it (and under supervision?) rather than battling for time and space at home. She was probably right, but I was dreadfully homesick, even with **Marie** there, as well as my cousin, Maureen, in the same year as myself. The last couple of years at St Bride's College, I settled down and really enjoyed life. **Marie** had moved on to teachers' college and my younger sister **Anne** joined me. There was a lot of encouragement from the nuns to take subjects that led us into professional jobs rather than commercial ones. I had plans of being a domestic science teacher in the senior years of primary school. It was during my senior year that one of the nuns, for whom I had great regard, asked me if I had ever thought of joining them. That took some thinking about. My parents were happy enough about it, but not so happy that it meant that I had to go to Sydney for three years. But with their blessing, I flew to Sydney in May 1963, with two other girls from the same school. We walked through the doors of the Brigidine Novitiate at St Ives (now Brigidine College for Girls) on 24 May 1963.

The next three and a half years were very lonely ones for me. I missed my family dreadfully. **Mum** used to write every week, which was an enormous blessing in keeping me in touch with my siblings and the wider family. As each letter arrived, I grieved over being the only member of the family missing the many family gatherings, and longed for the day that I would fly back home. Perhaps that wasn't as bad as for some of the Sydney-born novices who had their parents visit for a few hours once a month!

For the remainder of 1963, each school day I caught the bus from St Ives to Pymble Station with others who were already studying at Mount Street Catholic Teachers' College. Then the train to Lindfield with two of the nuns teaching in the small school at Bradfield Park, an Immigration Camp for New Australians. The entire camp was made up of army huts, as was the two-classroom school. I spent most of each morning helping where I was directed, then I caught the bus back to the school at Lindfield to help one of the nuns with her seven year olds with whatever they were doing.

The next two years were spent entirely on the property at St Ives. Then in Jan 1966 I was sent by the Lindfield community to attend the Catholic Teachers College at Mount Street, North Sydney. That was an experience. Day One, I was accompanied on the journey I would take each day, thereafter on my own. Imagine being left to do that, having absolutely no idea of the layout of Sydney, not knowing the names of suburbs or anything. So I set off on my first trip in Sydney on my own. You can imagine my delight at arriving at the gates of the college on time with no wrong turns. Returning to Lindfield wasn't quite so successful. I had walked to the station with other students who checked to see if I knew which train to catch. I said I did, but once on the train, I found myself heading for Milson's Point where I hopped off and was given directions to the right platform.

Joy of joys, I was sent back to New Zealand in January 1967 to begin teaching 45 seven year olds. Mum was at Wellington Airport, along with a couple of the NZ nuns. Tears! I was allowed to go home with Mum for a week or so — not to stay at home but to stay at a local convent and to visit family by day.

My first teaching appointment was at Porirua, housing commission 'city' to teach 45 darlings — they were a delight. Interestingly, there were five sets of twins in the class as well as a twin whose sister was in another class. One set of girls were identical, which caused a lot of fun. In those days teachers in Catholic schools were the ones who cleaned the classrooms, toilets etc. Other out-of-classroom tasks were for those of us who could play the piano, taking pupils for lessons as well as teaching religion to Catholic children who attended state schools, two of us cooked the evening meal for the community of 20 (one week the 1st course and next week, the 2nd course). On top of that I studied extramurally for the NZ Teachers' Certificate.

In 1968 I was appointed to a new community and school in Johnsonville, to teach a composite class of 8 and 9 year olds, with all the same extra duties as at Porirua.

In 1969 I found myself back at Porirua with 40 children of the same age group and extras as in 1967. Again I had a set of identical twin boys, as well as twin girls who were easily mistaken for each other. There were eleven sets of twins in the school of about 250 to 300 students.

In 1970 I remained in the same community in Porirua, but taught 8 year olds at Tawa which meant a drive of about half an hour morning and afternoon. This school had a smaller roll.

1971-72 I spent at Masterton, supervising boarders at the same school where I had boarded, as well as teaching 8 and 9 year olds the first year and 9 and 10 year olds the next, at St Pat's primary school. The second year of teaching at St Pat's was fantastic. At last I had a second year to build on to the first and for the first time in six years I felt great satisfaction. We had a great principal and a wonderful staff. I enjoyed my contact with the boarders, often outwitting them with my previous knowledge and experience of the place! We often laughed together about it. However it wasn't all 'beer & skittles' on staff of a boarding school. There was the occasion that some fellow one night decided to come and join us. He'd climbed up a fire escape and tried to open a window into the dormitory of which I was supervisor. Thankfully the girl whose bed was beside this window, had it bolted. A phone call to the local police solved that problem, but some of the girls as well as myself, didn't sleep too well that night. Then there was the time a couple of girls from my dorm left the property during the night. I was woken by a senior girl who alerted me to it. I immediately reported this to the nun in charge, and the two of us checked the property, not finding them; the police were again called upon. They found the girls, safe but scared, at about 2am in the Band Rotunda in the town park.

1973 saw another move to another community and another school. My class contained four different grades and it was this year that my hearing difficulties began following a bout of rubella. I found it a tough year. In 1974 I acted as a casual teacher for a couple of our schools while I completed some study.

For the period 1975-80, I was appointed to the staff of a college that had the last two years of primary school (intermediate) attached to a secondary college. I had a class of 11 year old girls and it was now that I found I was unable to hear the girls' answers to my questions. There were very many 'I beg your pardon's and 'What was that she said's. I was sent to an ear, nose and throat specialist, who referred me on to an audiologist who fitted me with a hearing aid for my almost-useless ear. I was now at the stage of considering giving teaching away because of my loss of hearing since the aid was of little help, if any!

In 1981 I was appointed to a small country school, nearer where I grew up, as the third teacher. This meant that I was able to spend lots more time with Mum and Dad who were still on the family farm. I had 18 delightful children in three grades, and found a woman who taught lip reading, but better still, she had a similar loss as mine and urged me to get a second opinion about my loss. Result – I was fitted with two hearing aids. Ouch! The noise people made, especially cutlery on plates. That hand bell used at school was horrendous. With a few adjustments... FANTASTIC! One youngster went home and said to his Mum, 'Sister can even hear us whisper'. What had been going on before?

After five great years there, by 1987 it was time for a change. I needed to take control of my own life and so had a year in Sydney for study – more like rest and reflection. I came to the decision that it was time for me to move on from life with the Brigidines, find my own place to live and for the first time ever, apply for a job. Scary stuff. I gained a job as Teacher Librarian at St. Thomas' Primary school at Lewisham, which I loved. This was followed by eventually moving to Taree and marrying **Terry**, whom I'd met some years before in NZ. And here I have stayed. Gaining a teaching position in St Joseph's was a huge plus and I loved every day I worked there. I spent almost all of my years there with either Year Three or Year Four – to me, the best age group of all to teach.

Monica with a few of her first class out on the playground in 1967.

Monica receiving her Australian Citizenship on 17 April 1989.

Monica, with her Grad. Dip. in R.E. certificate

In 1997, the Maitland-Newcastle Catholic Schools Office notified their teachers that they wanted us to become more knowledgeable and understanding of our religious beliefs. With encouragement from **Terry**, I took up the challenge and being a three-year trained teacher on Step 13, I was accepted by the Catholic University in Brisbane to begin my studies for a Graduate Diploma in Religious Education, extramurally. I felt that I could manage one unit a semester, while teaching full-time. This I was able to do except for 2nd semester in 1999 when **Terry** had retired and I took my 10 weeks long-service leave to take up our long-held dream to travel overseas. I submitted my final assessment task in 2nd semester 2001, graduating in Brisbane in April 2002, thanks to the support given me by **Terry**. He made it possible for me by being happy to discuss issues with me as a tutor would have done. He claims that he gained as much from it as I did. Again, a great sense of satisfaction.

I retired at the end of 2004 after 37+ years of teaching; or as I said when I retired, 'I have spent all of my life from the age of five in a classroom or study hall on one side of the desk or the other. It's time to stop.'

Retirement brought with it many blessings — biggest of all, to spend precious time with **Terry**. We made good use of spending time with my family in NZ and with **Terry**'s family along the eastern coast of Australia. I had time to make further discoveries on **Terry**'s family tree — both **Masons** and **Garretts** — and getting to know some of his distant relatives. As my new grandnieces/nephews arrived in NZ, I put my sewing skills to work — sometimes wool embroidered or appliqued cot blankets, sometimes patchwork cot quilts. All 26 of them, labelled with love. I also spent a fair bit of time doing voluntary work for the office staff at St. Joe's — filling out and filing record cards, refilling first aid kits for each classroom and many other jobs. My time there isn't so much these days, especially since **Terry** had a stroke in March 2009. Thankfully it didn't affect his speech or memory but did affect his left-side mobility. He gets around with a walking stick most of the time and is very cautious in unfamiliar places. Falls are to be avoided at all costs. He's had a few of those, with no damage, thank God!

We both continue to look forward to the future, whatever it may hold.

Chapter 5

The migrating Mason Daughters

Mary (Mason) Sheridan, Joanna (Mason) Tighe, Margaret (Mason) Creevey

Information for this segment from Monica Mason, Robyn Mason, Helen Mason Malcher, Norma McNamara and Patricia Keevers

Mary (Mason) Sheridan: b. c1813 d. 3 Mar 1873

DAUGHTER OF JOHN MASON II AND JOHANNA QUIGLEY
SISTER TO JOANNA, JOHN, OLIVER, MARGARET AND DANIEL
ARRIVED ON THE *CHINA* 19 DEC 1839
MARRIED THOMAS SHERIDAN 1840: B. C1768 D. 11 AUG 1848

Wedding record of Mary Mason and Thomas Sheridan

Husband	First Name	Wife	First Name	Date	Place
Sheridan	Thomas	Mason	Mary	1840	St Mary's Catholic Church, Sydney

Death record of Mary Sheridan

Reference	Died	Surname	First Name	Father	Mother	Location
6966/1873	1873	Sheridan	Mary	John Mason	Johanna	Tamworth

Mary Mason is in the shipping records in December 1839 as **John** and **Johanna (Quigley) Mason**'s eldest daughter, aged 26 when they arrived on the *China*, and listed as a housemaid. She was assigned to a Mr Harvey in Sydney, and presumably therefore went to work for him, together with her sister **Johanna**, then 16.

Only six months later, in May 1840, she married **Thomas Sheridan** at St Mary's Catholic Church in Sydney. He was an ex-convict and native of Connaught, Ireland, transported on the *Boyne* in 1826, sentenced for seven years for the crime of 'sacrilege'. Now having his Certificate of Freedom, he had served his sentence. We have no knowledge of how the couple met. He was then aged 52, she 27. The wedding ceremony was witnessed by her brother **Oliver Mason**, which would appear to indicate that the marriage had the family's blessing. She was illiterate, signing the wedding certificate with an X, and the couple moved to Victoria immediately after the wedding

It was this **Mary (Mason) Sheridan**, her young brother **Daniel's** 'sister **Mrs Sheridan**', who was to look after the 'absconding' **Daniel Mason**, some 20 years younger than herself, sought by an obviously furious father in 1850. She was at that time said by her father **John** to be living at Port Philip Bay.

Thomas Sheridan drowned in a waterhole in or near Maldron, Victoria, on 11 Aug 1848, according to an official record. A coroner's inquest found no suspicious circumstances. The couple had two children who died soon after birth. On 9 Oct 1847 their only surviving child, **James John Sheridan** was born to them in Coburg, Victoria, when the town was still called Pentridge, which confusingly became the name of the gaol built there. **James** was a shoemaker, had a large family of 12 children with his wife **Elizabeth**, and following generations followed the pattern of large families, as shown in the family tree. **James** died on 21 Oct 1918 at his home in Carthage St, Tamworth, aged 70.

Interestingly, **Mary** used the surname **Mason** when she was a sponsor for the birth of her cousin **Charles** in 1851, son of **Charles** and **Johanna (Quigley) Mason**, and in 1864 for her nephew **Oliver Peter**, son of her brother **John and Maria (Maher) Mason**, both in the Maitland district.

Mary and **Thomas Sheridan's** son **James** moved to NSW, marrying **Elizabeth Freeman** from Patricks Plain near Morpeth in 1851 (which may have something to do with his mother being in the area that year), and settling in Tamworth, where all his children were born.

Mary Sheridan died 3 Mar 1873 in Tamworth, aged 60. Her death certificate shows her occupation as housekeeper, which suggests, together with the use of her maiden name as witness at **Mason** family events, that she had been working to sustain herself in the area where her own family lived. Perhaps she felt herself to be more a **Mason** than a Sheridan.

Mary Sheridan's descendants.
Grave and memorial of father and son, both Oscar James Sheridan, at Tamworth.
One died 1954 at age 72, and the other in 1942 at age 20.

The following family tree is an indication of the extraordinary number of children from **James Sheridan**, the son of **Mary Mason** and **Thomas Sheridan**.

---

1 **Mary Mason** b. 1813 Tipperary IRL, m. **Thomas Sheridan** 6 May 1840 St Marys, Sydney d. 3 Mar 1873 Tamworth. Thomas b. 1796 Connaught IRL. d. 11 Aug 1858 Victoria.
  2 **James John Sheridan** b. 9 Oct 1847 Coburg/Brunswick, Vic d. 21 Oct 1918 Tamworth m. **Elizabeth Jane Freeman** 1868 Patricks Plain, Tamworth b. 1847 Sofala/Patricks Plain. d. 1919 Tamworth.
    3 **Thomas Sheridan** b. 1868 Patricks Plains m. **Martha Jane Mainwaring** 1904 Tingha, NSW b. 1886 Walcha, NSW d. 1963 Cessnock, NSW
      4 **William Thomas Sheridan** b. 1905 Tingha, NSW d. 1951 Petersham, NSW
      4 **Mary Sheridan**
      4 **Cecil Sheridan** b.1969 d. 1969 Cessnock, NSW
    3 **Mary Elizabeth Sheridan** b. 1870 Tamworth d. 1920 Newcastle, NSW
    3 **Leander Castleton Sheridan** b. 1872 Tamworth d. 1873 Tamworth
      4 **Annie Winton Sheridan** b. 1874 Tamworth, NSW d. 25 Nov 1964 Newcastle, m. **George Daniel Inkston** 1901 Tamworth, NSW d. 1936 Hamilton, NSW
      4 **Clifford William Inkston** b. 1901 Tamworth, NSW d. c1975 m. **Mary E Gleeson** 1926 Wickham
      4 **Eric James Inkston** b. 1905 Tamworth, NSW d. 1960 Campsie, NSW m. **Cecelia May Everett** 1933 Burwood, NSW d. 1974 Burwood, NSW
    3 **Ernest Emanuel Sheridan** b. 1876 Tamworth, NSW d. 1944 Tamworth, m. **Ellen Matilda Shearman** 1899 Newcastle, NSW b. 1876 Newcastle, NSW d. 1961 Kempsey
      4 **Stanley James Sheridan** b. 1900 Wickham, Newcastle, NSW d. c1974 Wickham
      4 **Thomas E Sheridan** b. 1902 Newcastle, NSW d. 1903 Newcastle
      4 **Elizabeth A Sheridan** b. 1911 d.1911 Newcastle
      4 **Frederick G Sheridan** b. 1904 Newcastle, NSW
      4 **Charles H Sheridan** b. 1906 Hamilton, NSW
      4 **Jack Sheridan** b. 1912 d. 1969 Sydney
    3 **Victor J Sheridan** b. 1877 Tamworth d. 1951 Tamworth m. **Mary A Robinson** 1900
      4 **Dorothy Sheridan** b. 1901 Newcastle d. 1903 New Lambton, NSW
    3 **Ethel May Sheridan** b. 1879 Tamworth d. 1952 m. **Joseph Enoch Gamble** 1905 Tamworth
      4 **Kathleen Gamble** b. c1909 m. **Ian P. Harvey** 1930 Hamilton, NSW
      4 **Richard Gamble** b. c1914 d. 1971 Newcastle, NSW m. **Rita Ada Robinson** 1942 Hamilton, NSW
      4 **Millie A Gamble** b.1915 d. 1915 Cessnock

3 **Loretta (Laura) Sheridan** b. 1880 Tamworth, d. 23 Jul 1967 Darlinghurst m. **Thomas Hammond** 1901 Tamworth
    4 **Thomas Hammond** b. 1901 Tamworth
    4 **Darrel D Hammond** b. 1903 Tamworth
    4 **Frank Victor Hammond** b.& d. 1946 Redfern, NSW
    4 **Arthur Hammond** b. 1907
    4 **Ruby R Hammond** b. c.1911 d. Aug 2001 Sydney m. **William Percy Tyndall** 1933 Paddington d. Jun 1984 Sydney
    4 **Harry Hammond** b. c1914
    4 **Miriam Hammond** b. c1917
    4 **James Hammond** b. c1919
    4 **Jack Hammond** b. c1920
    4 **Robert Hammond** b. c1926
3 **Oscar James Sheridan** b. 1882 Tamworth d. 21 Mar 1954 Tamworth, m. **Mary Jane Upson** 1907 Tamworth d.1965 Tamworth
    4 **Edna Sheridan** b. 1907 d. 1908
    4 **Ethel Frances (Dot) Sheridan** b. 1908 d. 1971 m1. **Aubrey Owen McNamara** 1929 m2.(df). **Norman Victor Hoskins (Hamper).** Had five children
[Children of Ethel Frances (Dot) Sheridan and Norman Victor (Hamper)]
      5 **Norma McNamara**
    4 **Glenville Sheridan** b. 1909 d. 1973 m. **Jean (Woods) Bell** Had 10 children plus 3 children in previous marriage b. 1904
      5 **Esther Sheridan** b. & d. 1945
      5 **Ethel Francis Sheridan** b.1945 d. 1954
    4 **Iris Laurel Sheridan** b. 1911 d. 1975 m. **Jack Judge**
    4 **Ruby Kathleen Sheridan** b. 1912 m. **David Clarence Addison**
    4 **Kathleen Sheridan** b. c 1913 m. **Harry Charles James Barnett**. Had 10 children
    4 **Anne Sheridan** b. 1915 d. 1916
    4 **Thelma Margaret Sheridan** b. 1917 m. **Clarence Bayliss**
    4 **Elizabeth Mary Sheridan** b. 1919 d. 1920
    4 **Richard Brimsley Sheridan** b. 1920 m. **Isabel Jane Warner**
    4 **James Oscar Sheridan** b. 1921 d. 10 Feb 1942
[Children of Mary Jane Upson]
    4 **Libby Upson**
3 **Mildred Lorne Sheridan** b. 1884 Tamworth NSW d. 1951 Balmain m1. (df) **Hector Israel** 6 children m2. **William James Frier** 1938 Rozelle d. 1963 Balmain
[Children of Mildred Lorne Sheridan and William James Frier]
    4 **Mavis Frier** b. 1929 d. 1929 Balmain
3 **Alonso Sheridan** b. 1886 d. 4 Sep 1908
3 **James John Sheridan** b. 1887 Tamworth BC. 34947 d. 21 Jun 1949, 118 Ann St, Enfield, Sydney. DC 10323 m. **Margaret J Hannon** 1910 Werris Creek, NSW .Occupation Fitter. Buried Rookwood.
    4 **Veronica Sheridan** b. 1910
    4 **Mary Sheridan** b. c1911 d. 1913 Quirindi, DC.16715
    4 **Ethel Sheridan** b. 1915
    4 **Joseph J Sheridan** b. c 1917 d. 1918 DC. 163
3 **Ronald Sheridan** b. 1920
    4 **Frederick Sheridan** b. 1924
    4 **Francis James Sheridan** b. c1926 d. 1927
    4 **John Sheridan** b. 1930
    4 **James E Sheridan** b.1949 d. 1949 DC. 10323
3 **Gordon Sheridan** b. 1889 Tamworth d. 1890 Tamworth
3 **Lynda K Sheridan** b. 1894 Tamworth d. 1894 Tamworth

Joanna (Mason) Tighe: b. 1823 d. 1885

DAUGHTER OF JOHN MASON II AND JOHANNA QUIGLEY
SISTER TO MARY, JOHN, OLIVER, MARGARET AND DANIEL
ARRIVED ON THE *CHINA* 19 DEC 1839
MARRIED CHARLES TIGHE/TYE 1841: B.1803 D. 1850

Joanna Mason came to New South Wales from Tipperary with her siblings and her parents, **John** and **Johanna (Quigley) Mason** on the *China* in December 1839. She was 16. She and her sister **Mary** were engaged off the ship to a Mr Harper in Sydney as housemaids and children's nurses.

The appointment to Mr Harper could not have lasted long, as on 20 Jun 1841 **Joanna** was in the Maitland district with her family, when she married an ex-convict, **Charles Tighe** (Tye, or even Callaghan). That her older brother **Oliver** was one of the witnesses at the marriage evidently gave the wedding gravitas, but does not explain it. **Charles** was a Protestant, so there must have been some arrangement with this Catholic family for the marriage. He was baptised as a Catholic two years later, in 1843, in the church where **Joanna** and he were married, as West Maitland's Roman Catholic Church records show.

More can be discovered of **Charles'** background as a convict than of **Joanna's**. He was transported on the *Royal Admiral* in 1833, the same convict ship as **Patrick Creevey** who later married **Joanna's** sister **Margaret Mason**. Both **Tighe** and **Creevey** were granted Certificates of Freedom, official recognition that they had completed their sentence and could return to England if they wished. **Tighe's**, No 40/1841, was on 7 Nov 1840, only seven months before he and **Joanna** married, which suggests a relationship between the two events – freedom and marriage. Land grants of 30 acres had previously been made to convicts as they completed their sentences, but this practice ceased in 1831. There is no evidence discovered in any land records that **Charles Tighe/Tye** had any land, though this would have provided a very neat start in life for them. Researcher **Patricia Keevers** believes **Charles** was granted 30 acres of land in Swan Reach after his sentence was completed. Marital opportunities for females at the time were excellent (in the East Maitland area there was a proportion of about 5 to 1 single men to women) so it is hard to understand why **Joanna** chose an ex convict (or he was chosen for her) without land, 20 years older than herself.

The Newcastle parish records, which cover the Maitland district where the family were, show that **Joanna** and **Charles Tighe** lived at Paterson in 1842. In 1845 they were at Swamps, and by 1852 (after **Charles'** death and that of their fourth child) at Swan Reach. The closeness of the families is demonstrated by the facts that **Patrick Creevey**, husband of **Joanna's** sister **Margaret**, was sponsor at the baptism of the short lived **Charles Junior** in 1845; and **Joanna's** older brother **John** sponsored the younger **Patrick**, in 1846 who died at under six years old.

Charles Tighe died in 1850, living only to age 41. When **Joanna** died some 35 years later in 1885, she was recorded as **Joanna Mason**, father **John Mason**, mother **Joanna**. We don't know why she was not recorded as **Joanna Tighe**. She had certainly lived much longer without her husband than with him, and raised her children presumably very much on her own.

---

1 **Joanna Mason** b. 1823, m. Protestant **Charles Tighe** 20 Jun 1841, witness **Oliver Mason**. **Tighe** arrived 1833 as a convict on *Royal Admiral* for 'stealing a shawl', baptised 1843 RC in West Maitland. Settler, previously convict, d. 1850. Recorded as Charles Tye, age 41. DC. V185038 36A
  2 **William Tighe**, b. 6 Apr 1842 BC. V1842 2145 61
  2 **Margaret Tighe**, b. 7 Jan 1844 m. **Edmund Brohan** Liverpool 1865
  2 **Charles Tighe**, b. 28 Jul 1845 Sponsors **Patrick Creevey, Mary Mahony**, d. 12 Dec 1845
  2 **Patrick Tighe**, b. 13 Dec 1846 Sponsored by **John Mason**, d. 19 Apr 1852

Chapter 5: The migrating Mason daughters

Margaret (Mason) Creevey: b. 1825 d. 8 Apr 1870

DAUGHTER OF JOHN AND JOHANNA MASON
SISTER TO MARY, JOANNA, JOHN, OLIVER AND DANIEL
BORN IN TIPPERARY IRELAND,
ARRIVED ON THE *CHINA* 19 DEC 1839
MARRIED EX-CONVICT PATRICK CREEVEY 15 APR 1844, B. 1809, D. 1871

From research and writings by Keith Creevey

Margaret Mason was only 14 when she arrived in Australia with her family on the *China* in 1839, and officialdom still considered her a child. On landing, she therefore went with her family to **William Bucknell**'s Paterson's River property to which they were allocated. At 18, she married **Patrick Creevey**, as his second wife, at Maitland on 15 Apr 1844. An ex-convict, **Patrick** arrived in Australia on the *Royal Admiral* in 1833 with 255 other convicts. Amongst them was the man who married **Margaret's** sister **Joanna** — **Charles Tighe/Tye**. The two families witnessed each other's ceremonies in following years and the convict ship voyage must have ensured **Patrick's** introduction to the family.

Patrick was born in Kilbeggan, Co Westmeath, Ireland in 1809, second son of **Patrick** and **Catherine (Rebet/Rabbitte) Creevey**. The township has several old substantial **Creevey** tombstones, which suggests the family was reasonably wealthy. However, his father was a farmer and the sons were farm servants. At 23 **Patrick** was transported to Botany Bay. He was 164 cm tall, had a ruddy freckled complexion, brown hair and hazel eyes. He had a large scar over his left temple and a large scar on his left leg. He was single and could read only.

The story of his crime is told by the investigating constable at the time:

Around 7 PM, Friday, 4th May 1832, an armed party of men entered the house of a James and Mary Quinn at Lara [not far from Kilbeggan]. They brought James outside his door, made him kneel, then fired 2 shots over his head, then gave him notice under the penalty of death, to leave the place by the next morning. Quinn left the following morning, and went to live at Moate. The Quinns were pensioners.

Signed Constable C. Ormsby, Kilbeggan.

The perpetrators were **Patrick Creevey**, his brother **John** and their cousin, **Lackey Creevey**, and the three stood trial on 12 Jul 1832. The offence was listed as 'Attempting to compel James Quinn by threats and menaces, to quit his place of abode'. **Patrick**, **John** and **Lackey** were what were known as 'Whiteboys', part of a secret agrarian society with increasing bitterness towards tithes and rackrent, poor harvests and a fall in the price of cereals in the 1830s. The tactics used by the Whiteboys included sending of threatening letters, digging up pasture land, mutilating livestock, burning estate property, intimidating landlords and assaulting stewards. Occasionally they resorted to murder. Convictions for these offences often resulted in death by hanging or transportation to Botany Bay for terms of between seven years and life. In this case, all three were charged with violent assault and sentenced to transportation for seven years.

Patrick, **John** and **Lackey** spent the best part of a year aboard the *Essex* hulk in Dublin harbour until they were transported on the *Royal Admiral* on 4 Jun 1833. The ship made only one stop at Cape Town on the way, arriving in Botany Bay on 20 Oct 1833. To ensure prisoners completed the voyage in reasonable health, ships' masters were paid a bonus of half a guinea per head for each convict delivered alive and well. The master's bonus for this trip would have been a very comfortable 105 guineas. It is on this voyage that **Patrick Creevey** and **Charles Tighe** met each other.

Sydney had only been established 45 years when **Patrick** arrived, and then had a population of about 45,000. It consisted of 1200 buildings of which nearly 75 were made from stone, 250 from brick and the remainder from timber or wattle and daub. Whale oil lamps illuminated the streets, electricity being another 60 years away. The streets were wide by English standards, but unsealed, so were dusty when dry and turned into a quagmire when wet. All land transport was dependent on either horse- or bullock-drawn vehicles as the first railway in NSW was 25 years away. **Patrick** was only one of 162,000 convicts overall, including 39,000 of his own countrymen.

Chapter 5: The migrating Mason daughters

Arrival of the Royal Admiral in 1833 and Patrick's later freedom:

Surname	First Name	Ship	Arrival	Certificate of Freedom	COF Issued	Ticket of Leave
Creevey	Patrick	Royal Admiral	1833	39/2229	10 Dec 1839	TL 37/1653

Patrick was fortunate in that he was disposed from the ship to **Campbell Drummond Riddell**, a Scot of high standing in the Sydney community. He was Colonial Treasurer and director of the Australian Colonial and General Life Assurance and Annuity Company of George St, Sydney. **Patrick**'s relations **John** and **Lackey** were also assigned to **Riddel**, as was another relative, **Bryan**, when he arrived in 1836.

At the time of **Patrick**'s arrival in the Colony, his bondsman **Riddell** had just acquired 17 acres at what was then known as Mrs Darling Point (later Darling Point), and was about to commence building an imposing sandstone residence on the site. **Patrick**, his brother and cousin were all sent to the building site as labourers and gardeners.

When it was completed, **Riddell** named his home *Lindesay* and it was, and still is, one of the showplaces of Sydney, the venue of many celebrity gatherings. It was the first home to be built at (now 1 Carthona St) Darling Point, and was clearly visible from passing ships as they sailed up the harbour. Fortunately, it is now under the care of the National Trust.

Patrick was granted a Ticket of Leave on 2 Dec 1837, four years after his arrival, stipulating that he reside in Maitland for the remaining three years of his sentence. **Riddell** actually petitioned by letter to the Governor that Patrick be allowed to stay in the Sydney area, in his service. **Riddell** wrote:

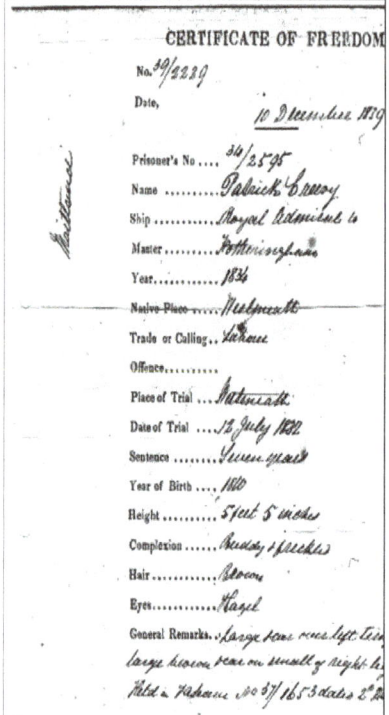

Patrick Creevey's Certificate of Freedom 1839

Sir, I have the honour to request that you obtain the sanction of the his Excellency the Governor to retaining in my service the convict named in the margin [Patrick Creevey] who has been lately gazetted for his Ticket of Leave but has not yet obtained it. It is understood that his Ticket of Leave is for the district of Maitland but he has been with me ever since he came to the Colony and has never been before a bench of Magistrates, altho' living in the immediate vicinity of Sydney at the time. I shall take it as a favour to be allowed to retain his services, and the man himself is anxious to remain with me. I have the honour to be Sir, your most obedient servant,

Signed C.D. Riddell April 20th 1838.

It is unclear what the result of that petition was, but **Patrick** was in the Maitland district in 1839, when he received his Certificate of Freedom, recognising that he had finished his sentence, and taking effect on 10th Dec 1839.

In 1840 **Patrick** married his first wife, **Catherine McManus**, when they were both 31 years old. **Catherine** was also a convict, arriving on the *Margaret* in January 1839 from Dublin. They settled near Morpeth in an area known as The Swamp where **Patrick** took up farming. Unfortunately, **Catherine** died 3 years later and was buried at East Maitland. It seems they had a son, who was born and died in 1842, so **Catherine** may have died in childbirth.

In loving memory of Margaret Creevey, died 8 April 1870, aged 44 years
And of Patrick her husband, who died 25 Nov 1871

Patrick sponsored **Charles junior**, son of **Charles** and **Joanna (Mason) Tighe** in 1841, but the youngster died at the age of only five months. **Charles Mason** and **Patrick Creepy** knew each other from being on the same convict transport. Later, **Patrick's** second wife **Margaret Mason Creevey** continued the practice of sponsorship by standing for nephew **John**, son of **John and Mary (Hickey) Mason** in 1852. Sponsorships of births or marriages demonstrate a status for the sponsor in the community. For **Patrick**, surely it shows he had outlived his background as Whiteboy and convict, and was making his way in the new land and community.

When **Patrick** married **Margaret Mason** in 1844, his father-in-law **John Mason** defined himself as a farmer in the Morpeth district. On the 1854 census **Patrick's** occupation is a carpenter, in 1863 he's a farmer, residing 1841-1859 in Swamps, Morpeth, before and after his marriage to **Margaret Mason**. His death certificate shows **Patrick** as a farmer.

Around 1863, with six children, **Patrick** and **Margaret** left the Morpeth district and moved to Dungowan, 16 kilometres south of Tamworth, according to the Liverpool Plains Electoral Rolls of 1869/70. They were the first of the family to move nearer Tamworth, perhaps giving impetus to the rest of the family to move there too. Grain crops and dairy farming supported the Dungowan district, although many came to the district in search of alluvial gold in nearby Dungowan and Swamp Creeks. In **Patrick**'s time, the township had one hotel, a baker, butcher, community hall, and a butter factory, which operated from 1860 until 1904.

Margaret died of tuberculosis on 8 Apr 1870, aged 44. **Patrick** died from dropsy (Oedema) on 23 Jan 1871, aged 61. Both are buried in the Roman Catholic section of East Tamworth Cemetery.

Death and burial records for Margaret (Mason) Creevey

Reference	Died	Born	Surname	First Name	Father	Mother	Location
5966/1870	8 April 1870	c1825	Creevey	Margaret	John Mason	Johanna	Tamworth

Death and burial records for Patrick Creevey

Reference	Died	Born	Surname	First Name	Location
5831/1871	25 Nov 1871	1810	Creevey	Patrick	Tamworth

Patrick and **Margaret's** children stayed on at Dungowan until some time between 1873 and 1875, with the exception of son **Patrick Francis**, who married in 1865 and by 1871 was living in Augathella, Queensland. **James, John, Malachy** and **Bernard** settled in the New England and Gwydir districts of NSW. **Johanna** lived in Dungowan from 1863 until just after the death of her parents in 1870 and 1871, then moved to Sydney. She married **Henry Moore (Harry) Richards**, producing five children to him, the first one being born and dying in 1879, when she was 22. Her marriage date, however, is recorded a bit later, as 1881.

We know little of **Patrick Creevey's** relatives' history in this country. **John** was married with three children and could read and write, and returned to Ireland after completing his sentence late in 1839. **Lackey** was 35, married with a son, could read and write, and was disabled in the left arm. Little is known of him after he received his Certificate of Freedom in December 1839. The third brother, **Bryan**, aged 25, was charged with a similar offence to his brothers and cousin and arrived on the *Surry* in 1836. As far as can be determined, he never returned to Ireland.

Margaret and **Patrick's** daughter **Johannah's** husband **Harry Richards** died at sea in 1890, widowing **Johanna** at 33. Their last two children died in infancy in 1890 and 1891. She then remarried, at the age of 37 in 1894, **William Norton,** to whom she produced two more children — both long-living and producing grandchildren. **Johannah** lived to the age of 77 in 1934, outliving her second husband **William Norton** by eight years.

Chapter 5: The migrating Mason daughters

Johannah Margaret Creevey b 1858 Dungowan d 1934 Fairfield and her first husband **Henry Moore Richards**, whom she married when she was 24. She was the daughter of **Patrick and Margaret (Mason) Creevey**

Death records of Johannah Creevey's husbands

Death Certificate	Surname	First Name	Father	Mother	Location
461/1890	Richards	Henry	Henry M	Johanna	Sydney
5226/1926	Norton	William	William	Sarah	Sydney

1 **Margaret Mason** b. 1825 Cahir, Tipperary, IRL d. 8 Apr 1870 Dungowan Creek m. **Patrick Creevey** 15 Apr 1844 Maitland b. 1809 Kilbeggan, Ireland d. 23 Jan 1871 Dungowan Creek
2 **John Patrick Creevey** b. 1845 East Maitland d. 18 Sep 1901 m. **Sarah Mary Frances Rowling** 1875 Tamworth b. 1856 Singleton, NSW d. 1945 Punchbowl
2 **Patrick Francis Creevey** b. 27 Feb 1847 East Maitland NSW d. 28 Jun 1928 Augathella Qld m. **Jane Preston/Thompson** 1865 b. 8 Aug 1847 Sydney d. 27 Feb 1906 Iva Downs, Augathella Qld
2 **James William Creevey** b. 26 Mar 1849 East Maitland d. 1 Mar 1884 Lonewood, Singleton m. **Harriet Smith** c1874 Tamworth NSW b. 1855 UK d. 1926 Warialda
2 **Malachi Creevey** b. 1851 East Maitland d. 1921 Chiltern, Vic m. **Mary Coyle** 19 Jan 1873 Dungowan, Tamworth MC. 3973/1873 (his name spelt Mallick)
2 **Bernard Creevey** b. 9 Jan 1854 East Maitland, d. 26 Dec 1936 Base Hospital, Tamworth
2 **Johannah Margaret Creevey** b. 19 Nov 1857 Lochinvar d. 4 May 1934 Fairfield Westm. **Henry Moore Richards** 7 Dec 1881 Registry Office b. 1848 London, d. 1890 at sea m2. **William Norton** 1894
[Children of Johannah Margaret Creevey and Henry Moore Richards]
    3 **Annie Richards** b. 1879 Benevolent Asylum, Sydney d.1879
    3 **Mabel Richards** b. 1881 Dubbo NSW
    3 **Beatrice Ann Richards** b. c1883 Launceston, Tasmania d. 1956 Kogarah Hospital m. **John Thomas Creevey** 1906 Redfern b. 1883 Inverell d. 1952 Hurstville NSW
    3 **Daphne Ann Creevey** b. 1911 Randwick d. 1912
    3 **Raymond John Creevey** b. 1912 Kingsford NSW d. 2007 Mt Lofty Nursing Home, Toowoomba Qld m. **Stella Eva Mitchell** 1933 Randwick NSW b. 1912 Boolaroo, NSW d. 1970 Calgary Hospital, Kogarah
    3 **Ronald Dardenelles Creevey** b. 1915 Randwick d. 1971 Sydney m. **Joyce** 1948 Hurstville b. 1916 Maitland d. 1993 Greenacre
    3 **Gloria Mary Creevey** b. 1917 Randwick d. 2006 Alice Springs, NT m. **Vincent Dennis Seymour** 1939 Randwick b. 1920 Kensington
    3 **Patrick Charles Creevey** b. 1920 Randwick NSW d. 2003 Falls Creek, Vic m. **Joyce Ellen Williams** 1945 Kogarah NSW b. 1921 Lismore NSW d. 2000 Falls Creek Vic
    3 **Aubry Joseph Creevey** b. 1925 Randwick NSW
    3 **Anthony John Creevey** b. 1938 (adopted)
    3 **Henry Moore Richards** b. 1889 Benevolent Asylum Sydney d. 1890 Sydney
    3 **Florence I Richards** b. 1891 d. 1891
[Children of Johannah Margaret Creevey and William Norton]
    3 **Sydneyora Richards/Norton** b. 1896 North Sydney d. 1973 North Rocks NSW m. **James Alfred Berwick Liebs** 1920 Sydney b. 1879 Brisbane d. 1949 Granville
    3 **Willoughby R N Creevey/Richards/Norton** b. 1897 St Leonards d. 1950 Berry NSW m. **Annie** d. 1934

Three Convicts

It is difficult to understand why all three daughters of this migrating family from Tipperary married ex-convicts.

Mary, 27, to **Thomas Sheridan**, 44, married in 1840, 12 months after arrival, in Sydney town.
Joanna, 18, to **Charles Tighe**, 38, married in June 1841, 18 months after arrival, in Maitland.
Margaret, 18, to **Patrick Creevey**, 31, married in 1844, 4 years after arrival, in Maitland

Marriageable females were short in the colony — part of the reason Caroline Chisholm, a philanthropist and reformer who worked very hard for the general safety of women's lives in the 1840s, bringing out many single girls to marry and settle here. These three Mason girls were young, presumably strong and healthy — no evidence to the contrary appears in the immigration records — so it is hard to explain. Love is unlikely to have come into the equation in all cases, and land grants to emancipated convicts no longer existed, so land ownership was not the drawcard. Tighe and Creevey had arrived on the same transport, the *Royal Admiral*, in 1833, which established a relationship between them. Sheridan had been here since the transport *Boyne* arrived in 1826. One wonders for whom these marriages were advantageous.

Then finally one realises the class and the country that the family came from. Poor and Irish, with no doubt memories of the injustice and oppression that they left behind them. The new husbands came from much the same background — Creevey as a 'Whiteboy', demonstrably against oppression; Sheridan for 'sacrilege' of whatever sort; and Tighe for 'stealing a shawl' for unknown reasons.

The 'crimes' which these fellow-Irish convicts had committed included, in a very generous view, demonstrable opposition to the much disliked powers in Ireland, as well as thefts to provide sustenance for their families. Thus the ex-convicts were seen with empathy by the Irish here. Companions in thought, rather than 'convict' and 'free' opposites.

Chapter 6

The Mason Bible

Oliver and Ann (Fitzgerald) Mason's Bible.

The printed work, brass decorated, is dated 1748.

Inherited from the **Oliver Masons** by their son **Charles**, then his son **Oliver Alphonsus Mason**, then **Marie (Mason) Lyons**, and now **Terry** and **Monica (Murphy) Mason**

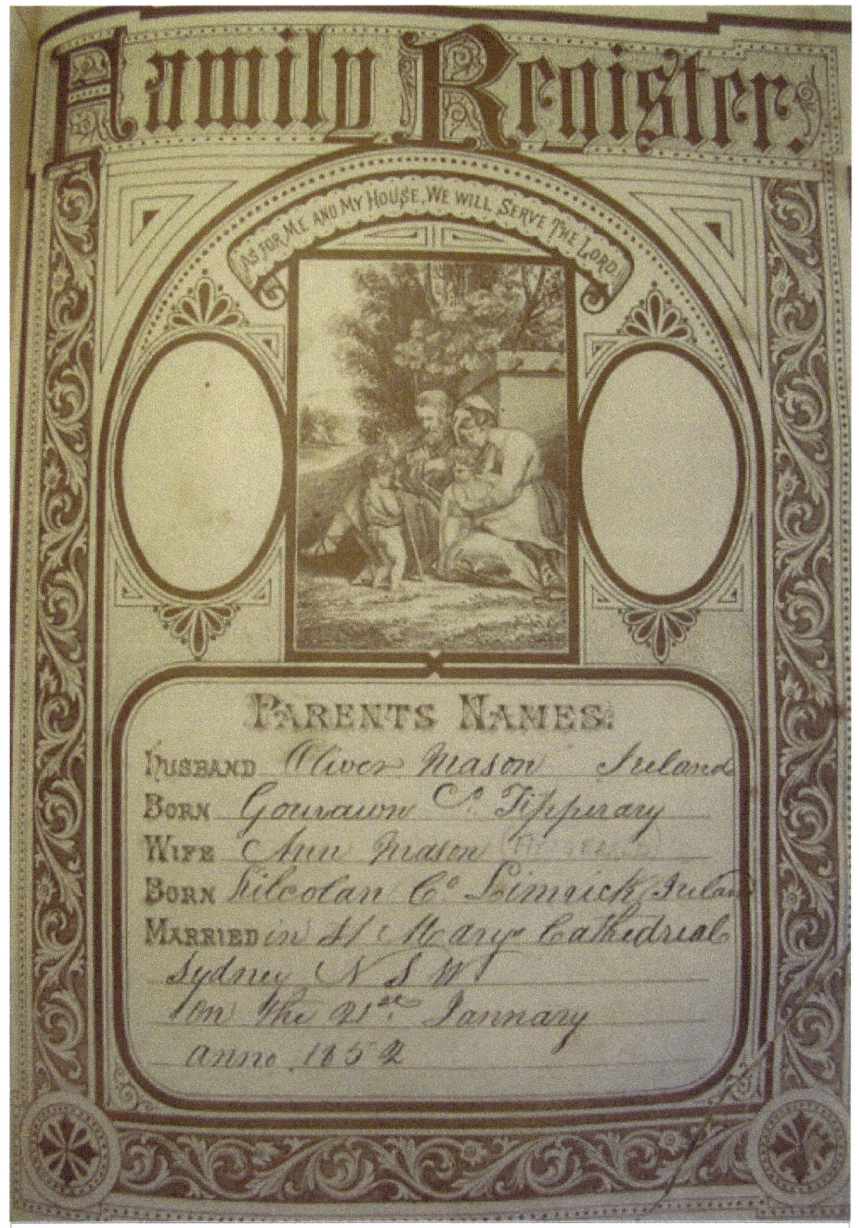

**Family Register
Parents Names**
Husband - Oliver Mason Ireland
Born - Gourawn [Golden] Co Tipperary
Wife - Ann Mason (Fitzgerald)
Born - Kilcolan Co Limerick, IRL
Married - in St Mary's Cathedral Sydney NSW
on the 21st January 1852

Chapter 6: The Mason Bible

Children's names
John b. Morpeth Dec 14 1853
Oliver b. Williams Rd 9? Apr 1858
Patrick b. Raymond Tce 9 May 1859
Charles b. Port Stephens 13 Jul 1862
James b. Raymond Tce 21 May 1856
Terrence b. 14 Dec 1863

Children's Names
Joseph born 29 March 1865
Josephine b 19? February in Hornsby 1930
to Rosemary Lollbach & Oliver Mason
Colleen Mason b. 6 January 1943
in Hornsby NSW to Rosemary & Oliver Mason
Annette Mason born Hornsby NSW 1932
to Netta Garrett & Oliver Mason
Catherine Mason b. Hornsby NSW 1933
to Netta Garrett & Oliver Mason
Clare Mason b. 29 Dec 1931 in Hornsby
to Netta & Oliver Mason
Rubie Mason b. 1 June 1888
Charles Mason b. 12 April 1893

Chapter 6: The Mason Bible

Marriages
Patrick married 6 September 1883
St Nicholas Tamworth
Hannah Mason b. 9 (?) 1885
Bartholomew Mason b. 6 April 1887
Margaret Mason b. 1 May 1885
John Mason b. 8 Dec 1886
Jane Mason b. 1 Feb 1895
Rubie Mason b. 1 June 1888
Charles Vincent Mason b. 12 April 1893

Marriages
James married in St Michaels Tamworth
Mary Terese born Cockburn River Jun 12 1879
Ann Mason born 13 October 1881
Patrick Daniel born Glengarvon 29 Oct 1880
Hannah May Mason born 9 May 1885
Ann Mason born 13 October 1881

Chapter 6: The Mason Bible

Sacred to the Memory of
Oliver Mason who died on 7 April 1891
Mrs Ann Mason who died on 1 August age 66
Ruby Mason died on 8 August 1890

Sacred to the Memory of
Charles Vincent born 12 April 1893
John Cecil Mason born 30 May 1893
James Augustine born 23 Dec 1894
Irene born 18 July 1897

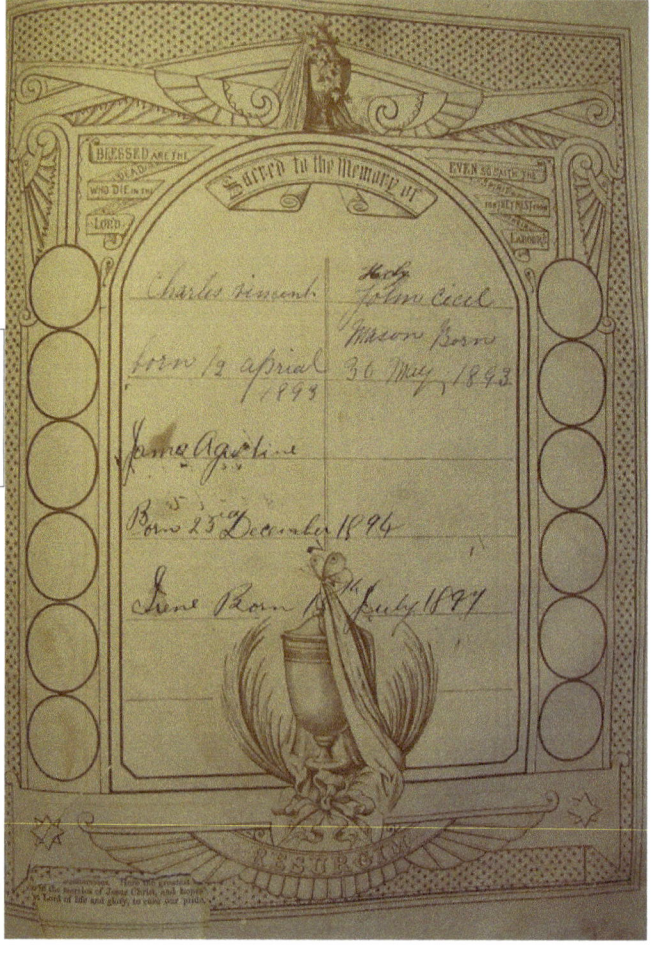

Chapter 7

The Full Mason Family Tree

> The following family trees are of
> John Mason III and his brother
> the migrating Oliver Mason,
> as well as their migrating sisters.
>
> They show the forebears and ALL the
> descendants to enable readers
> to work out their own ancestors.
>
> ENJOY!

Chapter 7: The Full Mason Family Tree

The full Family Tree of John Mason III of Tipperary, Ireland.

Red text defines a writer/contributor to this family history

1. **John Mason I** was born in Cahir Tipperary, Ireland c1760, and died c1798. He married **Margaret O'Connor**, and did not migrate to Australia.
    2 **John Mason II** was born c1793 Cahir, Tipperary, Ireland, married **Joanna (Johanna, Hannah) Quigley** 1811 Cashel, migrated to Australia in the China, arriving in December 1839, and died here on 10 Jan 1858 Swan Reach, NSW, from a 'coup de soleil'. **Joanna** was born 1792 in Cashel, Tipperary, Ireland, migrated with him, and died 6 Apr 1857 Swan Reach, Morpeth.

---

3 **John Mason III** b. 1816 Golden, Tipperary, IRL. Gravestone d. 12 Oct 1879 Tamworth DC 9059/1879 m1. **Mary Hickey** 14 Jan 1850 b. 1827 Tipperary? d. 21 Jun 1860 Morpeth NSW. m2. **Maria Maher** 3 Aug 1863 Singleton, NSW b. 1844, Thurles, Tipp IRL d. 27 May 1905 Tamworth
   [Children of John Mason III and Mary Hickey]
   4 **John Mason IV** b. 10 Dec 1852 BC 1080 Vol. 70. d. 1858 DC 4071/1858 Maitland
   4 **Cornelius Mason** b. 2 Aug 1854 BC 1128 Vol. 71. Morpeth. d. 18 Sep 1934 Kiola Pte Hospital, Armidale m. **Janet Mitchell** 1 Jul 1878 MC 2213/1878 Cameron's Creek, Armidale. d. 9 Jul 1933 Armidale NSW
      5 **Matilde Mary Mason** b. 5 Oct 1879 BC 08539 Armidale d. 5 Oct 1964 Neringah Home of Peace, Wahroonga m. **Percival Charles Drew** 1905 Armidale b. 1870 Armidale d. 21 Dec 1953 State Hospital, Lidcombe
         6 **Dorothy Janet Drew** b. 1907 Armidale d. m. **Frank B Lopez** 2 Feb 1929 Ref 1052/1929 Rockdale: St Pauls Anglican Church, Kogarah, NSW b. 1876 London, England d. c1956 Rockdale.
      5 **William George Mason**, renamed **Thomas Mitchell Mason** b. 1881 BC 24360/1881 at Walcha (66km from Armidale) d. 24 Apr 1970 Armidale & New England Hospital, Armidale m. **Mary Barry** 1905 Armidale
         6 **Cornelius A Mason**
         6 **Kathleen E Mason** b. 1907 d. early, Armidale
   4 **Matilda Mason** b. 1857 d. 1857
   4 **Johanna Mason** b. 23 Oct 1857 Windermere BC 8509/1857. d. 20 Nov 1930 tuberculosis, Randwick. m. **William Henry Hill** 28 May 1881 Sydney. MC 731/1881, St Barnabas Anglican Church, George St Sydney b. 18 Aug 1858 Pitt Town NSW d. 28 Sep 1888 Cholera, at his home in Eden St, St Leonards
      5 **William Hill** b. 1882 St Leonards BC 9335/1882 d. 1949 DC 0975/1949
      5 **Edith Hill** b. 1884 Redfern BC 9934/1884 d. 1964 DC 30894/1964 m. **Frederick Mashford** 1902 St Leonards MC 7619/1902 d. 1946 Mosman NSW
         6 **William Frederick Mashford** b. 1903 St Leonards district BC 34099/1903 d. 1958 Chatswood m. **Harriett Patricia Madden** 1926 MC 6336/1926 d. 1958 Chatswood, Sydney DC 9875/1958
            7 **Beverley Mashford** b. c1905 d. 1930 Mosman
         6 **Gladys E(dith?) Mashford** b. 1906 m. **Albert E Bryant** 1928 St Leonards
         6 **Ivy E(dith?) Mashford** b. 1909 (twin Myrtle) St Leonards BC 18915/1909 d. 1909 at less than one year old in St Leonards DC 7079/1909
         6 **Myrtle May Mashford** b. 1909 St Leonards BC 18914/1909 m. **Reginald Hamilton Tippett** 1937 North Sydney MC 2325/1937
         6 **Thomas Henry Mashford** b. c1912 d. 1972 Neutral Bay Convalescent Hospital m. **Emily ?**
            7 **Thomas Mashford** b.? d. 1951 DC 13272/1951
               8 **Thomas Mashford** b.? d. 1946 DC 25557/1946
         6 **Joyce Gwendoline Mashford** b.? d. 1941 DC 12096/1941 Randwick m. **Charles Campbell** 1939 North Sydney MC 10554/1939
      5 **Emily Hill** b. 1886 Sydney BC 470/1886 d. 23 Mar 1956 Newington State Hosp, Newington m. **John (Jack) Crighton** 1908 Chatswood d. 1955 Parramatta
         6 **Arthur E Crighton** b. 1910 Ref 43268/1910 d. 1911
         6 **Myra Crighton** b.? d. 1922 very young
         6 **Mildred Catherine Crighton** b.? d. 1949 North Sydney
      5 **John Hill** b. 1888 St Leonards BC 12931/1888 d. 1907
      5 **Arthur Edward Hill** b. 1889 or 1892 not registered d. 1969 Mater Hospital Crows Nest m. **Olive Irene Jahns** 1916 b. 1895 Tamworth d. 1956
         6 **Lillian Hill** b. 1916 d. 2007 m. **Cyril Adrian Muir** 1939 North Sydney b. 1906 d. 2002
         6 **Audrey Olive Mavis Hill** b. 1920 Tamworth d. 2004 m. **Frederick Jamison Gibbes** 1943 North Sydney b. 1909 d.1981

   7 **Stephen Gibbes** b. 1953
[Children of John Mason III and Maria Maher]
 4 **Oliver Peter Mason** b. 29 Jun 1864 Dunmore NSW d. 12 Apr 1935 DC 7880/1935 m. **Annie Bezant** 23 Apr 1905 Tamworth, b. 11 Jan 1862 Braidwood NSW d. 26 Dec 1957 Nazareth House, Tamworth.
  5 **Mary Mason** b. 1908 Tamworth d. 1 Feb 1929 Marius St, Tamworth
 4 **Patrick P Mason** b. 20 Apr 1866 Morpeth, BC 10986, reg Dunmore d. 17 May 1881 age 15
 4 **Dennis (Dan) Mason** b. 7 May 1868 Singleton, Patricks Plain. d. 10 Aug 1932 Lismore, m. **Emily Maude Smith** 1893 MC 84785 East Maitland b. 1871 Armidale 9 Apr 1947 Lismore
  5 **Arthur Mason** b. 1900 BC 28843 d. 1902
 4 **William John Mason** b. 7 Aug 1870 Hannahton (now Wittingham) reg. Singleton d. 11 Jan 1935 Bankstown m. **Priscilla Ann Smith** 25 Apr 1898 Tamworth MC 4209 b. 24 Aug 1878 Bullawa Creek (Narrabri) d. 23 Dec 1968 Bankstown
  5 **Arthur William Mason** b. 29 Jul 1898 Tamworth d. 1968? 1946? England? US?
  5 **Ethel Mason** b. 1900 d. 1902 Rubella?
  5 **Victor Oliver Mason** b. 3 Oct 1902 d. 6 Apr 1985 Tugun, Qld m. **Catherine Florence (Cath) Hogan** 31 Oct 1931 Sydney. MC 14624 b. 6 Apr 1905 Brewarrina, NSW d. 30 Nov 1983 Tugun, Qld [daughter of John Bernard Hogan and Jessie Maude Douglass]
   6 Janet Claire (Jan) (Mason, Fagan) O'Donnell b. 14 Oct 1932 Windermere Private Hospital, Melbourne m1. **Arthur Fagan** 8 May 1955 Rose Bay, Sydney b. 24 Jul 1930 Divorced d. <1970 m2. **Cyril Francis (Cy) O'Donnell** 12 Dec 1968 Lae, New Guinea b. 27 Jul 1922 New Zealand d. 11 Jun 2006 Macleay Island, Qld [son of Francis Leonard O'Donnell and Lilla Cecilia (Dot) Brewer]
   6 Helen Marie (Mason) Malcher b. 24 Sep 1935 Rose Bay Hospital m. **Heinrich Carl (Harry) Malcher** 8 Apr 1961 Sydney b. 1Apr 1925 an Austrian, born in Turramurra, NSW [son of Franz Xaver Ernst Malcher and Hedwig Barbara Malik]
    7 Victoria Frances (Vicki) Malcher b. 16 Aug 1964 Sydney m1. **Timothy Martin Brown** 28 Nov 1992 div. Apr 1997 Sydney b. 31 Oct 1961 Middlesborough, England m2.(df) **Scott William Richardson** 28 Jul 1999-30 Sep 2013 b. 11 Sep 1963 Helensburgh, Scotland
    7 Alexandra Jane Louise (Sandy, Alex) (Malcher, Mitchell) Fullerton b. 18 Sep 1966 Sydney m1. **Graeme Paul Mitchell** 14 Jan 1989 div. 3 Nov 2004 Sydney b. 22 Sep 1964 Maidenhead, England [son of Gary Donald Mitchell and Ann Camille Fowler] m2. **Ian Neil Fullerton** 20 Nov 2014 Maleny, Qld b. 10 Jun 1956 Nambour, Qld [son of Hector Fullerton and Daisy Lillian Cross]
    [Children of Sandy Malcher and Graeme Paul Mitchell]
     8 **Flynn Oliver Gary Mitchell** b. 13 Jan 1998 Buderim, Qld
     8 **Elouise Victoria (Ella) Mitchell** b. 18 Nov 2000 Nambour, Qld
    [Children of Ian Neil Fullerton]
     8 **Kate Daisy Fullerton** b. 2 Mar 1989, identical twin
     8 **Sarah Jill Fullerton** b. 2 Mar 1989, identical twin
     8 **Laura Rose Fullerton** b. 15 Nov 1990
     8 **Ellen Amelia Fullerton** b. 12 Nov 1992
     8 **James Ian Fullerton** b. 4 Nov 1995
    7 **Christopher Charles (Chris) Malcher** b. 14 Nov 1968 Sydney m. **Giang Le Truong** 5 Dec 2009 Sydney b. 24 Nov 1972 Hung Yen, Vietnam [daughter of Truong Viet Hung and Le Thuy Dau]
     8 **Oliver Truong Malcher** b. 24 Jun 2012 Canberra
     8 **Emily Le Malcher** b. 2 July 2014 Canberra
  5 **John Edward (Jack) Mason** b. 21 Oct 1905 Waterloo d. 17 Jun 1976 Sydney m. **Carmela (Mella) Macare** 2 Dec 1930 Bankstown NSW, b. 11 Oct 1908 High St, Loanhead, Scotland. d. 7 Mar 1981
   6 **Clarice Margaret Mason** b. 12 Oct 1931 Lakemba, NSW m. **John Arthur (Blade) Reid** 1 Oct 1954-1997 St Andrew's, Summer Hill NSW b. 24 Mar 1932
    7 **Ross James Reid** b. 5 Jul 1956 'Ross Reid' Subiaco, Perth, WA. m1. **Christine Helen Street** 4 Dec 1980, St Ives,b. 20 Aug 1959 Murwillumbah, NSW. Divorced. m2. **Fariba Soltani** 26 Jun 1993 Wahroonga
    [Children of Ross Reid and Christine Street]
     8 **Melanie Jane Reid** b. 9 Aug 1984 Hornsby
     8 **Caroline Michelle Reid** b. 27 Feb 1987
     8 **Nicholas James Reid** b. 10 Aug 1990 Hornsby
    [Children of Ross James Reid and Fariba Soltani]
     8 **Sam Reid** b. 26 Aug 1998 NSH St Leonards
    7 **Glenn John Reid** b. 19 Apr 1958 Subiaco, Perth, WA m. **Jennifer Margaret Stanley** 1 Dec 1984 St James, Turramurra, NSW b. 17 Mar 1962 Wahroonga, NSW

Chapter 7: The Full Mason Family Tree

        8 **Jessica Nicole Reid** b. 23 Feb 1989 Newcastle, NSW (fraternal twin)
        8 **Kate Elizabeth Reid** b. 23 Feb 1989 Newcastle NSW (fraternal twin)
        8 **Eliza Margret Reid** b. 16 Apr 1993 Wahroonga, Sydney Adventist Hospital
    7 **Brett Mathew Reid** b. 2 Oct 1960 South Perth m. **Judith (Jude) Bowen Triemer** 8 May 1982 Christ Church, St Ives NSW b. 4 Apr 1963 St Leonards
        8 **Michael John Reid** b. 26 Apr 1996 Wahroonga, Sydney Adventist Hospital
        8 **Andrew Jules** b. 17 Oct 1997 Wahroonga Sydney Adventist Hospital
5 **Eric Francis Donald Mason** b. 12 Jun 1910 Waterloo d. 31 Jul 1968 Corrimal m. **Thelma Mary Davies** 6 Feb 1937 Punchbowl, NSW. b. 17 Dec 1912 d. 25 July 1999 Killarney Vale Nursing Home NSW
    6 **William Eric (Bill) Mason** b. 2 Sep 1937 Wollongong, NSW m. **Sally Anne (Anne) Benjamin** 18 Apr 1960 Corrimal NSW b. 21 Dec 1940 Wollongong NSW
        7 **Sharon Narelle Mason** b. 6 Feb 1961 Bulli m. **James Richard Salatnay** 19 Sept 1998 Ingleside, NSW b. 15 Sep 1965
            8 **Zachary Mason** b. 4 May 1998 Mona Vale
            8 **Zoe Kathleen Salatnay** b. 28 Nov 1999 Mona Vale
        7 **Glenn Anthony Mason** b. 18 Feb 1962 Bulli
    6 **John Robert Mason** b. 14 Sep 1941 Corrimal NSW m1. **Dorothy Callahor** Wollongong m2. **Robyn Grant** m3. **Sue Ballard** 1994 Perth WA m4. **Lorraine Donaldson**
[Children of John Robert Mason and Dorothy Callahor]
        7 **Debbie Mason** b. 13 Nov 1962 Wollongong
        7 **Mark Mason** b. 29 Jan 1965 Wollongong
[Children of John Robert Mason and Sue Ballard]
        7 **Joshua Mason** b. 1994 Perth, WA
    6 **Rhonda Mason** b. c1944 Fostered. Returned to Institution.
    6 **Dennis James Mason** b. 25 Sep 1948 Corrimal, NSW m. **Marilyn Sweeney** b. 22 Sep 1949
        7 **Kylie Mason** b. 16 Nov 1974 Wollongong m. **Scott Osborne** 19 Feb 2000 Moorooduc Vic
            8 **Ella Louise Osborne** b. 19 Jan 2003 Melbourne
            8 **Abby Georgia Osborne** b. 28 Sep 2005 Melbourne Cabrini Hospital, Brighton
        7 **Bradley Mason** b. 15 Jun 1977 Wollongong NSW m. **Katie Hewitt** 28 Feb 2009 Eltham, Vic
        7 **Grant Mason** b. 5 Apr 1979 Frankston Vic m. **Sarah Cannon** 30 Aug 2009 Sydney, NSW
    6 **Eric John Mason** b. 22 Feb 1950 Corrimal, m. **Linda Giles** 1970 Wollongong
        7 **Adam Mason** b. 2 Jan 1971 d. 1994 Wollongong
        7 **Chantel Mason** b. 17 Aug 1972
        7 **Heath Mason** b. 15 Aug 1973
5 **Hilton Matthew Mason** b. 24 Feb 1913 Redfern, NSW d. 16 Sep 1981 m. **Thelma Mabel Denny** 5 Oct 1940 St Saviors Church, Punchbowl b. 1 Dec 1914 d. 23 Sep 1988 Hurstville, Sydney
    6 **Pamela Mason** b. 26 April 1941 Royal Hospital for Women, Paddington, Sydney d. 8 July 1941
    6 **Lynette Joywyn Mason** b. 12 Sep 1945 Paddington m1. **Paul Evan Lillington** 25 Aug 1967 b. 18 Jun 1948 m2. **Roger Newman** 12 Dec 1992 b. 20 Nov 1942 New Zealand d. 17 Mar 2014
[Children of Lynette Mason and Paul Evan Lillington]
        7 **Wade Evan Lillington** b. 21 Dec 1971 m.(df) **Megan Edwards**
            8 **Aidan Manning Lillington**
        7 **Amanda Lillington** b. 16 Nov 1973 m. **Paul Platt** Jan 1999 England
            8 **James Paul Evan Platt**
            8 **Alexander David Platt**
    6 **Robyn Gai Mason** b. 3 April 1947 Royal Hospital for Women, Paddington, Sydney
5 **Robert Joseph (Bob) Mason** b. 19 Aug 1923 Rickard Road, Bankstown NSW d. 10 Jun 1979 DC 13570 m. **Audrey Patricia Parker** 14 Feb 1948 b. 17 Oct 1925 d. 10 Oct 2014
    6 **William David (Bill) Mason** b. 15 Dec 1948 Sydney m. **Barbara deSorcy** 2 Nov 1985 Toronto, Canada b. 13 Apr 1951 Toronto, Canada
    6 **Suzanne (Sue) Marie Mason** b. 17 Aug 1950 Sydney m. **William Thomas Davies III** 14 Feb 1976 b. 17 Nov 1951 Wales
        7 **William Thomas Davies IV** b. 3 Apr 1978 in Cefn Hengood, South Wales m. **Renee** 14 Feb 1975
            8 **Jye Davies**
            8 **Luke Davies**
            8 **Jake Davies**
            8 **Ellie Davies**
        7 **Robert Gareth Davies** b. 2 Aug 1979 m. **Vanessa**

Chapter 7: The full Mason Family Trees

        8 **Shayla Davies**
        8 **Kyuss Davies**
   6 **Linda Louise Mason** b. 8 Aug 1952 m. **Bruce Alexander Parr** 10 Apr 1972 Sydney b. 17 Nov 1951 Wales
      7 **Shane Alexander Parr** b. 16 Oct 1972 Sydney m. **Alison Mary Reid** 13 Jul 2002 Shropshire, UK b. 6 Dec 1969 Bangor, Anglesey, Wales
        8 **Euan Alexander Parr** b. 30 Nov 2002 Manly
        8 **Finnley Stewart Parr** b. 14 May 2004 Shropshire, UK
      7 **Daniel Parr** b. 5 Nov 1974 Upper Hutt NZ m. **Renee Lee Carton** 5 Jan 2007 Carterton
        8 **Riley George Parr** b. 10 May 2008 Lower Hutt
        8 **Mason William Parr** b. 10 May 2010 Lower Hutt NZ
      7 **Katherine Parr** b. 17 Sep 1976 NZ, twin
      7 **Louise Parr** b. 17 Sep 1976, older twin m.(df) **Cesar Concha de Rurange** b. 8 Mar 1981 Santiago, Chile
        8 **Emily Katherine de Rurange** b. 26 Mar 2010 Manly, NSW
        8 **Vivienne Monica de Rurange** b. 29 Sep 2011 Manly, NSW
   6 **Terece Ivy Mason** b. 28 Sep 1954 m. **Gareth Davies** 28 Oct 1990 b. 4 Sep 1954 Wales
      7 **Deinyon Davies** b. 2 Aug 1994 Sydney
4 **Arthur Edmund Mason** b. 29 Apr 1872 d. 9 Sep 1939 118 Victoria St Ashfield. m. **Maude Bailey** 14 Nov 1917 Muswellbrook. b. 9 Aug 1893 Oberon, NSW d. 25 Dec 1974 8 Union St, Lidcombe, NSW. **Maude** married **Tom Nicholls** 6 Nov 1942, after Arthur's death
  5 **Margaret (Peg) Mason** b. 14 Aug 1918 m. **Albert Butt** 31 Mar 1945 b. 5 Jul 1923 d. 5 Jan 1981
    6 **Diana Butt** b. 19 Jul 1947 m. **Kevin Duff**
      7 **James Duff** b. 21 Jan 1971
      7 **Amanda Duff** b. 2 Feb 1972
      7 **Graham Duff** b. 2 Jan 1977
    6 **Kriss Butt** b. 20 Apr 1950 m. **Reg Feutrill** 12 Jan 1973
      7 **Sarah Feutrill** b. 24 Nov 1976
      7 **Reon Feutrill** b. 12 Mar 1979
      7 **Wade Feutrill** b. 1981
    6 **John Butt** b. 9 Jun 1951 m1. **Judith Gates** 19 Jan 1974 b. 29 Aug 1954 m2. **Debbie Janssen** Aug 1984 b. 9 Nov 1960
    [Children of John Butt and Judith Gates]
      7 **Joel Butt** b. 7 Jun 1974
      7 **Megan Butt** b. 9 Aug 1975
      7 **Amy Butt** b. 23 Feb 1977
      7 **Luke Butt** b. 6 Apr 1979
    [Children of John Butt and Debbie Janssen]
      7 **Jerri Butt** b. 21 Sep 1987
      7 **Tameka Butt**
      7 **Reon Butt**
    6 **Robert Butt** b. 28 Jul 1956 m. **Mona Lisa (Lisa, Moni) Reimitz** b. 22 Sep 1955
      7 **Vienna Butt** b. 25 Oct 1981
      7 **Jordan Butt** b. 19 Feb 1983
  5 **John Arthur (Jack) Mason** b. 16 Nov 1920 d. 10 Mar 2010 Lidcombe, NSW m. **Kathleen O'Connor** 11 Nov 1949 d. 15 Nov 2004
    6 **John Mason** b. 19 Jul 1951
  5 **Robert Oliver (Bob) Mason** b. 13 Feb 1924
  5 **Dorothea Anne (Dorothy) Mason** b. 12 Dec 1929 d. 23 May 1991 Calvary Hospital, Kogarah m. **Leslie (Jack) Loveridge** 11 Oct 1956 b. 19 Mar 1929 d. 5 Apr 2009
    6 **Peter Loveridge** b. 18 Sep 1957 m. **Mary Anne Clemson** b. 24 Apr 1964
      7 **William Loveridge** b. 11 Sep 1999
      7 **Maitland Loveridge** b. 4 Mar 2001
    6 **Stephen (Bruce) Loveridge** b. 1 Nov 1958 m. **Julie Paget** b. 26 Jul 1958 Sydney
      7 **Vikki Loveridge** b. 31 Oct 1990
      7 **David Loveridge** b. 29 Mar 1993
      7 **Nicole Loveridge** b. 29 Aug 1995
    6 **Paul Leslie Loveridge** b. 13 Dec 1962 m. **Helen Carroll** b. 3 May 1965
      7 **Amelia Loveridge** b. 13 Apr 2005
      7 **Eloise Loveridge** b. 13 Sep 2006
    6 **Andrew Loveridge** b. 26 Feb 1971 m. **Lynda Claxton** b. 7 Aug 1973
      7 **Matthew Loveridge** b. 13 Jan 2005
      7 **Megan Loveridge** b. 30 Sep 2006
      7 **Jack Richard Loveridge** b. 21 Jul 2008

Chapter 7: The Full Mason Family Tree

The full Family Tree of Oliver Mason of Tipperary, Ireland

1. **John Mason I** was born in Cahir Tipperary, Ireland c1760, and died c1798. He married **Margaret O'Connor**, and did not migrate to Australia.
   2 **John Mason II** was born c1793 Cahir, Tipperary, Ireland, married **Joanna (Johanna, Hannah) Quigley** 1811 Cashel, migrated to Australia in the China, arriving in December 1839, and died here on 10 Jan 1858 Swan Reach, NSW, from a 'coup de soleil'. **Joanna** was born 1792 in Cashel, Tipperary, Ireland, migrated with him, and died 6 Apr 1857 Swan Reach, Morpeth.

   3 **Oliver Mason** b. Feb 1818 Golden, near Cashel, Tipperary, IRL. d. 7 Apr 1885 Tamworth, NSW. DC 14440 (2525) m. **Ann Fitzgerald** 21 Jan 1853 St Mary's Cathedral, Sydney. b. 1825 Stonehall, Limerick, IRL d. 1 Aug 1891
      4 **John Fehian Mason** b. 14 Dec 1853 Morpeth, NSW. d. 24 Aug 1926 Gayndah, Qld m. **Ada Evelyn Burnes** 1888 Narrabri, NSW. b. 1872 Murrurundi d. 9 May 1959
         5 **Oliver Patrick Mason** b. 1889 Baan Baa, NSW (between Tamworth and Narrabri), d. 15 Mar 1944 Qld m. **Amelia Emily Bourne** 21 Apr 1930 Qld
         5 **Robert Joseph Mason** b. 1891 Boggabri BC 7224 1891
         5 **Ann Mason** b. 1892 Narrabri BC 24416 1892 d. 1893 Narrabri DC 9839 1893
         5 **John Leo Mason** b. 1894 Narrabri BC 23093 1894 d. c1934. m. **Freda Kathleen Hunting** 17 Jul 1933 Qld. b. c1912 d. 21 Apr 2004 Mudgeeraba, Qld
         5 **Zillah May Mason** b. 1895 Gunnedah, NSW d. 5 Feb 1949 Caboolture m. **Bernard Patrick McErlane** 20 May 1937 Qld, d. 22 Nov 1985 Caboolture, Qld
            6 **Bernard McErlane** b. c1938 d. 15 May 1939 Qld
         5 **Mary Philomena Veronica Mason** b. 1898 Gunnedah, NSW m. **Bertrand Frederick Evans** 11 Jun 1924 Qld d. 23 Sep 1957 Qld
            6 **Bruce Evans** b. c1925 d. 25 Feb 1957 Qld
         5 **James Edward Mason** b. 9 Jul 1900 Quirindi, NSW d. 1962 Qld m. **Helen Isabel Leslie** 23 Mar 1929
         5 **Joseph Charles Mason** b. 12 Apr 1903 Baan Baa, near Narrabri, NSW d. Record not found in Qld
         5 **Edward John Mason** b. 12 Jul 1905 Quirindi, NSW m. **Hilda Rosa Taylor** 22 Apr 1937 Qld. b. c1915 d. 30 Sep 2003 Pullenvale, Qld
         5 **Ada Anne Mason** b. 1909 Quirindi
      4 **Patrick Arthur Mason** b. 29 May 1855 Raymond Terrace NSW d. 1913 Temora m. **Margaret Toohey** 6 Sep 1883 St Nicholas Church, Tamworth NSW
         5 **Hannah May Mason** b. 9 May 1885 Tamworth NSW (Family bible) d. 23 May 1937 20 Martin Place, Mortdale from cerebral thrombosis. m. **Edward J Smalley** 1914 Glebe b. 1884 Waterloo d. 1962
            6 **Edward J Smalley**
         5 **Bartholomew Theobald Mason** b. 16 Apr 1887 Tamworth (Family bible) d. 6 Dec 1906 Drowned in billabong, Marsden, NSW, age 19.
         5 **Veronica Pearl Mason** b. 1889 Tamworth, NSW d. 1956 Narrabeen, NSW m. **Charles Oldham Johnson** 1916 Balmain South, NSW, b. 1892 Bathurst d. 1955 Ashfield, NSW
      4 **James Mason** b. 21 May 1856 Stroud, Raymond Terrace, NSW d. 9 Mar 1915 m. **Jane E Purtell** 15 Sep 1878 St Nicholas' Church, Tamworth MC 4843/1878 (family bible). b. 1860 West Maitland, NSW. d. 7 Mar 1936 Quirindi, NSW
         5 **Mary Therese Mason** b. 12 Jun 1879 Cockburn River Tamworth, NSW. BC 'Mary Thelma' d. 9 Jul 1965 Sacred Heart Hospice, Darlinghurst, m. **John Francis Joseph (Jack) Purcell** 15 Oct 1912 Tamworth, NSW. b. 1884 Morpeth, NSW d. 1952 Petersham, Sydney, NSW
            6 **John Francis Dominic Purcell** b. 1913 d. 1988 m. **Joyce Gladys Clarke** 1945 Marrickville. NSW
               7 **Gabrielle Purcell** m. **Warren Goodyer**
                  8 **Joseph Goodyer**
                  8 **Luke Goodyer** m. **Evette** 1998
                     9 **Stephanie Goodyer**
                  8 **Paul Goodyer** m. **Julie**
                     9 **Dominic Goodyer** b. 11 Jan 1995
                  8 **Elizabeth Goodyer**
                  8 **Brendan Goodyer**
                  8 **Kathleen Goodyer**
               7 **Michelle Purcell** m. **Owen Ihlein**
                  8 **Rebecca Ihlein** m. **Barry Newman**
                  8 **Lucas Ihlein**
                  8 **Joshua Ihlein**

8 Jonathon Ihlein
    7 **Mark Purcell** m. **Jennifer (Jenny)**
        8 **Elsie Purcell**
        8 **Monica Purcell**
    6 **James Vincent Purcell** b. 7 Feb 1915 Tamworth, NSW d. 18 Oct 1995 St Anne's Nursing Home, Hunters Hill, Sydney
    6 **Marie Dolores Purcell** b. 21 Dec 1916 Werris Creek, NSW d. 27 Mar 2000
5 **Patrick Daniel Mason** b. 27 Dec 1880 Glengarvon Station, Tamworth, NSW. d. 1 Dec 1937 m1. **Elizabeth Gilmore** 22 May 1916 Mission Hall, Roselle, NSW d. 7 Mar 1917 m2. **Martha Austin** c1918 b. c1877 Liverpool, Lancashire, England d. 15 Jun 1951 26 Roscoe Street, Bondi Beach
[Children of Patrick Daniel Mason and Martha Austin]
    6 **Arthur Daniel Mason** b. 1919 d. 8 Apr 1991 Collombatti, NSW, m. **Isobel Armstrong** 31 Aug 1940 Dissolved by decree by wife 3 days after wedding. b. 1918 Fifeshire, Scotland
5 **Ann Mason** b. 18 Oct 1881 Narrabri, NSW d. 7 Apr 1942? Mental Hospital, Perth
5 **Margaret Mason** b. 1 May 1885 Tamworth d. 29 Dec 1921 St Joseph's Province, Albert St, East Melbourne
5 **John Charles (Jack) Mason** b. 8 Dec 1886 Tamworth d. 1943 Warwick, Queensland m. **Alice Mary (Mary) Heyman** 1914 Tamworth d. 27 Sep 1954 Balmain NSW DC 17141/1954
    6 **Patricia Amelia Thomasine Mason** b. 17 Oct 1915 m. **Clifford Edward Keating** b. 15 Feb 1910 Coonamble, NSW d. 20 Oct 1990 Cardinal Gilroy Retirement Village, Merrylands, Sydney
        7 **Michael Keating** b. 1 Sep 1944 m. **Colleen Boylan**
            8 **Nicholas Keating**
            8 **Joshua Keating**
            8 **Elizabeth Keating**
            8 **Bernadine Keating**
            8 **Jessica Keating**
            8 **Sarah Clare Keating**
        7 **Timothy John Keating** b. 7 Jan 1949 d. 30 Mar 2006 Amity Nursing Home, New Farm, Qld m. **Kathleen Quinn** 2 Sep 1978 Lake Alexandra, Vic b. 28 Oct 1954
            8 **Rebecca Keating** b. 4 Jun 1980
            8 **Siobhan Keating** b. 26 Jul 1981
            8 **Nathaniel Keating**. 31 Oct 1982
            8 **Brigid Keating** b. 8 Aug 1984
        7 **Patrick Keating** b. 26 May 1956 m1. **Karen** m2. **Lorraine**
        [Children of Patrick Keating and Karen]
            8 **Amy Keating**
            8 **Nicole Keating**
        [Children of Patrick Keating and Lorraine]
            8 **Aishling Keating**
            8 **Jack Keating**
5 **Ruby Myrtle Mason** b. 1 Jun 1888 Tamworth, NSW d. 18 Aug 1890 West Tamworth, NSW
5 **Jane (Sister Thomasene) Mason** b. 2 Feb 1891 Tamworth, NSW d. 24 Jul 1963 Hunters Hill
5 **(Unnamed male) Mason** b. 14 Mar 1892 Tamworth, NSW d. 17 Mar 1892 West Tamworth, NSW
5 **Charles Vincent (Vin) Mason** b. 12 Apr 1893 Tamworth d. 10 Nov 1963, Richmond, Sydney m. **Winifred Margaret Mary Fletcher** 28 Jan 1920 St Mary's, Scone, NSW b. 8 Jan 1903 Scone, NSW d. 17 Feb 1994
    6 **James William Mason** b. 28 Jul 1921 Scone, NSW d. 21 Aug 1942 Tamworth, NSW DC 22810/1942
    6 **Noel John Mason** b. 30 Sep 1924 Scone, NSW d. 30 Jan 2005 Sydney m. **Eileen Patricia Conroy** 12 Jan 1949 St Mary's Cathedral, Sydney b. 28 Jul 1924 Northbridge, Sydney
        7 **Stephen Lawrence Mason** b. 31 Jul 1949 Mater Hospital, Sydney m. **Margaret O'Connor** Sep 1970 b. 8 Jul 1949
            8 **Dominic Bernard James Mason** b. 27 Dec 1973 Sydney d. 11 Dec 2007 Belmont, Newcastle, NSW m. **Michelle**
                9 **Rebecca Mason** b. c2002
                9 **Nicholas Mason** b. c2004
            8 **Daniel Mason** b. 2 Apr 1977 Sydney
            8 **Timothy Mason** b. May 1979 Darwin
        7 **Andrew James Mason** b. 1 Oct 1951 m1. **Anna Armstrong** m2. **Carol Reid** Canberra b. 30 Jun Scotland
        [Children of Andrew James Mason and Anna Armstrong]
            8 **Joshua Mason** b. 24 Mar 1975 d. Nov 2002 Freak Accident

8 **Zachary Mason** b. 29 Aug 1978 Sydney
[Children of Andrew James Mason and Carol Reid]
    8 **Jessica Mason** b. 28 Aug 1987 Sydney
    8 **Hamish Mason** b 13 Jun 1990
7 **Catherine Anne Mason** b. 16 Jun 1956 Port Moresby m. **Mark Ryan**
    8 **Felix Malachy Ryan** b. 18 Nov 1997
7 **Peter Daniel Charles Mason** b. 22 May 1959 Port Moresby
7 **Paul Vincent Mason** b. 16 Apr 1964 Port Moresby m. **Christina Alverez**
    8 **Vincent John Alverez Mason** b. 14 Jun 1998 Sydney
6 **Mary Monica Mason** twin b. 25 Jun 1929 Quirindi, NSW d. 25 Jun 1987 m. **Vincent Jeffery Keen** 12 Jun 1957 St Nicholas', Tamworth, NSW d. 26 Aug 2007 Narrabri, NSW
    7 **Jeffery James Keen** b. 28 Dec 1959 d. 1989 m. **Rosemary Waddle**
        8 **Peter Keen**
        8 **Benjamin Keen**
    7 **Martin Edward Keen** b. 22 Jun 1961 d. 23 Aug 2009
6 **Margaret Joan Mason** twin b. 25 Jun 1929 Quirindi m. **Maxwell Thomas Keevers** 14 Apr 1951 St Mary's Scone
    7 **Anne Keevers** b. 11 Jun 1952 Scone, NSW
    7 Patricia Keevers b. 1 Aug 1953 Scone, NSW
    7 **Michael Keevers** b. 24 Apr 1958 Scone, NSW m1. **Melissa Keogh** 20 Apr 1989 Armidale, NSW m2. **Louise McArdle** 12 Apr 2000
        [Children of Michael Keevers and Melissa Keogh]
        8 **Thomas Keevers** b. 23 Oct 1992
        8 **Henry Keevers** b. 15 Aug 1995
        8 **Charlotte Keevers** b. 23 May 1998
  5 **James Augustine Mason** b. 23 Dec 1894 Tamworth d. 19 Feb 1911 Tamworth Hospital
  5 **Blandine Mason** b. 5 Mar 1896 Duri, NSW Reg. Quirindi, d. 20 Nov 1896 West Tamworth
  5 **Irene Mason** b. 18 Jul 1897 Duri, NSW, Reg.Quirindi d. 20 Dec 1897 Duri
  5 **Dorothy Mason N** b. 1900 Tamworth d. 11 May 1900 West Tamworth
4 **Oliver Mason** b. 24 Apr 1858 Burrowell, nr Seaham, Raymond Terrace NSW d. 28 Aug 1932 Cornwall Rd, Sandringham, NZ m1. **Elizabeth English** 27 Feb 1878 Tamworth NSW b. 1857 Tamworth NSW d. c1879 Lismore, from childbirth? m2. **Honoria (Nora) Dunn** 1907 Pukekohe, NZ b. 11 Dec 1872 Auckland, NZ d. 24 Oct 1943, 5 Egerton St., Eden Terrace, Auckland
[Children of Oliver Mason and Elizabeth English]
    5 **Margaret Ann Mason** b. 6 Dec 1878 d. 1879 Tamworth
[Children of Oliver Mason and Honoria (Nora) Dunn]
    5 **Charles Gerald Mason** b. 28 Jan 1908 Auckland d. 9 Dec 1970 Howick, Auckland, NZ. Left a Will. Cremated.
4 **Charles Mason** b. 25 Oct 1862 Wards River, reg. Port Stephens NSW, d. 4 Apr 1954 North Sydney m. **Catherine Theresa Morris** 18 Jan 1888 b. 27 Jul 1858 Louth Park, Ward's River. nr Port Stephens. d. 29 Aug 1927 Cooroy, near Noosa, Qld.
    5 **Oliver Alphonsus Mason** b. 24 Nov 1888 Woolamol, Tamworth d. 4 Jul 1987 m1. **Netta Olga Garrett** 4 Sep 1920 Temp Catholic Church, Lithgow, NSW b. 27 Mar 1895 Hartley, near Lithgow d. 28 Apr 1935. m2. **Rosemary Lollbach** 4 Apr 1947 Holy Family Church Lindfield b. 17 Sep 1914 d. 12 Feb 1996 Coffs Harbour. Buried Northern Suburbs Lawn Cemetery.
    [Children of Oliver Alphonsus Mason and Netta Olga Garrett]
      6 **Marie Olga (Mick) Mason** b. 11 Jul 1921 Junee NSW d. 4 Nov 2002 Hornsby m. **Bernie Lyons** 12 May 1947 Our Lady of the Rosary, Waitara NSW b. 3 Apr 1917 Coogee, NSW d. 29 Apr 1997 Hornsby
        7 **Peter Lyons** b. 6 Feb 1947 Hornsby m. **Jayne Boyd** 27 Apr 1991 Gulgong b. 25 Dec 1959 Gulgong
            8 **Peter Sercombe** b. adopted
        [Children of Jayne Boyd]
            8 **Renae Boyd** b. 15 Jan 1981
        7 **Michael Lyons** b. 14 Mar 1948 m. **Christine Cormie** b. 29 Oct 1950 Catholic Church Waitara
            8 **David Michael Lyons** b. 7 Sep 1971
            8 **Melissa Lyons** b. 13 Jul 1974
                9 **Joshua Lyons-Finch** b. 7 Oct 1995
                9 **Samson** ?
            8 **Katie Louise Lyons** b. 14 Mar 1976
            8 **Sarah Patricia Lyons** b. 24 Apr 1977
            8 **Patrick Kevin Lyons** b. 5 Jun 1979
            8 **Thomas John Walter Lyons** b. 7 Dec 1982
        7 **John Lyons** b. 19 Feb 1950 Hornsby m. **Pauline McKay** 29 Jul 1975 b. 25 May 1950

Chapter 7: The full Mason Family Trees

       8 **Jeffery Michael Lyons** b. 9 Feb 1973 m. **Katherine McRae** 12 Oct 2000 Normanhurst
          9 **Rose Elizabeth Lyons** b. 9 Oct 2002 Melbourne
          9 **Annabelle Lyons** b. 2005
          9 **Oliver Lyons** b. 19 Mar 2007
       8 **Timothy Paul Lyons** b. 22 Jan 1974 m. **Amy Baird** Jan 2006
          9 **Louis Lyons** b. 13 Feb 2007
       8 **Christopher John Lyons** b. 9 May 1977 m. **Kim Ellem**
          9 **Bernard Christopher Lyons** b. 9 Nov 2004
          9 **Angus Lyons** b. Dec 2005
       8 **Jane Elizabeth Lyons** b. 23 Oct 1981
7 **Mary Lyons** b. 2 Mar 1951 Hornsby
7 **Joseph (Joe) Lyons** b. 25 Oct 1954 m. **Elizabeth (Beth) Collins** 9 Oct 1987 Cath Church Waitara, NSW b. 13 Sep 1958
    8 **Benjamin Thomas Lyons** b. 8 Aug 1990
    8 **Emily Lyons** b. 7 Jul 1994
7 **Carmel May Lyons** b. 5 May 1956 Hornsby m. **Doug Adams** 8 Nov 1999 Ourimbah b. 18 Dec 1955
    8 **Daniel Patrick Lyons** b. 22 Feb 1976 m. **Susie Duke** 22 Mar 2008 Auckland NZ b. 20 Jan 1979
       9 **Samuel Patrick Lyons** b. 7 Aug 2009 Sydney
7 **Jennifer (Jenny) Lyons** b. 26 May 1958 Hornsby
7 **Kevin Lyons** b. 20 Apr 1960 m1. **Elizabeth van Leuwen** c1987, divorced, m2. **Denise Joan Buchii**. 8 Sep 1990 USA b.12 Jan 1963 USA
    [Children of Kevin Lyons and Denise Joan Buchii]
    8 **Joseph Keon Woo-Lyons** b. 26 Jun 2001 Seoul, Korea
7 **Angela Lyons** b. 29 Jun 1963 Hornsby m. **Greg Crawley** (divorced) Catholic Church, Waitara
    8 **John Crawley** b. 10 Oct 1985
       9 **? Crawley** b. 2009
    8 **Luke Crawley** b. 31 Dec 1986 Hornsby
    8 **Sally Crawley** b. 7 Sep 1996 Tamworth
    8 **Kate Elizabeth Crawley** b. 30 Apr 1998 Tamworth
    8 **Patrick Joseph Crawley** b. 7 Jul 2001 Moss Vale NSW
6 **Charles Francis (Chick) Mason** b. 4 Feb 1923 Blayney NSW d. 23 Feb 2007 Public Hospital Muswellbrook m. **Marj Norma Daniels** Muswellbrook b. 6 Aug 1927
    7 **Julianne Mason** b. 13 Mar 1954 m. **Russell Butel** divorced
    7 **Dianne Kay Mason** b. 14 Feb 1958 m. **Gordon Lawrence Elliott**
       8 **Kristy Louise Elliott** b. 17 May 1990
6 **Leila Monica Mason** b. 12 Dec 1924 Blayney NSW d. 8 Apr 2009 Holy Spirit Home, Carseldine, Brisbane, m. **Neville Gilbert** 5 Oct 1946 Waitara b. 11 Jan 1921 Wynnum Central, Brisbane
    7 **Caroline Gilbert** b. 7 Jul 1947 m. **Peter Gustafson** c1976 b. 20 Apr 1944 Queensland
       8 **Andrew Gustafson** b. 7 Jun 1978 Canberra
       8 **David Gustafson** b. 1 Apr 1981 Melbourne Vic
    7 **Christine Gilbert** b. 18 Apr 1950 Brisban m. **William (Bill) Webb** Redcliff, Brisbane b. 2 Jul 1946 St Therese, Kedron
       8 **Simon Webb** b. 12 Jul 1974 Brisbane
       8 **Damien Webb** b. 17 Oct 1975 Brisbane m. **Vivienne (Ruth) Engeman** 22 Jun 2003 Kedron
          9 **Harrison Victor Webb** b. 19 Dec 2005 Brisbane
          9 **Grace Lily Webb** b. 2 Jul 2007 Brisbane
       8 **Christopher Webb** b. 23 Jun 1980 Brisbane m. **Monica Maria Grazzi Iozzi** Jun 2006 St Therese Church, Kedron, Brisbane b. 12 Dec 1974 Brisbane
          9 **Olivia Grace Webb** b. 28 Jun 2007 Brisbane
          9 **Matilda Elizabeth Webb** b. 28 Jun 2008 Brisbane
    7 **Michael Gilbert** b. 30 Nov 1951 Brisbane m. **Berna ?** Brisbane
       8 **Elspeth Gilbert** b. 21 Feb 1984
       8 **Camille Gilbert** b. 21 Feb 1984
       8 **Hugh Gilbert** b. 2 Sep 1988
       8 **Madeline Gilbert** b. 9 Sep 1992
    7 **Annette Gilbert** b. 6 Mar 1957 Brisbane m. **Michael Roggenkamp** b. 21 Feb 1952
       8 **Mathew Roggenkamp** b. 17 Sep 1985
       8 **Daniel Roggenkamp** b. 19 Aug 1988
       8 **Patrick Roggenkamp** b. 18 Sep 1993

Chapter 7: The Full Mason Family Tree

6 **Kathleen Patricia (Pat) Mason** b. 17 Sep 1926 Blayney NSW m. **John Edward O'Grady** b. 6 Nov 1919 Fremantle d. 19 Sep 1989 Hospital, Katoomba
    7 **Annette Michelle O'Grady** b. 5 Jun 1953 m.(df) **Richard Peter Wilson** Coffs Harbour b. 6 Jun 1960
        8 **Julian Edward Wilson-O'Grady** b. 13 Nov 1993
    7 **David John O'Grady** b. 1 Dec 1954 Sydney
    7 **Peter Charles O'Grady** b. 23 May c1956 m. **Kim Pattison** Wentworth Falls b. 19 May ?
        8 **Kate O'Grady** b. 6 Aug 1981
        8 **Matthew O'Grady** b. 28 Aug 1982
    7 **Kerrin Mary O'Grady** b. 15 Dec 1958 Wentworth Falls
    7 **Christopher Oliver O'Grady** b. 16 Apr 1960 m.(df) **Verena Alleman** b. 8 Oct 1967 Switzerland
        8 **Oliver O'Grady** b. 3 Apr 1991 Katoomba
        8 **Claudia O'Grady** b. 6 Dec 1995
    7 **Renee Patricia O'Grady** b. 28 Jan 1962 Coffs Harbour m.(df?) **Chris Schweikurt**
        8 **Tom Schweikurt-O'Grady** b. 29 Oct 1995
    7 **Denise Clare O'Grady** b. 16 Jun 1963 Crescent Head
        8 **Benjamin John O'Grady** b. 22 Oct 1982
    7 **Louise Veronica O'Grady** b. 25 Jan 1966 m. **John Paul Collins**
        8 **Anika Collins b.** 13 Mar 1993
        8 **Vincent Collins** b. 5 May 1997
    7 **Jane Elizabeth O'Grady** b. 17 Nov 1967 m. **James Jones** Wentworth Falls, NSW b. 2 May 1967
        8 **Haylee Jones** b. 30 Jun 1999 Wentworth Falls
        8 **Sophie Jane Jones** b. 15 Oct 2001
        8 **Lachlan Jones** b. 2003

6 **Oliver Benedict (Brother Claudius) Mason** b. 28 Feb 1928 Hunter St. Hornsby

6 **Terence Joseph (Terry) Mason** b. 7 Sep 1929 Hornsby NSW m. **Monica Clare Murphy** 5 Jul 1988 Taree NSW b. 4 May 1945 Waipukurau, NZ

6 **Claire Frances Mason** b. 14 Jan 1931 m. **Michael (Kazimerz) Kurzawaski** 27 Apr 1968 Our lady of the Rosary Waitara, NSW b. 22 Dec 1927 Poland d. 27 Mar 1990 Gwandalin, NSW
    7 **Helen Kurzawaski** b. 5 Jan 1955 Ryde
    7 **Peter Kurzawaski** b. 22 Aug 1956 m. **Cheryl** Sydney
        8 **Daniel Kurzawaski** b. 29 Jun 1984
        8 **Simone Kurzawaski** b. 12 May 1988
        8 **Jessica Kurzawaski** b. 7 Aug 1990

6 **Annette Philomena (Anne) Mason** b. 10 Aug 1932 Hornsby NSW m. **Peter (Pius) Hartman** 16 Apr 1968 St Mary's Catholic Church, North Sydney b. 11 Jul 1929 Switzerland d. 12 Aug 1990 Nabiac NSW
    7 **Paul Hartmann** b. 7 Aug 1970 Adopted m. **Melinda Woodhouse** 17 Oct 1999
        8 **Eliza Rose Hartman** b. 29 Sep 2001 Forster NSW
        8 **Emily Louise Hartman** b. 27 Jan 2003 twin
        8 **Lucy Anne Hartman** b. 27 Jan 2003 twin
    7 **Maria Hartmann** b. 15 Sep 1972

6 **Catherine Eileen (Cath) Mason** b. 29 Dec 1933 Hornsby NSW m. **Maurice Tully** 21 Jan 1963 Catholic Church, Kirribilli NSW b. 28 Aug 1937
    7 **Michelle Anne Tully (O'Shaunessy)** b. 11 Nov 1964 m. **Bob Vidler**
    7 **Mark Oliver Tully** b. 18 Apr 1969 Valentine, Newcastle m. **Christine Gemmell**
        8 **Joshua Tully** b. 7 May 1997 Newcastle
        8 **Georgia Rose Tully** b. 4 Apr 2003 Newcastle
    7 **Andrew Maurice Tully** b. 18 Dec 1970 m. **Kelly Daunt**
        8 **Summer Bree Tully** b. 22 Dec 1992 Newcastle
        8 **Amber Tully** b. 9 Mar 1998 Newcastle
    7 **Rebecca Carmel Tully** b. 8 Jun 1972 Sydney
    7 **Jeremy Michael Tully** b. 12 Oct 1973 Newcastle m. **Jill** 18 Oct 2007 Mermaid Beach, Qld
    7 **Jonathon Paul Tully** b. 18 Jan 1976 Valentine, Newcastle m. **Angela Speirs**
        8 **Tara Belle Tully** b. 8 Jul 2003 Newcastle
        8 **Jet Jaxson Tully** b. 1 Apr 2006 Newcastle
    7 **David Anthony Tully** b. 12 May 1978 Valentine

[Children of Oliver Alphonsus Mason and Rosemary Lollbach]
    6 **Colleen Mary Mason** b. 6 Jan 1948 d. 13 Oct 2011 m. **Brian Lester** 13 Dec 1969 Waitara b. 21 Nov 1946 Mater Hospital, North Sydney

Chapter 7: The full Mason Family Trees

       7 **Kylie Anne Lester** b. 27 Aug m. **Sean Burns** 8 Jul 2000, Emu Plains NSW b. 25 Oct 1969 Belfast, Ireland
          8 **Aidan William Burns** b. 28 Nov 2003 Penrith
          8 **Neve Alica Burns** b. 17 Mar 2006 Penrith
       7 **Mark Geoffrey Lester** b. 28 Nov 1975, Wahroonga m. **Alana Jones** 21 Aug 2004 Loxley Kurrajong, NSW b. 23 Apr 1981 Penrith
          8 **Tristan Lester** b. 1 Nov 2006 Sydney
          8 **Teyan Lester** b. 18 Nov 2008 Sydney
   6 **Josephine Gertrude Mason** b. 19 May 1950 m. **Paul Parrish** Our Lady of the Rosary, Waitara b. 19 Aug 1956
       7 **Daniel Paul Parish** b. 11 Jan 1976 m. Belinda **Dowsett** 3 Sep 2005 Tweed Heads,NSW
       7 **Rebecca Mary Parrish** b. 7 Aug ? m. **Jamie Brindley** 17 Jan 2009 Tweed Heads NSW
   6 **Judith Rosemary Mason** b. 1 Jul 1951 m. **Merrick Rhone** 9 Dec 1980 Gosford b. 14 Nov 1952 Central Coast NSW
       7 **Levi John Rhone** b. 26 Oct 1980
       7 **Erin Jennifer Rhone** b. 29 Feb 1984
       7 **Joshua Alexander Rhone** b. 11 Apr 1988
   6 **Anthony John (Tony) Mason** b. 29 May 1954 Sydney m. **Deborah (Debbie) Robb** 12 Mar 1987 Lowanna b. 20 Feb1963 Coffs Harbour
       7 **Lucy Matilda Mason** b. 4 Nov 1990
       7 **Tracey Mason** b. 11 Sep 199, twin, Coffs Harbour
       7 **Katie Rose Mason** b. 11 Sep 1993, twin, Coffs Harbour
   6 **James Oliver Mason** b. 25 Apr 1958 m. **Wendy Barnard** 16 May 1985 Durham House, Carlingford, NSW b. 13 Jul 1954 Auckland
       7 **Hamish Oliver Mason** b. 16 May 1986
       7 **Jasmine Margaret Mason** b. 10 Jul 1987
5 **Mary Monica (May) Mason** b. 23 Mar 1890 Tamworth NSW d. 30 Jun 1938 Hornsby
5 **Annie Veronica (Sister M Irenaeus) Mason** b. 24 Apr 1891 Tamworth BC 33718/1891 d. 3 Mar 1976 Wagga
5 **Catherine Gertrude (Sister M Regis) Mason** b. 4 Aug 1892 Woolomin NSW d. 20 Jul 1977 Newcastle
5 **Richard Percy (Dick) Mason** b. 8 Oct 1894 Tamworth 1894 d. 6 Jul 1965 Newcastle m. **Alice Eileen Scannell** 29 Oct 1926 East Maitland b. 1898 Moree NSW d. 1956 Mayfield NSW
   6 **Margaret Mason** b. 21 Jun 1930 m. **Gerhard (Gerry) Bergholcs** 18 Dec 1958 b. 6 Jan 1930
       7 **Richard Bergholcs** b. 27 Mar 1959 m. **Anne Mountain** 15 Dec 1987 b. 13 Mar 1960
          8 **Nicholas Bergholcs** b. 27 May 1988
          8 **Zachary Bergholcs** b. 26 Apr 1990
          8 **Kieran Bergholcs** b. 21 Jun 1994
       7 **Justin Bergholcs** b. 31 Aug 1961
       7 **Simone Bergholcs** b. 26 Jul 1968 Newcastle
   6 **Paul Patrick Mason** b. 17 Dec 1931 m. **Robin Vidler** 9 Apr 1960 St Canice Church, Darlinghurst, NSW b. 19 Dec 1938 Tamworth
       7 **Michael Mason** b. 21 Jan 1961 Sydney m. **Karen Sherman** Hawaii
       7 **Tracey Mason** b. 21 Dec 1963 Tamworth m. **Luke Dawson** 9 Apr 1988, North Sydney
          8 **Laura Dawson** b. 20 Jun 1990 Forestville NSW
          8 **Spencer Dawson** b. 28 Jul 1996 Forestville NSW
       7 **Felicity Mason** b. 6 Jun 1974 Sydney m. **Andrew Coleman** 9 Apr 2001 Forestville
          8 **Liam James Coleman** b. 17 May 2005 RNS Hospital, North Sydney
5 **Charles Morris (Morrie) Mason** b. 16 Dec 1896 Tamworth d. 29 May 1965 Brisbane, m. **Valerie Campbell** 1924 b. 27 May 1896 Ballina, NSW d. 16 Nov 1956
   6 **Brian Mason** b. 20 Feb 1926 Cooroy, Qld m. **Joyce Albury** 1958 Kingscliff, Murwillumbah b. 8 Jul 1929 d.17 Jan 2012 Banora Pt, Tweed Heads.
       7 **Christopher Mason** b. 29 Apr 1959 m. **Angela Jenner** b. 13 Dec 1959 Canberra
          8 **Joshua Mason** b. 20 Nov 1987
          8 **Timothy Mason** b. 1992
       7 **Maria Mason** b. 8 Jul 1960
       7 **Frances Mason** b. 13 Jul 1961 m. **Barry Stegeman**
          8 **Tonita Stegeman** b. 1987
       7 **Kathleen Mason** b. 1965
   6 **Carmel Catherine Mason** b. 24 Oct 1927 Cooroy, Qld d. 24 Jul 2011 Canberra m. **Arthur William Bullman** 1949 Murwillumbah b. 1925
       7 **Valerie Mary Bullman** b. 11 Jun 1950 m. **Bernard Ramsey** 9 May 1970
          8 **Paul Andrew Ramsey** b. 14 Mar 1972 m. **Marion**
             9 **Matilda Ramsey** b. 13 Jun 2006

Chapter 7: The Full Mason Family Tree

    8 **David Robert Ramsey** b. 4 Dec 1973
    8 **Christine Maree Ramsey** b. 20 Oct 1976 m. **Daniel Lubrinski**
   7 **William Gerard (Bill) Bullman** b. 22 Nov 1951 m. **Elaine Austin** Aug 1974
    8 **Chantelle Bullman** b. 17 Jun 1977
    8 **Gregory Bullman** b. Apr 1981
    8 **Scott Bullman** b. 10 Oct 1983
   7 **Gabrielle Therese (Gay) Bullman** b. 10 Jan 1956 m. **Robert Deeker** 27 Apr 1990
   7 **Patrick Charles (Pat) Bullman** b. 24 Mar 1957 m. **Therese Thompson**
    8 **Jessica Kate Bullman** b. 24 Aug 1984
    8 **Matthew Charles Bullman** b. 30 Sep 1987
    8 **Michael Bullman** b. 14 Feb 1992
   7 **Janelle Catherine Bullman** b. 30 Sep 1958 m. **Paul Levett** 30 Dec 1994
    8 **Luke Levett** b. 2000
    8 **Adam Levett** b. 2004
  6 **Valerie May Mason** b. c1929 Cooroy or Roma, Qld d. c1929 (stillborn)
  6 **Val (Sister Frances Regis) Mason** b. 1 Nov 1931 Roma, Qld d. 20 May 2007 Hunters Hill
 5 **James Kevin (Jim) Mason** b. 18 Feb 1898 Tamworth d. c1985 m. **Margaret Mary Josephine (May) Day** 2 Feb 1928 St Augustine's Coolangatta b. 1904 Cattle Gully, Darling Downs, Qld
  6 **Monica Mason** b. 25 Dec 1928 Terranora NSW d. 4 Dec 2002 Toowoomba Qld m. **Terence O'Neill** Toowoomba, Qld.
   7 **John Vincent O'Neill** m. **Pauline**
   7 **Mary O'Neill** b. Aug 1957 m. **Warren**
   7 **Gerald O'Neill** b. 1960 m. **Alison**
   7 **Anne O'Neill** b. 1962
   7 **Damien O'Neill** m. **Julie**
  6 **Kevin James Mason** b. 15 Jul 1931 Coolangatta Qld d. 8 Jan 1997 m. **Denise McCarthy** 12 Oct 1957 Ashgrove Qld b.6 Nov 1935 Ashgrove Qld
   7 **Peter Mason** b. 24 Apr 1958 m. **Karen** 11 Sep 1970
    8 **Scott Mason** b. 14 Jun 1981, twin
    8 **Keith Mason** b. 14 Jun 1981, twin
    8 **Luke Mason** b. 8 Oct 1985
   7 **Michael James Mason** b. 5 Dec 1960 m. **Ros**
   7 **Paul Kevin Mason** b. 28 Jul 1962
    8 **Timothy Mason** b. 11 Aug 1989
    8 **Hannah Mason** b. 15 Sep 1990
    8 **Bernadette Maree Mason** m. **Chris Ratcliffe** 23 Jul 1994
     9 **Samantha Ratcliffe** b. 29 Mar 1999
     9 **Nicholas Ratcliffe** b. 3 Aug 2003
   7 **Patricia Jean (Trish) Mason** b. 19 Apr 1967
  6 **Leo Mason** b. 4 Jul 1935 Tweed Heads m1. **Gloria** 21 Feb 1959 Camp Hill, Sydney, divorced m2. **Dianne Davies** 18 Apr 1987 Gold Coast
[Children of Leo Mason and Gloria]
   7 **Brett Andrew Mason** b. 11 Mar 1976 Brisbane
   7 **Lisa Jane Mason** b. 17 July 1977 Lae, PNG, m. **Phillip Norman** 10 Oct 1998 Brisbane
    8 **Lucy Lily Anne Mason** b. 11Jan 2005
 5 **Irene Clementine (Rene) Mason** b. 4 Feb 1900 Tamworth d. 26 Jul 1988 Nazareth House, Turramurra NSW m. **Sydney Mostyn** 10 Jul 1937 St Mary's North Sydney. b. 7 Feb 1899 Helensburg NSW d. 6 Apr 1964
 5 **Clement Odillo (Clem) Mason** b. 4 Jul 1902 Tamworth BC 26686/1902 d. 12 Oct 1987 Kiama NSW m. **Winifred Kelly** 19 Oct 1935 St Patrick's Sydney, b. 4 Mar 1903 Launceston, Tasmania d. 17 Feb 1994 Kiama, NSW
4 **Terence Mason** b. 13 Dec 1863 Port Stephens NSW 1864 d. Mar 1928 Yeppoon, Qld.
4 **Joseph Paul Mason** b. 19 Mar 1865 Tamworth NSW d. 4 May 1918 Auckland m. **Catherine Purtell** 29 Jun 1892 Tamworth, MC 7121 b. 1870 Albury, NSW
 5 **John Cecil (Jack) Mason** b. 30 May 1893 Tamworth d. 11 Oct 1956 Pukekohe, Auckland, m. **Ellen Genevieve (Cissy) Smith** 22 Jun 1919 Auckland b. c1887 Auckland d. 13 Jul 1963 Auckland
 5 **Oliver Louis Joseph (Brother Herman) Mason** b. 23 Jul 1895 Tamworth d. 21 Jun 1937 Naililili, Fiji
 5 **Ronald Joseph Mason** b. Jul 1897 Auckland d. 31 Jan 1898 Auckland
 5 **James Aubrey Mason** b. 1900 Auckland m. **Winifred Evelyn Nixon** 19 May 1962 Auckland b. c1900 Wanganui NZ d. 6 Nov 1986 Auckland
 5 **Joseph Mary Hillary Mason** b. 3 May 1903 Auckland NZ d. 23 May 1969 Wellington NZ m. **Olga Alice Raunes** 26 Aug 1924 Sacred Heart Church, Ponsonby, Auckland b. 1902 Balclutha d. 9 Nov 1971 Wangere area m. **Fiona Marion McClure Walker King** 17 Mar 1943 Wellington

Chapter 7: The full Mason Family Trees

[Children of Joseph Mary Hillary Mason and Olga Alice Raunes]
    6 **Shirley Alice Mason** b. 1 Jan 1926 Ponsonby Auckland m. **Duncan Kitchener Grant** 7 Feb 1948 Auckland
    6 **James Audus Mason** b. 22 Oct 1927 Grey Lynn, Auckland d. 7 Nov 1998 Auckland m1. **Leslley Emma Deadman** 1947 Auckland m2. **Lorraine Frieda Woods** 1954 Auckland
    [Children of James Mason and Leslley Deadman]
        7 **Robert Mason** b. 1948 Auckland
    [Children of James Audus Mason and Lorraine Frieda Woods]
        7 **Geoffrey James Mason** b. 23 Jul 1955 Auckland m. **Louise Ann Thornton**
            8 **Richard James Mason** b. 1984
        7 **Ashley James Mason** b. 1960 m. **Bridget Ann Sheeny**
            8 **Rebecca Louise Mason** b. 1988
[Children of Joseph Mary Hillary Mason and Fiona Marion McClure Walker King]
    6 **John Bernard Muir** b. 8 Oct 1935 Wellington, born **Hilary Joseph Bernard Mason** d. 17 Dec 2010 Busselton, WA m. **Barbara Mary Rouse** 8 Dec 1959 Balmoral, Auckland
        7 **Erin Adaire Muir** b. 22 May 1961 Whangarei, NZ m. **Arnold Wilhelmus Malta** 28 Apr 1984 Como, Perth
            8 **Taara Jada Muir** b. 22 Feb 1980 Subiaco WA
                9 **Radelle Boseilala** b. 7 Jan 2005 NZ
            8 **Robert John Kyle Muir** b. 18 Aug 1981 Bunbury, WA m. **Leanne Marie Lewis** b. 5 Oct 2006 Auckland
                9 **Hermione Rose-Marie Muir** b. 12 Dec 2007 Northshore, Auckland d. 24 Jan 2008 Orewa, Auckland
                9 **Amberleigh Faith Muir** b. 3 Mar 2009 Auckland
            8 **Joseph Troy Malta** b. 23 Jul 1986 Maitland
        7 **Donna Mary Muir** b. 1 Aug 1962 Palmerston North, NZ m. **Thomas George Hicks** 20 Aug 1979 Roebourne, WA
            8 **Mary Elizabeth Hicks** b. 25 Feb 1981 Karratha WA, m. **George Raymond Metcalfe**
                9 **Eloise Mary Metcalfe** b. 1 May 2003
                9 **George Raymond Metcalfe** b. 14 May 2005
            8 **Wesley Thomas Hicks** b. 27 Aug 1982 Ballina, NSW
            8 **Hannah Rose Hicks** b. 3 Sep 1984 Scone NSW m. **Scott Lloyd Woodhouse**
                9 **Natalie Rose Woodhouse** b. 16 Oct 2007
        7 **Troy George Joseph Muir** b. 28 Jul 1965 Palmerston North, NZ d. 19 Sep 1994 Darwin
    6 **Lorna Mason** b. 3 Jan 1938 Wellington m. **Frank Bryant Taylor** 1955 Wellington
        7 **Robyn Taylor**
            8 **Carl Taylor**
            8 **Julian Taylor**
        7 **Erin Taylor** m. ? **Smith**
            8 **Cindy Smith**
            8 **Jolene Smith**
            8 **Calvin Smith**
        7 **Christopher Taylor**
            8 **Shane Taylor**
        7 **Angela Taylor** m. ? **King**
            8 **Eliana King**
            8 **Cassandra King**
5 **Mary Dolores (Sister Mary Consiglio) Mason** b. 14 Mar 1905 Auckland d. c1981

Chapter 7: The Full Mason Family Tree

The full Family Tree of the migrating daughters of Tipperary, Ireland

1. **John Mason I** was born in Cahir Tipperary, Ireland c1760, and died c1798. He married **Margaret O'Connor**, and did not migrate to Australia.
    2 **John Mason II** was born c1793 Cahir, Tipperary, Ireland, married **Joanna (Johanna, Hannah) Quigley** 1811 Cashel, migrated to Australia in the China, arriving in December 1839, and died here on 10 Jan 1858 Swan Reach, NSW, from a 'coup de soleil'. **Joanna** was born 1792 in Cashel, Tipperary, Ireland, migrated with him, and died 6 Apr 1857 Swan Reach, Morpeth.

Mary Mason Sheridan: 1813 – 1873

3. **Mary Mason** b. 1813 Tipperary IRL, m. **Thomas Sheridan** 6 May 1840 St Marys, Sydney MC. V1840561 90/1840. Witnessed by her brother Oliver Mason. d. 3 Mar 1873 DC. 6966 Tamworth. Thomas b. 1796 Connaught IRL. He died after the birth of James John Sheridan, who produced very many progeny. d. 11 Aug 1858 Victoria - drowned in a waterhole - coroner's inquest had no finding. Son James informant on DC.
    4 **James John Sheridan** b. 9 Oct 1847 Coburg/Brunswick, Vic (formerly Pentridge) d. 21 Oct 1918 Carthage St. Tamworth NSW m. **Elizabeth Jane Freeman** 1868 Patricks Plain, Tamworth b. 1847/52/55 Sofala/Patricks Plain. BC. 5131/1859 d. 1919 Tamworth. [Daughter of George and Margaret Freeman]
        5 **Thomas Sheridan** b. 1868 Patricks Plains m. **Martha Jane Mainwaring** 1904 Tingha, NSW b. 1886 Walcha,NSW d. 1963 Cessnock, NSW
            6 **William Thomas Sheridan** b. 1905 Tingha, NSW d. 1951 Petersham, NSW
            6 **Mary Sheridan**
            6 **Cecil Sheridan** b.1969 d. 1969 Cessnock, NSW
        5 **Mary Elizabeth Sheridan** b. 1870 Tamworth d. 1920 Newcastle, NSW
        5 **Leander Castleton Sheridan** b. 1872 Tamworth d. 1873 Tamworth
            6 **Annie Winton Sheridan** b. 1874 Tamworth, NSW d. 25 Nov 1964 Newcastle, m. **George Daniel Inkston** 1901 Tamworth, NSW d. 1936 Hamilton, NSW BC. 19722/1874 MC. 2174/1901 DC. 35785/1964 Newcastle. **George** DC. 15012/1936 Hamilton. Son of George and Charlotte Inkston
            6 **Clifford William Inkston** b. 1901 Tamworth, NSW d. c1975 m. **Mary E Gleeson** 1926 Wickham. NSW BC. 36267/1901 Tamworth. MC. 5645/1926 Wickham NSW DC. 105395/1975
            6 **Eric James Inkston** b. 1905 Tamworth, NSW d. 1960 Campsie, NSW m. **Cecelia May Everett** 1933 Burwood, NSW d. 1974 Burwood, NSW BC. 17835/1905 Tamworth. DC. 946/1974 Daughter of James and Cecelia Everett
        5 **Ernest Emanuel Sheridan** b. 1876 Tamworth, NSW d. 1944 Tamworth, m. **Ellen Matilda Shearman** 1899 Newcastle, NSW MC. 8587/1899 b. 1876 Newcastle, NSW d. 1961 Kempsey DC. 27928/1944
            6 **Stanley James Sheridan** b. 1900 Wickham, Newcastle, NSW d. c1974 BC. 8778/1900 Wickham, Newcastle DC. 48720/1974
            6 **Thomas E Sheridan** b. 1902 Newcastle, NSW d. 1903 Newcastle, BC. 14797/1902 Newcastle DC. No. 2823/1903
            6 **Elizabeth A Sheridan** b. 1911 BC 33814/1911. d.1911 Newcastle, DC. 12271/1911 Tamworth
            6 **Frederick G Sheridan** b. 1904 Newcastle, NSW BC. 5471/1904 Newcastle
            6 **Charles H Sheridan** b. 1906 Hamilton, NSW BC. 24491/1906
            6 **Jack Sheridan** b. 1912 BC 35286/1912 d. 1969 Sydney, DC. 3633/1969
        5 **Victor J Sheridan** b. 1877 Tamworth d. 1951 DC. 31103/1951, Tamworth m. **Mary A Robinson** 1900. Divorced? Or he left home when the baby died.
            6 **Dorothy Sheridan** b. 1901 Newcastle d. 1903 New Lambton, NSW
        5 **Ethel May Sheridan** b. 1879 Tamworth d. 1952 m. **Joseph Enoch Gamble** 1905 Tamworth, MC. 7942/1905
            6 **Kathleen Gamble** b. c1909 m. **Ian P. Harvey** 1930 Hamilton, NSW MC. 12824/1930
            6 **Richard Gamble** b. c1914 d. 1971 Newcastle, NSW m. **Rita Ada Robinson** 1942 Hamilton, NSW, MC. 30106/1942 DC. 81862/1971
            6 **Millie A Gamble** b.1915 d. 1915 Cessnock, DC. 1839/1915
        5 **Loretta (Laura) Sheridan** b. 1880 Tamworth, d. 23 Jul 1967 Sacred Heart Hospice, Darlinghurst m. **Thomas Hammond** 1901 Tamworth, BC. 25048/1880, MC. 7645/1901, DC. 3858 Sydney. Thomas was a well-known trainer of champion horses.
            6 **Thomas Hammond** b. 1901 Tamworth, BC. 26778/1901
            6 **Darrel D Hammond** b. 1903 Tamworth, BC. 16383/1903
            6 **Frank Victor Hammond** b.and d. 1946 Redfern, NSW DC. 21408/1946
            6 **Arthur Hammond** b. 1907

  6 **Ruby R Hammond** b. c.1911 d. Aug 2001 Sydney m. **William Percy Tyndall** 1933 Paddington d. Jun 1984 Sydney, MC. 15316/1933
  6 **Harry Hammond** b. c1914
  6 **Miriam Hammond** b. c1917
  6 **James Hammond** b. c1919
  6 **Jack Hammond** b. c1920
  6 **Robert Hammond** b. c1926
5 **Oscar James Sheridan** b. 1882 Tamworth d. 21 Mar 1954 Tamworth, m. **Mary Jane Upson** 1907 Tamworth. MC. 2546 She already had a daughter **Libby** (m. Robert Ritchie) when she married Oscar b. 1882 Mother's maiden name Daly d.1965 Tamworth. Buried Tamworth
  6 **Edna Sheridan** b. 1907 d. 1908
  6 **Ethel Frances (Dot) Sheridan** b. 1908 d. 1971 m1. **Aubrey Owen McNamara** 1929 m2. (df). **Norman Victor Hoskins (Hamper).** Had five children, including **Norma McNamara**)
[Children of Ethel Frances (Dot) Sheridan and Norman Victor (Hamper)]
    7 **Norma McNamara**
  6 **Glenville Sheridan** b. 1909 d. 1973 m. **Jean Bell (nee Woods)** Had 10 children plus 3 children in previous marriage b. 1904
    7 **Esther Sheridan** b. and d. 1945
    7 **Ethel Francis Sheridan** b.1945 d. 1954
  6 **Iris Laurel Sheridan** b. 1911 d. 1975 m. **Jack Judge**
  6 **Ruby Kathleen Sheridan** b. 1912 m. **David Clarence Addison**
  6 **Kathleen Sheridan** b. c 1913 m. **Harry Charles James Barnett**. Had 10 children
  6 **Anne Sheridan** b. 1915 d. 1916
  6 **Thelma Margaret Sheridan** b. 1917 m. **Clarence Bayliss**
  6 **Elizabeth Mary Sheridan** b. 1919 d. 1920
  6 **Richard Brimsley Sheridan** b. 1920 m. **Isabel Jane Warner**
  6 **James Oscar Sheridan** b. 1921 d. 10 Feb 1942 WWII, Malaya Army NX854, Pte. Killed in action. Buried with his father in Tamworth.
[Children of Mary Jane Upson]
  6 **Libby Upson**
5 **Mildred Lorne Sheridan** b. 1884 Tamworth NSW d. 1951 Balmain m1. (df) **Hector Israel** 6 children m2. **William James Frier** 1938 Rozelle MC. 6116/1938 d. 1963 Balmain DC. 2689/1963
[Children of Mildred Lorne Sheridan and William James Frier]
  6 **Mavis Frier** b. 1929 d. 1929 Balmain
5 **Alonso Sheridan** b. 1886 d. 4 Sep 1908
5 **James John Sheridan** b. 1887 Tamworth BC. 34947 d. 21 Jun 1949, 118 Ann St, Enfield, Sydney. DC 10323 m. **Margaret J Hannon** 1910 Werris Creek, NSW .Occupation Fitter. Buried Rookwood.
  6 **Veronica Sheridan** b. 1910
  6 **Mary Sheridan** b. c1911 d. 1913 Quirindi, DC.16715
  6 **Ethel Sheridan** b. 1915
  6 **Joseph J Sheridan** b. c 1917 d. 1918 DC. 163
5 **Ronald Sheridan** b. 1920
  6 **Frederick Sheridan** b. 1924
  6 **Francis James Sheridan** b. c1926 d. 1927
  6 **John Sheridan** b. 1930
  6 **James E Sheridan** b.1949 d. 1949 DC. 10323
5 **Gordon Sheridan** b. 1889 Tamworth d. 1890 Tamworth
5 **Lynda K Sheridan** b. 1894 Tamworth BC. 13026, d. 1894 Tamworth

Joanna Mason Tighe: 1823 – 1885

3 **Joanna Mason** b. 1823, m. Protestant **Charles Tighe** 20 Jun 1841, witness **Oliver Mason**. **Tighe** arrived 1833 as a convict on *Royal Admiral* for 'stealing a shawl', baptised 1843 RC in West Maitland. Settler, previously convict, d. 1850. Recorded as Charles Tye, age 41. DC. V185038 36A
 4 **William Tighe**, b. 6 Apr 1842 BC. V1842 2145 61
 4 **Margaret Tighe**, b. 7 Jan 1844 BC .V1844 2913 121B m. **Edmund Brohan** Liverpool 1865 MC. 2327/1865
 4 **Charles Tighe**, b. 28 Jul 1845 BC. V1845 2522 62. Sponsors **Patrick Creevey, Mary Mahony**, d. 12 Dec 1845 DC. V185038 36A
 4 **Patrick Tighe**, b. 13 Dec 1846 BC. V1846 3088 64, baptised 21 Feb 1847. Sponsored by **John Mason**, d. 19 Apr 1852

Chapter 7: The Full Mason Family Tree

Margaret Mason Creevey: 1825 – 1870

3 **Margaret Mason** b. 1825 Cahir, Tipperary, IRL d. 8 Apr 1870 Dungowan Creek, near Tamworth. DC. 5966/1870. m. **Patrick Creevey** 15 Apr 1844 Maitland MC. V1844222 123/1844 b. 1809 Kilbeggan, West Meath, Ireland near border Offaly d. 23 Jan 1871 Dungowan Creek, Tamworth, NSW (gravestone 25 Nov 1870). Patrick's first marriage to **Catherine McManus** had produced one son, **John** who was born and died in 1841. Son of Patrick Creevey and Catherine Rebet/Rabbitte.
   4 **John Patrick Creevey** b. 1845 East Maitland d. 18 Sep 1901 On the rail line, by a train at Redfern Station, in Sydney, at age 56. m. **Sarah Mary Frances Rowling** 1875 Tamworth b. 1856 Singleton, NSW d. 1945 Punchbowl
   4 **Patrick Francis Creevey** b. 27 Feb 1847 East Maitland NSW d. 28 Jun 1928 Augathella Qld m. **Jane Preston/Thompson** 1865 b. 8 Aug 1847 Sydney d. 27 Feb 1906 Iva Downs, Augathella Qld
   4 **James William Creevey** b. 26 Mar 1849 East Maitland BC. VC1849878 66 d. 1 Mar 1884 Lonewood, Reedy Creek, NE of Singleton DC. 10315 m. **Harriet Smith** c1874 Tamworth NSW b. 1855 UK d. 1926 Warialda
   4 **Malachi Creevey** b. 1851 East Maitland d. 1921 Chiltern, Vic m. **Mary Coyle** 19 Jan 1873 Dungowan, Tamworth MC. 3973/1873 (his name spelt Mallick)
   4 **Bernard Creevey** b. 9 Jan 1854 East Maitland, BC. V185452 71/1854 d. 26 Dec 1936 Base Hospital, Tamworth
   4 **Johannah Margaret Creevey** b. 19 Nov 1857 Lochinvar, Maitland BC. 8579/1858 d. 4 May 1934 Hamilton Road, Fairfield West, NSW m. **Henry Moore Richards** 7 Dec 1881 Registry Office MC. 1675/1881b. 1848 London, d. 1890 at sea DC. 461/1890 m2. **William Norton** 1894
[Children of Johannah Margaret Creevey and Henry Moore Richards]
      5 **Annie Richards** b. 1879 Benevolent Asylum, Sydney d.1879
      5 **Mabel Richards** b. 1881 Dubbo NSW
      5 **Beatrice Ann Richards** b. c1883 Launceston, Tasmania d. 1956 Kogarah Hospital m. **John Thomas Creevey** 1906 her first cousin (both grandchildren of Patrick Creevey, 1809-1871), in Redfern NSW b. 1883 'Lonewood', Reedy Creek, Inverell NSW d. 1952 Hurstville NSW Son of James William Creevey and Harriet Smith.
      5 **Daphne Ann Creevey** b. 1911 Randwick d. 1912
      5 **Raymond John Creevey** b. 1912 Kingsford NSW d. 2007 Mt Lofty Nursing Home, Toowoomba Qld m. **Stella Eva Mitchell** 1933 Randwick NSW b. 1912 Boolaroo, NSW d. 1970 Calgary Hospital, Kogarah
      5 **Ronald Dardenelles Creevey** b. 1915 Randwick d. 1971 Sydney m. **Joyce** 1948 Hurstville b. 1916 Maitland d. 1993 Greenacre
      5 **Gloria Mary Creevey** b. 1917 Randwick d. 2006 Alice Springs, NT m. **Vincent Dennis Seymour** 1939 Randwick b. 1920 Kensington
      5 **Patrick Charles Creevey** b. 1920 Randwick NSW d. 2003 Falls Creek, Vic m. **Joyce Ellen Williams** 1945 Kogarah NSW b. 1921 Lismore NSW d. 2000 Falls Creek Vic
      5 **Aubry Joseph Creevey** b. 1925 Randwick NSW
      5 **Anthony John Creevey** b. 1938 (adopted)
      5 **Henry Moore Richards** b. 1889 Benevolent Asylum Sydney d. 1890 Sydney
      5 **Florence I Richards** b. 1891 d. 1891
[Children of Johannah Margaret Creevey and William Norton]
      5 **Sydneyora Richards/Norton** b. 1896 North Sydney d. 1973 North Rocks NSW m. **James Alfred Berwick Liebs** 1920 Sydney b. 1879 Brisbane d. 1949 Granville
         6 **Essie Beatrice Liebs** b. 1921 d. 2003 Carramar Hospital, NSW m. **Charles Frederick Lewis** 1942 Parramatta b. 1922
         6 **James Norman Liebs** b. 1923 d. 2000 m. **Evelyn Alethea Jones** 1945 Parramatta. b. 1919
         6 **Mavis Aelia Liebs** b. 1924 m. **Thomas Charles Greenhalgh** 1943 Liverpool NSW b. 1920
         6 **Heather Lillian Liebs** b. 1928 m. **Ronald William Ley** 1951 Parramatta b. 1928 d. 2005
      5 **Willoughby R N Creevey/Richards/Norton** b. 1897 St Leonards d. 1950 Berry NSW m. **Annie** d. 1934
         6 **Daphne Josephine Norton** b. 1921 d. 1973 m. **Cecil Leo Blackall** b. 1943 Kogarah d. 1975
         6 **Donald Norton** b. 1923 d. 1960